History *of* Science
Selections *from* ISIS

GENERAL EDITOR, Robert P. Multhauf

Philosophers
and
Machines

Philosophers
and
Machines

Otto Mayr

Editor

Science History Publications

New York · 1976

First published in the United States by
Science History Publications
a division of
Neale Watson Academic Publications, Inc.
156 Fifth Avenue, New York 10010

© Science History Publications 1976

First Edition 1976
Designed and manufactured in the U.S.A.
LC 75-39528
ISBN 0-88202-044-7

Contents

Introduction

For the historian of science reflecting on technology, the question naturally arises: how is technology related to science? Is one part of the other, or are they opposites? Is technology merely the applications of science, or is it, on the contrary, its matrix, source of the experiences, skills, challenges and funds from which scientific enterprises grow?

The question about the relationship between science and technology has been the subject of a long and wearying discussion, a discussion made difficult by confusions of language and by differences in background and motive among the participants. In the end one feels a craving for factual information instead of further debate, and for the testimony of historical sources instead of special pleading. Testimony of precisely that kind may perhaps be obtained by the following prescription: take a representative journal for the history of science and screen its published volumes for historical research dealing with this issue, the science-technology relationship and technology per se.

If we apply this test to *Isis* the results are partly predictable and partly unexpected. In its past sixty-odd volumes, *Isis* has published a considerable number of studies dealing with the invention of scientific instruments and their role in the advance of science, and more than a few discussions of the interaction between science and society through the medium of technology. What is surprising, however, is the far greater number of articles concentrating on the history of technology directly and for its own sake. This latter category then, where historians of science discuss technology, is of particular interest, and it is from it that the following collection of articles is chosen.

The task of selecting involves considerations of quality as well as of topic. A first criterion for an article to be included was that it must appear fresh and readable in the light of current scholarship. That is not the same, of course, as requiring it to represent the latest word on the subject, or to be an achievement of timeless value. It only should, and this is the second criterion, constitute an effective historical statement on the essence and the character of technology. With this latter requirement the relatively few articles on scientific instruments and on the social impact of science, regardless of their quality, had to be excluded: at bottom they are concerned with science, not with technology.

Nevertheless, the tension between science and technology that is of such central interest to us will not be sacrificed by this method. Although insisting in our selection on a strictly technological focus, the point of view from which technology is regarded here is expressly or unconsciously that of science, if only for the reason that the material selected here was written and published by and for students of the history of science.

The resulting selection is noteworthy in two regards. First, these articles record encounters between science and technology in a manner that is refreshingly free of received ideology and public posture. The historians writing here have lowered their guards, giving free rein to their fascination with the phenomena themselves. The second aspect is even more intriguing: the great majority of *Isis* articles dealing with technology converge on a single theme that is perhaps best described by the title "Philosophers and Machines." To be sure, for this purpose, the terms "philosopher" and "machine" will have to be interpreted liberally. The word "philosopher" will cover not only the natural philosopher and his successor, the modern "scientist;" it will be stretched to include poets. The concept "machine," whose most archetypical manifestation is perhaps the steam engine, is used flexibly enough to include simple devices like stills and spectacles, as well as such a static and in some sense negative structure as the tunnel.

Thus defined, the motif of "philosopher and machine" recurs in the volumes of *Isis* with great frequency and variety. Virtually every one of the nineteen articles represents a different variation on this theme.

Some of them, like those on the still, the waterclock, and the eyeglass, deal with the origins of devices that are useful tools in practical life as well as fascinating demonstrations of natural phenomena. The debate devoted to the tunnel of Eupalinus investigates the share of mathematical method in one of the great feats of ancient engineering; incidentally, it demonstrates how opposing historical theories can be argued with great persuasiveness. The short article on floating docks in the Renaissance shows that even a historian of science of such elitist tastes as George Sarton was not immune to the appeal of machinery. The study of the transmission of Hero's *Pneumatics* traces the enormous impact of this greatest of ancient machine books on European engineers as well as natural philosophers at the outset of the Scientific Revolution. Two case studies in Baroque machinery, namely of the cannon and the gear transmission, describe how these benefited from the help of mathematics. A brief discussion of Joseph Black's contribution to James Watt's steam engine leads to the subtle observation that occasionally a scientist may help an engineer more through the method of his approach than the substance of his discoveries. Sadi Carnot, the engineer whose *Reflections on the Motive Power of Heat* reshaped not only thermal engineering but also cosmology, is the subject of two articles: One deals with the curious heat engine of Cagnard that possibly had a decisive influence on the formation of Carnot's theory; the other explores the reasons for the initial reluctance of practical engineers to accept Carnot's results. An article on Maxwell's theory of centrifugal governors argues that Maxwell's work was inspired by his experience with practical machinery, but motivated by purely scientific goals. Another article refutes the legend that Heinrich Hertz, discoverer of electromagnetic waves, had denied any practical utility of his discovery. Two articles, finally, deal with pessimistic premonitions of two great Romantic poets about the approaching machine age.

The common theme of this collection of articles is self-evident. But to appreciate its significance one must realize that the theme is inherent in the material and not an artificial result of editorial choice. Our selection represents the bulk of such work on the history of technology as *Isis*, a journal to which this subject is of necessity somewhat peripheral, has published, almost in spite of itself, over the years. The selection certainly represents no conscious policy on the part of successive *Isis* editors. All the more remarkable, therefore, is the consistency with which they all focus, in various ways, on the encounter between the philosophic mind and the machine.

Where does the machine stand in the relationship between science and technology? The distinction between science and technology lies in their characteristic aims: science is dedicated to the explanation of the riddles of nature's phenomena; technology to the solution of material problems in man's life. Such neat distinctions in abstract principle, however, are blurred in the mixed and conflicting motivations of the actual practitioners, whose activities are the results of a complex of ethical, economic, and other drives, activities that only seldom can be classified as pure science or technology.

Is it sufficient, then, to discuss the science-technology relationship on the level of goals, purposes, motivations alone? On that level there would be no room for the discussion of the concept "machine."

But what is the machine? A crucial distinction between the concepts "tool" and "instrument" on one side, and "machine" on the other is marked by the question: "does the thing serve a purpose?" Tools and instruments are contrivances for accomplishing a task. We will not call an artifact "tool" or "instrument" unless we know that it has a purpose, and what that purpose is.

This requirement does not apply to the concept "machine." When we call a structure "machine" we do not ask about its purpose. In order to qualify for the title "machine," a structure—apart from being mechanical, i.e. involving forces or motions—must only satisfy two criteria: it must possess a certain amount of complexity (otherwise it would be a so-called "simple machine") and, more important, it must be ingenious.

The importance of ingenuity as an essential characteristic of the concept is highlighted by the ancient double meaning of the Greek and Latin words for machine, mechanism, engine, engineer, and their counterparts in modern languages: in addition to their customary technical meaning they often have the figurative connotation of ingenious artifice, clever trick, deception, a fact heatly illustrated by the word "machination."

But a strong intellectual component is also part of real machines, artifacts of metal and wood; by virtue of this feature the machine participates in a unique way in the two worlds of mind and matter.

The intellectual substance that characterizes machinery is of a peculiar kind. It varies in texture and flavor with the nature of the particular machine to which it belongs: the ideas incorporated in clocks and mechanical automata tend to be related to geometry and kinematics, while thermal and electrical machines lead to abstract thought processes that transcend the boundaries of the existing mathematics and philosophy. In all cases, however, such ideas are in essence nonverbal: they cannot be described and communicated in words. Even the traditional language of engineers, the drawing, fails to convey the composition and mode of functioning of complex machines. Philosophers have devised symbolic languages and algebras to meet that challenge and have failed. Modern technology communicates through a large number of special purpose languages invented as the need arises, while the literary world, recognizing that its tools are ineffective in the face of this problem, prefers to employ machines in metaphors. Perhaps machines owe their unique charm to this very difficulty of grasping their intellectual substance in terms of conventional forms of communication.

3

The appeal of machines works in two directions: it affects philosophers as much as engineers. Examples are familiar of philosophers who dreamed of inventing magical machines, and of others who struggled with the actual construction of clocks, computers, regulators; who introduced mechanical conceptions into abstract speculations, or who used machinery as a favorite analogy.

The intellectual, almost spiritual appeal of machinery becomes evident to everyone who experiences machines directly. It is this curious fascination more than the wish to build something useful or the hope for material rewards that makes men devote their lives to machinery. Constructing, operating, even watching machines provides satisfactions and delights that can be intense enough to become ends in themselves. Such delights are purely aesthetic. Our culture displays an ambivalent attitude towards the delights of machinery. We strongly recommend them to boys, but in adults we discourage excessive indulgence. The works of a classical inventor like Hero of Alexandria that were obviously inspired by a nonutilitarian delight in machines we often call "frivolous," "useless," or "mere playthings," and among our contemporaries we describe devotees of such pleasures as "gadgeteers." To point this out is not to demand a revision of our culture's scale of aesthetic pleasures. It should be recognized, however, that the fascinations and delights of machinery are a historical force, insufficiently appreciated perhaps because of a cultural bias, but nevertheless real, a force that has affected not only technology but also philosophy, science, literature, or in short, our culture at large.

The above reflections cannot claim to be fully supported by evidence contained in the following selection of *Isis* articles. Their purpose is only to explain how the selection was made, to suggest the spirit in which it should be read, and to stimulate a discussion that may prove interesting and profitable. For the problem of the science-technology relationship mentioned at the start we have discovered no solution, but the selection should make it clear that between science and technology, or perhaps rather between the worlds of thought and action, or mind and matter, the machine constitutes a unique link.

The Earliest Stages in the Evolution of the Still

by Martin Levey*

IT HAS BEEN clearly demonstrated from Greek alchemical texts that distillation apparatus was well known in the early centuries of the Christian Era.[1] Not only are there a number of diagrams of distillatories in the Greek manuscripts but these show a high technical order of development.[2] In fact, the stills used then are not too different from those in use in chemical laboratories today.

As to the evolution of the still, this has largely been a matter of conjecture. The main reason for this has been a complete lack of evidence for the existence of the still prior to Alexandrian times. As a result, F. Sherwood Taylor, from the facts at hand in 1945, described the possible course of evolution of the still head with the body of the still remaining almost the same from the very beginning.

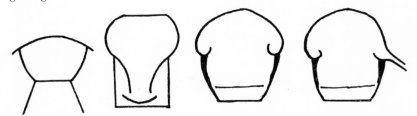

Fig. 1. Possible origin of the still according to Taylor. After *Annals of Science*, 5.

According to Taylor (fig. 1) the vapor was originally caused to condense on a lid or cup or on a suspended fleece in the neck of the still. In succession, the rim of the alembic, the upper part of the still, was turned in, then a spout was added and the still head elevated, and finally a trough was added to cool the alembic.

Since the publication of Dr. Taylor's work, new data has been brought to light. Although it does not necessarily controvert the possibility of the evolution of the still head espoused by him, it points to another line of development, that of the still body itself. To support this new idea on the evolution of the

* The Institute for Advanced Study and Temple University.

[1] F. Sherwood Taylor, "The Evolution of the Still," *Annals of Science*, 1945, *5:* 185-202.

[2] For drawings of early Alexandrian stills,

cf. M. Berthelot, *Collection des Anciens Alchimistes Grecs* (Paris, 1887), *passim.;* F. S. Taylor, "A Survey of Greek Alchemy," *J. Hellenic Studies*, 1930, *50:* 109.

still, the evidence may be brought forward not only from Arabic times but also for the first time from an era much earlier than even the Alexandrian period, i.e., from *ca.* 3500 B.C. in ancient Mesopotamia, just before the beginning of the earliest historical period.

Since the preparation of aromatic substances was one of the most important industries in ancient Mesopotamia[3], it is logical, therefore, that one should search for distillatory artifacts in this region and perhaps look for written evidence for distillation in the cuneiform literature of the Sumerians or the later Akkadians. This has been done with interesting results.

In the excavation at Tepe Gawra, in northeast Mesopotamia, in levels going back to the middle of the fourth millennium B.C., earthenware pots of a peculiar construction have been found which must drastically change previous ideas as to the history of ancient chemistry. In this excavation, both extraction and distillation apparatus have been unearthed. All of these are of the double-rimmed type as shown in the accompanying figures.

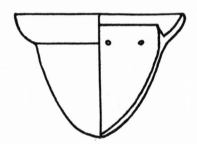

FIG. 2. Extraction apparatus from Tepe Gawra.
Courtesy University Museum, Philadelphia.

The vessels intended for the process of extraction (fig. 2) have their inner rims pierced in a number of places so that the extracted material may run down through these drainage holes back into the mixture. These pots are well suited for either aqueous or oil extraction. In operation, the comminuted raw material of botanical or zoological origin was placed in the channel between the rims while, in the bottom of the pot, the volatile solvent was boiled. The vapor then struck the cooler lid, condensed, ran down into the trough to dissolve the sought-for ingredients in the raw material, then drained through the holes of the inner rim to the bottom of the vessel. In this way, a continuous extraction operation was affected.

It is but a short step to an understanding of the operation of the still which, in principle, is the same vessel without the drainage holes. In the tablet literature of Mesopotamia of ca. 1200 B.C., there is evidence for the use of a still such as that found at Tepe Gawra (fig. 3). It is written in Akkadian.

In an account of perfumery manufacturing techniques, the tablet reads:[4]

[3] M. Levey, *Chemistry and Chemical Technology in Ancient Mesopotamia* (Amsterdam: Elsevier, 1959), 132-146.
[4] E. Ebeling, "Parfümrezepte und Kultische

Texte aus Assur," *Orientalia*, 1948-1950, *17*: 129-145, 299-313; *18*: 404-418; *19*: 265-278. In Istanbul text II, rt. col., lines 1-6.

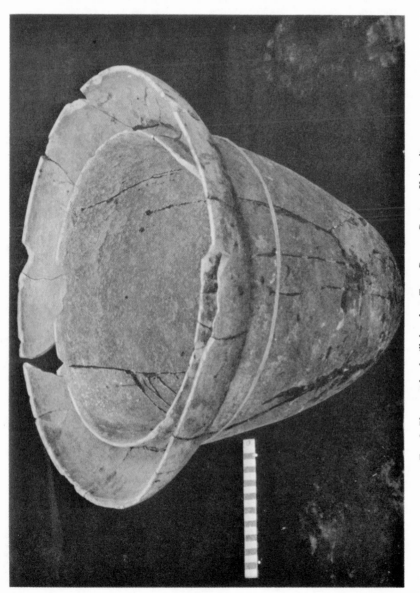

FIG. 3. Photograph of still found at Tepe Gawra. Courtesy University Museum, Philadelphia. The scale is in centimeters.

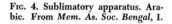

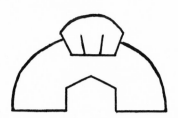

FIG. 4. Sublimatory apparatus. Arabic. From *Mem. As. Soc. Bengal,* I.

FIG. 5. Still used by Al-Kindi. After Karl Garbers, *op. cit.*

At the thirteenth time of pouring the ingredients together, you remove the oil and purify the still body. You heat water, clean out a *ḫariu* [Akkadian: "storage vessel"] pot, pour it (the water) into the *ḫariu* pot and then pour in two cup measures of balsam condensate. It thus remains all day. In the evening, you transfer it to a shallow bowl and add 3 *qa* [Akkadian: about .35 liter] measures of balsam. It stands overnight and at dawn you wipe out a *diqaru* [Akkadian: "distillatory"] pot (the still body) and place the soaked aromatic material which was in the shallow bowl overnight in the *diqaru* pot. You kindle a fire under the *diqaru* pot; the aromatic material becomes hot. You pour in the oil, stir, and cover up. You do not remove the (botanical) material and do not take away the charcoal. The fire rises; the oil throws up bubbles. You will repeatedly wipe up the innerstructure[5] (the trough) of the *diqaru* vessel[6] with a handcloth.

In much later Arabic times, in the early part of the tenth century, al-Rāzī gave a description (fig. 4) of a sublimatory which had a wide brim or lip with a slight depression in it all around to retain the sublimate which condensed upon the cooler lid and then coursed down into this channeled brim or ledge.[7]

> There are several ways of performing the rising up in the aludel and the substances which the chemists sublime in it are Mercury, Arsenic sulfide, Sulfur and Sal-Ammoniac. They are placed after treatment in the aludel, and the cover being fitted in position over it, a fire is lit. Then the substance rises up, and settles on the shelf.[8]

Al-Kindī, in the ninth century A.D., had used essentially the same procedure although much simpler[9] (fig. 5). In the thirteenth century, in a work by

[5] L. Dennefeld, *Babylonische-Assyrische Geburts-Omina* (Leipzig, 1914), p. 30a, obv. line 31.

[6] M. Levey, "Evidence of Ancient Distillation, Sublimation and Extraction in Mesopotamia," *Centaurus,* 1955, *4:* 23-33.

[7] E. Ebeling, *op. cit.,* in KAR 222, obv. left col., line 15 mentions the "lip of the still body."

[8] H. E. Stapleton, R. F. Azo, and M. H. Husain, "Chemistry in Iraq and Persia in the Tenth Century A.D.," *Mem. Asiatic Soc. Bengal,* 1922-29, *8:* 359.

[9] Karl Garbers, "Kitāb Kīmiyā Al-'Iṭr Wat-tas'īdāt von Yaqūb b. Isḥaq Al-Kindī," *Abhandlungen f.d. Kunde des Morgenl.,* 1948, *30.*

M. LEVEY

Geber,[10] there is a drawing of a still which is based on the same principal as that of the ancient Mesopotamian forbear. The still body is almost an exact replica (fig. 6). Here, the trough to catch the distillate is outlined clearly.

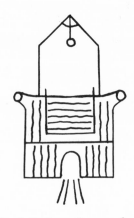

FIG. 6. Developed trough on the still body. From Geber, "Summa Perfectionis Magisterii" after Latin MS No. 6504, Bib. Nat.

FIG. 7. Jar inverted over a beaker placed in a hearth base. From Geber, op. cit.

Another example is also found in Geber (fig. 7). In this case, the still body is a beaker inverted over a smaller one. These are sealed in over the hearth base. The trough is thus formed partly by the still body and partly by the aludel.

Therefore, the evidence for the evolution of the still would seem to be complete with attempts having been made in three directions to build and improve the apparatus. In the first place, the trough was developed as part of the still body itself, later as part of the still head,[11] and, third, as an intermediate combination with the still body and head helping to form the channel to catch the sublimate or distillate.

[10] E. J. Holmyard, The Works of Geber Englished by Richard Russell (London, 1928).

[11] F. S. Taylor, "A Survey of Greek Alchemy," J. Hellenic Studies, 1930, 50, 135.

Egyptian water clocks

ABSTRACT

Reconstruction of a prismatic prototype of cylindrical inflow clocks. Operating with the simplest fractions, 1/2 and 1/3, and drawing straight lines only, we may construct a prismatic diagram which accounts for the unusual features of the cylindrical diagram of the Edfu inflow clock. The new diagram points to an Egyptian—not Greek— origin of several passages of classical literature dealing with the rate of increase of the length of the day.

Reproduction and discussion of hitherto unpublished items connected with water clocks, such as the prismatic model in the Metropolitan Museum (Acc. No. 86.1.93) and the Medinet Habu astronomical ceiling. It is shown that the decanologue of the Karnak outflow clock is closer related to the Senmut decanologue than to those of the Ramesseum and of Medinet Habu.

1. *Introduction.*

A detailed treatment of Egyptian methods for measuring time—by the flow of water or the apparent motions of the sun and of the stars—will be found in L. BORCHARDT's (1) monumental Altägyptische Zeitmessung; a good survey of the more important problems is given in R. W. SLOLEY's (2) papers on the same subject. The present paper will be devoted to some of the neglected aspects of the problems presented by Egyptian water clocks.

2. *Kircher.*

" The theories of KIRCHER as to the content of the hieroglyphic inscriptions exceed all bounds in their imaginative folly " (3);

---

(1) Die Geschichte der Zeitmessung und der Uhren, hrsg. von E. v. BASSERMANN-JORDAN. Bd. I, Lieferung B : LUDWIG BORCHARDT, Die Altägyptische Zeitmessung. Berlin, 1920.

(2) Ancient clepsydrae. *Ancient Egypt*, 43-50. London, 1924. Primitive methods of measuring time, with special reference to Egypt. *The Journal of Egyptian Archaeology*, 17, 166-78. London, 1931.

(3) ALAN H. GARDINER, Egyptian Grammar, p. 11. Oxford, 1927.

this harsh statement is, unfortunately, fully justified; occasionally, however, the vivid imagination of ATHANASIUS KIRCHER (1601-1680) could lead to scientific discoveries. When a fragment of a granite vase was excavated, in Rome, near Santa Maria sopra Minerva, he thus described (4) this valuable addition to the growing Museum Kircherianum :

" Hoc eodem loco erutum fuit vasis Nilotici fragmentum hieroglyphicis notis refertum, ex quo apertè Niloticorum vasorum ratio & forma dignoscitur. Videtur illic linea in duodecim partes distributa, in qua per interiorem vasis superficiem, vsque in fundum, duodecim ordine aequaliter inter se distantes veluti termini quidam eminentes disponuntur; qui termini haud dubiè vel ad incrementum decrementumque fluminis, vel ad horas in hydrologio commonstrandas, deputabantur. In exteriori verò vasis superficie, ad extremum vasis limbum, circulus est in 365 stellas diuisus..."

Although KIRCHER's fragment contained but two incomplete monthly scales, he arrived at the conclusion that a complete scale must consist of 12 parts; one of the two fragments in the Museum Gaddianum, in Florence, contained a complete scale, which may account for KIRCHER's generalization. On p. 385 of Oedipus Aegyptiacus is reproduced a plate borrowed from GIOVANNI NARDI's edition of LUCRETIUS (Florence 1647); see facsimile of pp. 384 and 385 of Oedipus in *Isis*, 24, 431, 1936. KIRCHER, not NARDI, deserves full credit for the interpretation of the two fragments from the Museum Gaddianum. To appreciate the value of KIRCHER's hypothesis—that the " Nilotic vases " were either Nilometers or " hydrologia," i.e., water clocks,—it is necessary to compare it with the status of the clepsydra problem in the beginning of the present century. Incidentally, it is a curious coincidence—which does not excuse KIRCHER's " imaginative folly " where hieroglyphic inscriptions were concerned—that his " Nilotic vase," found near Santa Maria sopra Minerva, originally came from a temple of the Nile-god.

3. *From Kircher to the Karnak clepsydra.*

In the beginning of the present century, little was known

(4) A. KIRCHER, Oedipus Aegyptiacus, v. 3, p. 384. Rome, 1654 (colophon : 1655).

about Egyptian water clocks, despite literary references and the presence of more than a dozen fragments in European museums. Thus, in 1901, A. WIEDEMANN (5) published a paper containing a description of fragments of six water clocks; here are his conclusions (6) :

"There must exist a connection between these vessels and the months of the year, as is shown by the month divinities they bear, and by the number 12 playing a *rôle* in the point-lines engraved in their inside. Perhaps the purification-water in them stood under the protection of the cycle of these divinities. The gods named in the dedication formulas may have been the gods out of the temples of which the vessels originally came. But, in all cases, I believe, we have to see in them the type of the purification-vessels, of which Heron (7) speaks in the passage quoted at the beginning of this communication."

In 1901, G. MASPERO found, in Edfu, a water clock of the inflow type; this specimen, of the Roman period (ca. A.D. 100), is now in Cairo, and seems to be the only inflow clock extant. A description of the Edfu water clock was published by G. DARESSY (8) in 1902; he considered (9) the " grand vase en pierre avec graduations " as belonging to the " catégorie des vases récemment étudiés par M. WIEDEMANN comme ayant servi aux purifications," not as a water clock. Long after it was recognized as an inflow clock, Sir FLINDERS PETRIE (10) wrote, in 1924 :

" Regarding the Edfu cylinder, it is very difficult to regard it as an inflow vessel, because the lines start from a uniform level at the top, and vary greatly between the months below. The idea of beginning each night by a variable filling up to a given mark seems very unlikely. There is one way in which it would work truly as an outflow vessel like the Karnak vessel..."

In 1903, the Oxyrhynchus (11) papyrus fragment 470 was published; it deals, in lines 31 to 87, " with the construction of a ὡρολόγιον or time-piece, shaped something like a flower-pot " (12); in his interpretation of this papyrus fragment of the

---

(5) Bronze circles and purification vessels in Egyptian temples. *Proceedings Soc. Biblical Archaeol.*, 23, 263-74. London, 1901.

(6) *Loc. cit.*, p. 274.

(7) Pneumatica, II, 32, p. 148, ed. SCHMIDT.

(8) Grand vase en pierre avec graduations. *Annales du service des antiquités de l'Égypte*, 3, 236-39. Cairo, 1902.

(9) *Loc. cit.*, p. 236.

(10) *Ancient Egypt*, p. 50. London, 1924.

(11) The Oxyrhynchus papyri, Part III. Ed. by B. P. GRENFELL and A. S. HUNT. London, 1903.

(12) *Loc. cit.*, p. 142.

third century of our era, J. G. SMYLY (13) uses the following cautious expression (14) : " if the instrument in question were a water clock, a knowledge of this volume would be of great importance "; apparently, he failed to study the dimensions and the water-level scales of the fragments of WIEDEMANN's " purification vessels." A complete analysis of lines 31 to 87 of the Oxyrhynchus fragment 470, with facsimile, emendated transcription, translation, computations, diagrams, etc., will be found in BORCHARDT (15). The " flower pot " discussed in the papyrus had an upper diameter of 24, a lower diameter of 12, and a height of 18 δάκτυλοι (fingerbreadths); the duodecimal graduation was limited to the upper two-thirds of the vessel.

The problem of Egyptian water clocks appeared in a new light, in 1904, when G. LEGRAIN discovered, in Karnak, the magnificent translucent alabaster outflow clock which is now in Cairo; it has an upper diameter of 24, a lower diameter of 12, and a height of 18 Egyptian fingerbreadths (16); the duodecimal graduation covers the upper two-thirds of the vessel. The Karnak clepsydra was made about 1400 B.C., during the reign of AMENHOTEP III (XVIIIth dynasty); it is, therefore, more than a thousand years older than the oldest known fragments of an outflow clock (ca. 330 B.C.; BORCHARDT's Auslaufuhr 2).

G. DARESSY's (17) paper on the two clepsydrae in Cairo—the Edfu inflow clock and the Karnak outflow clock—appeared in 1916. KIRCHER's hypothesis that the three fragments known to him were parts of " hydrologia," water clocks, became an obvious fact—but KIRCHER did not get credit for his vision.

The following tabulation will help the reader to see the development of Egyptian chronometry and calendariography in the right perspective.

---

(13) *Ibid.*, p. 141 : " For the interpretation of this papyrus we are indebted to Mr. J. G. SMYLY."
(14) *Ibid.*, p. 145.
(15) Altägyptische Zeitmessung, p. 10,ss.
(16) An Egyptian fingerbreadth is 18.75 mm., about 3/4 in.
(17) Deux clepsydres antiques. *Bulletin de l'Institut égyptien*, 5e série, 9, 5-16, 1915. Cairo, 1916.

TABLE I

Calendars, water clocks, and ceiling decorations

Item	Year (approx.)	Dynasty
Asyut calendars	2000	IX-XI
AMENEMHET's clepsydra	1550	XVIII
SENMUT's ceiling	1500	XVIII
Karnak clepsydra	1400	XVIII
SETI's ceiling	1350	XIX
Ramesseum ceiling	1250	XIX
Medinet Habu ceiling	1175	XX
ALEXANDER's clepsydra	330	
Edfu clepsydra	A.D. 100	
Oxyrhynchus papyrus 470	250	

4. *Prismatic inflow clocks.*

No satisfactory explanation has been given for the distribution of the vertical lines engraved in the cylindrical inflow clock from Edfu. The distances of these lines vary as follows :

$$3:2:1; \qquad 1:2:3; \qquad 3:2:1; \qquad 1:2:3,$$

if one begins with the longest scale of 14 fingerbreadths or with the shortest scale of 12 fingerbreadths ; see Figure 2.

The ratio 14:12 for the lengths of the scales corresponding to the longest and to the shortest nights, respectively, did not change from the time of AMENEMHET until the end of Egyptian history; this implies, of course, that the length of the scales corresponding to the equinoxes should be 13. The maker of the Karnak outflow clock probably followed AMENEMHET in making the further simple assumption that the lengths of the scales between 12 and 13, 13 and 14, 14 and 13, and 13 and 12, vary uniformly, 1/3 of a fingerbreadth per month. The next step in the development of water clocks—made, apparently, by a designer of an inflow clock—was the correct observation that the length of the nights changes slowly during the month immediately preceding and during the month immediately following the shortest or the longest night; the advanced design of sun dials made such an observation possible at a relatively early date.

Here is a simple method for incorporating this observation

into the scales of a prismatic inflow clock with a square base; see Figure 1. The corner scales of the prism ADGJ are 14, 13, 12, and 13 fingerbreadths, respectively; each corner scale is divided into 12 equal parts, and the corresponding points are joined by inclined straight lines which form "stripes" on

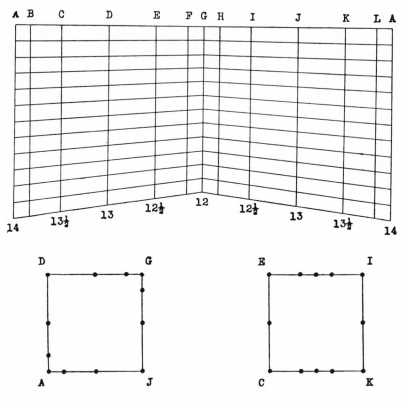

Fig. 1. — Graduation of the 1:2:3 type for a square prismatic inflow clock. Enlarged five times, the diagram would fit the Edfu clock.

all four walls; additional vertical lines are then drawn through the centers, C and K, and E and I, of the sides of the prism, and form the 13 1/2 and the 12 1/2 scales, respectively; finally, the distances AC and AK, and GE and GI, are divided into thirds, and the vertical lines B and L, and F and H, form the 13 5/6 and the 12 1/6 scales, respectively.

Here is another method for drawing the diagram of Figure 1

on the inside of a square inflow clock. The corner scales of the prism CEIK are 13 1/2, 12 1/2, 12 1/2, and 13 1/2 fingerbreadths, respectively; the equinoxial scales, D and J, occupy the middle of the side walls of the prism, while the solstitial scales, A and G, with their satellites B and L, and F and H, are drawn on the inside

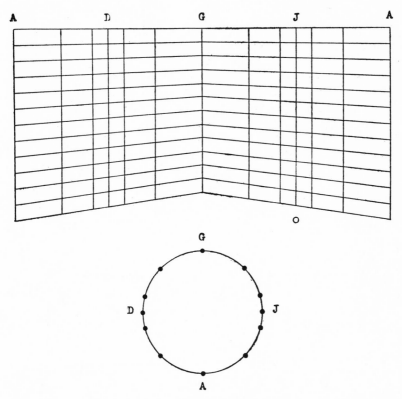

FIG. 2. — Graduation scheme of the cylindrical inflow clock from Edfu. One-fifth of the size of the original.

of the front and back walls, respectively; the inclined lines form " chevrons " on the front and back walls, and ordinary " stripes " on the side walls.

5. *Obsolescence of rim inscriptions.*

It is, practically, indifferent whether the scales of an outflow or of an inflow clock are assumed to be correct at the beginning

or in the middle of an Egyptian month of 30 days; the water
clocks completely disregard the 5 epagomenal days, but even

TABLE II

The civil year and the seasons

Year B.C.	Civil New Year's Day	Vernal equinox	Vernal equinox	Summer solstice	Autumnal equinox	Winter solstice
1617	Oct. 1	Apr. 4				
			VII	X	I	IV
1497	Sep. 1	Apr. 3				
			VIII	XI	II	V
1373	Aug. 1	Apr. 2				
			IX	XII	III	VI
1249	July 1	Apr. 1				
			X	I	IV	VII
1129	June 1	Mar. 31				
			XI	II	V	VIII
1105	May 1	Mar. 30				
			XII	III	VI	IX
885	Apr. 1	Mar. 29				
			I	IV	VII	X
761	Mar. 1	Mar. 28				
			II	V	VIII	XI
648	Feb. 1	Mar. 28				
			III	VI	IX	XII
524	Jan. 1	Mar. 27				
			IV	VII	X	I
401	Dec. 1	Mar. 25				
			V	VIII	XI	II
281	Nov. 1	Mar. 25				
			VI	IX	XII	III
157	Oct. 1	Mar. 24				
			VII	X	I	IV
37	Sep. 1	Mar. 23				

Note.—Roman numerals refer to Egyptian months.

The first two columns show the rapid recession, through the Julian calendar,
of the civil New Year's Day, i.e., of the 1st day of the 1st month of the *ȝḫt* season,
or, in the post-Persian period, of the 1st day of the month Thōuth.

The first and third columns show the slow recession, through the Julian
calendar, of the date of the vernal equinox.

The last four columns indicate, roughly, the Egyptian months of the equinoxes
and solstices. Thus, during the fifteenth century, the civil year began in August,
and the winter solstice fell on dates advancing through the 1st month of the *prt*
season; in the fourth century, the civil year began in November, and the winter
solstice progressed through the month Phaōphi.

this is of little importance; what matters, in the long run, is the neglected difference of about 1/4 of a day between the length of the tropical or of the stellar year, on the one hand, and the length of the civil year of 365 days, on the other. This difference amounts to one day in four years, or one month in about 120 years; in the course of centuries, the names of the months marked on the upper rim of a water clock cease to correspond to the scales which are engraved immediately below them; see Table II. Let us take the case of a prismatic inflow clock, ADGJ or CEIK, which was " correct," according to Egyptian standards, about 700 B.C.; the twelve months are so distributed over the rim that

XI (3rd m. of $šmw$) appears over the winter-solstice scale A;
II (2nd m. of $ȝḥt$)   ,,   ,,   ,, vernal-equinox   ,, D;
V (1st m. of prt)   ,,   ,,   ,, summer-solstice   ,, G;
VIII (4th m. of prt)   ,,   ,,   ,, autumnal-equinox ;, J.

After the lapse of about 120 years, there was a discrepancy of one month between the names on the rim and the scales of the clock.   By the middle of the fifth century B.C., the discrepancy amounted to two months.   At the time of ALEXANDER the Great, the readings on our clock had to be made as follows :

during II (Phaophi), on the winter-solstice scale A;
,,   V (Tybi),   .,   ,, vernal-equinox   ,, D;
,, VIII (Pharmouthi) ,,   ,, summer-solstice   ,, G;
,,   XI (Epiphi)   ,,   ,, autumnal-equinox ,, J.

The simple process of erasing and shifting the names of the months on the rim, in order to keep an old water clock " up-to-date " was actually used, as some of the preserved fragments of outflow clocks reveal.   In most cases, however,   the reading was simply done, during the lifetime of a generation, on scales removed, say, two or three or five months, from the names engraved on the rim.   When a new clock was made, correct names would be engraved on the rim, over the scales; the maker of the new clock would, of course, preserve the arrangement of the scales on the walls of the prism, but would engrave the correct name of the month with the shortest night over the shortest scale, and shift the other names correspondingly.

6. *The Edfu diagram.*

When prismatic inflow clocks were replaced by cylindrical ones, the diagram remained unchanged, and the distances between the scales,

$$1:2:3; \quad 3:2:1; \quad 1:2:3; \quad 3:2:1,$$

preserved on the cylindrical diagram of the Edfu clock, point, it seems to me, clearly to the prismatic prototypes of the cylindrical inflow clocks. The Edfu diagram, Figure 2, is a somewhat careless and not too intelligent copy of a diagram of the type reproduced in Figure 1; it was copied either directly from an obsolete prismatic inflow clock, or, more likely, from a cylindrical inflow clock which was " out-of-date." The fact that the Edfu diagram begins the 1:2:3 count from the autumnal-equinox scale placed over the cynocephalos orifice seems to indicate that the maker of the clock was trying to copy a diagram which originated on the inside of a prismatic clock of the " chevron " type, CEIK, where the cynocephalos orifice was placed, for reasons of symmetry, below a solstitial scale; the engraver of the Edfu diagram did not realize that the 1:2:3 count of distances between the scales must begin at a solstitial scale, and that the position of the cynocephalos orifice is irrelevant; he saw that the diagram he was trying to copy started the 1:2:3 count from the orifice, and he faithfully reproduced this irrelevant detail. The lengths of the Edfu scales increase and decrease by the traditional amounts, 1/12, 1/6, and 1/4 of the difference between the longest and the shortest night, but the wrong starting point of the 1:2:3 count leads to slow changes of the lengths of the scales near the equinoxes, and to rapid changes near the solstices—an absurdity which failed to shock the maker of the Edfu clock; apparently, like many an Asyut coffin decorator who did not understand the meaning of the calendar table he was copying, this clock maker of the Roman period did not understand the meaning of the 1:2:3 diagram.

7. Cleomedes' duodecimal rule.

Our prismatic diagram reproduced in Figure 1 accounts not only for the cylindrical diagram of the Edfu clock—it throws new light on several passages of classical literature (18) dealing

---

(18) CLEOMEDES, Κυκλικὴ θεωρία μετεώρων, I, 6. The text of CLEOMEDES is unusually clear and well preserved. Other references may be found in G. BILFINGER, Die antiken Stundenangaben, p. 153, Stuttgart, 1888.

with the seasonal rate of increase and decrease of the length of the day and of the night. CLEOMEDES (19), who lived, in all probability, in the first century B.C., states that the difference between the longest and the shortest day is thus distributed on the six months which follow the winter solstice :

during the 1st month, the day increases by 1/12 of the difference;
during ,, 2nd ,,   ,, ,,   ,,   ,, 1/6 ,, ,, difference;
during ,, 3rd ,,   ,, ,,   ,,   ,, 1/4 ,, ,, difference;
during ,, 4th ,,   ,, ,,   ,,   ,, 1/4 ,, ,, difference;
during ,, 5th ,,   ,, ,,   ,,   ,, 1/6 ,, ,, difference;
during ,, 6th ,,   ,, ,,   ,,   ,, 1/12 ,, ,, difference.

The numerators of these fractions immediately suggest an Egyptian origin of CLEOMEDES' rule. A glance at our diagrams

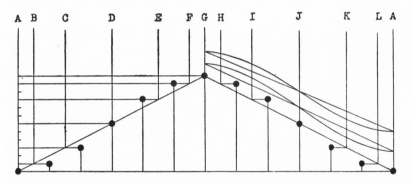

FIG. 3. — CLEOMEDES' duodecimal rule and the prismatic diagrams of the 1:2:3 type.

reproduced in Figures 1 and 3 shows that these six fractions are the direct result of the 1:2:3 process of distributing the twelve monthly scales on the four inside walls of a square inflow clock; it was the intention of the Egyptian inventor of the 1:2:3 diagram to produce scales showing slower monthly variations near the solstices and faster ones near the equinoxes; the monthly rates, 1/12, 1/6, and 1/4, happen to be an inevitable consequence, for the ordinates of the diagram, of a simple and symmetrical geometrical construction based on the favorite Egyptian fractions, 1/2 and 1/3, applied to the abscissae.

The numerical example given by CLEOMEDES is, obviously,

(19) *Loc. cit.*, I, 6.

of his own making, and throws no light on the country of origin of his duodecimal rule; he uses the simplest possible fraction, 1/2 hour, for the smallest monthly increase, and, therefore, 6 hours for the total difference between the longest and the shortest day —a difference which exists under latitude 41° or 42°, if we count the days from sunrise to sunset, disregarding twilight. It is obvious that CLEOMEDES did not care about the latitude implied in his numerical example, as long as the monthly increase and decrease rates could be expressed in a simple way, 1/2 hour, 1 hour, and 1 1/2 hour. CLEOMEDES gives no mathematical proof of his statement; apparently, he had none to offer, and was quite satisfied with a numerical example. We may assume that the duodecimal rule was of Egyptian origin, and was derived from the lengths of the scales of prismatic inflow clocks—not from mathematical considerations involving |the successive positions of the sun in the ecliptic. Figure 3 shows the straight sloping lines of a prismatic diagram and the sinusoidal distribution of CLEOMEDES' values plotted on equidistant ordinates; both the Egyptian inventor of the 1:2:3 diagram for prismatic inflow clocks and the Egyptian astronomer who first formulated the duodecimal rule concerning the monthly rate, were so close to the true solution of the problem that their achievements deserve a place of honor in the history of Egyptian science.

The traditional dimensions of outflow clocks offer us another example of the expression of a physical law by the judicious use of simple numerical relations. A " flower pot " with a bottom radius of 6, an upper radius of 12, and a height of 18 fingerbreadths —again a 1:2:3 construction rule—differs but little, in its graduated upper two-thirds, either from the paraboloid or from the truncated cone with an inclination of 77° which are characterized, in their upper two-thirds, by levels which sink uniformly—theoretically in the case of the paraboloid, practically in the case of the 77° frustum (20).

8. *Models of inflow clocks.*

In the case of the prismatic inflow clocks—as distinguished from the case of the " flower-pot " outflow clocks mentioned

(20) BORCHARDT, *loc. cit.*, p. 16.

in the preceding paragraph,—the ratio of the width to the height was dictated by practical and aesthetical rather than by theoretical considerations : it was a compromise between the tendency to lengthen the scales by reducing the cross section, and the necessity of reducing the depth, in order to simplify the engraving and reading of the scales. We shall see that the simple ratios of 1:1, 1:2, and 1:3, between the width and the height, must have been in use. The longest scale of the prism being, traditionally, 14 fingerbreadths, the side of the rim had to be, in the case of the 1:2 ratio, 7 fingerbreadths; the cylinder of Edfu is 14 fingerbreadths deep, and the developed horizontal length of its diagram is 28 fingerbreadths.

The emptying of an inflow clock offered architectural and sculptural opportunities which could not have escaped the Egyptians. In the case of an outflow clock, its very operation, during the night, left but a small amount of water, in the lower third of the " flower pot," at sunrise; since the clock had to be filled to the upper level, in the evening, this " residual " water was, probably, drained off but occasionally. In the case of an inflow clock, the result of a night's running was a prism full of water which had to be drained, before the next evening, to the bottom of the scale corresponding to the current month; the evacuation of the water, through the cynocephalos squatting at the base of the prism, could be easily adjusted in such a manner that it lasted until evening; the decreasing volume of the outflow was irrelevant, since no measurement of time was involved. A little rectangular basin at the foot of the prism, in front of the cynocephalos, could, therefore, become a decorative as well as a useful part of the draining arrangement; it was but natural to incorporate, into the design of the rectangular basin, a sun clock of the " flight-of-stairs " type, if the prismatic inflow clock happened to be located in a court.

Almost a century ago, C. LEEMANS (21) gave the following description of the Leiden model of an inflow clock :

" *Terre émaillée.* CYNOCEPHALE, accroupi entre deux réservoirs, dont

---

(21) Monumens égyptiens du Musée d'antiquités des Pays-Bas à Leide, p. 16, Pl. XIX, no. 47. Leiden, 1842. Dutch edition, p. 17.—Pl. XIX, no. 23 represents a squatting cynocephalos, on a slab, with an opening below the cynocephalos; apparently, a fragment of a water clock or of a model of a clock.

24　　　　　　　A. POGO

le plus grand se trouve derrière l'animal, l'autre, plus petit, devant ses pieds; un trou est percé de l'un dans l'autre de ces réservoirs et un escalier de six gradins conduit sur le bord du dernier. Ce petit monument nous offre peut-être le modèle d'une *clepsydre* Égyptienne, analogue à celles que décrit HORAPOLLON, *Hierogl.* I. 16."

The Leiden model, shown in Figure 4, is made of green faience; it is 44 mm. high; the water clock is formed by a low, rectangular prism; there is no graduation, of course; the rectangular shape indicates that the model represents an inflow clock which must have been different from the sqaure prototype of the Edfu clock. The outside walls of the Leiden model show some tapering.

The GRÉAU-MORGAN model of a rectangular inflow clock is reproduced on Plate 4, top, left; see also the excellent reproduction

FIG. 4. — Leiden model of a prismatic inflow clock. Height, 44 mm. After : C. LEEMANS, Monumens égyptiens, P. XIX, no. 47. Leiden, 1842.

in the catalogue of the GRÉAU-MORGAN collection, Pl. 294.6; green faience; the height of this (late dynastic?) model is 55 mm. According to FROEHNER's (22) description, it is a " gaine carrée, portant sur le devant un cynocéphale accroupi "; the Metropolitan Museum (23) lists it as a " Nilometer. In the form of a tank, with 6 steps and with figure of ape sitting on the front." The

---

(22) Collection JULIEN GRÉAU. Verrerie antique. émaillerie et poterie appartenant à M. JOHN PIERPONT MORGAN. Texte rédigé par W. FROEHNER. Page 234 and Pl. 294.6. Paris, 1903.

(23) Acc. No. 17.194.2341.

Models of inflow clocks and a votive offering. Late dynastic?
Top, left : GRÉAU-MORGAN model. Acc. No. 17.194.2341. Height, 55 mm.
Top, right : MASPERO model. Acc. No. 86.1.93. Height, 87.5 mm.
Bottom : *šb.t* from Sakkāra. Acc. No. 10.176.45. Height, ca. 4 5/8 in.

Courtesy of The Metropolitan Museum of Art.

pl, 4.   A. POGO.

Medinet Habu. XXth dynasty. Astronomical ceiling. Western part.

Courtesy of The Oriental Institute,
The University of Chicago.

pl. 5.   A. Pogo.

Medinet Habu.   XXth dynasty.   Astronomical ceiling.   Eastern part.

Courtesy of The Oriental Institute,
The University of Chicago.

pl. 6.   A. Pogo.

Ramesseum. XIXth dynasty. Astronomical ceiling. East is on the right.

Courtesy of Dr. Siegfried Schott.

A. Pogo.

hollow rectangular inflow clock rests on a base which has, in front of the cynocephalos, a shallow rectangular basin; the cynocephalos sits on a small rectangular block pierced by the draining orifice. The front wall of the main base is slightly inclined, and a double row of steps ascends to the rim of the basin; the double row of steps below the cynocephalos is marked on a vertical wall; these four rows may be considered as symbolizing the 24 hours, and originally they must have belonged to a sun clock of the " flight-of-stairs " type leading up to the cynocephalos. The inside of the clock is prismatic, the outside shows a slight tapering (the side walls are 40 mm. high, 40 mm. at the base, and 38 mm. at the top).

The Cairo model has been reproduced and discussed by BORCHARDT (24) and by SLOLEY (25). It will, therefore, suffice to state that the inside walls of the clock seem to be vertical; the horizontal cross section is a square; the ratio of the width to the height is about 1:2; the tapering of the outside walls is pronounced; the total height is 108 mm.; the overflow of the shallow basin in front of the cynocephalos runs down three steps. Like the other models, it has no graduation on the inside; the fact, however, that its cross section is square and its width-to-height ratio is 1:2, permits us to assume that the full-size clock represented by the Cairo model could have been 7 fingerbreadths wide and 14 fingerbreadths deep; it is, therefore, possible that the Edfu diagram originated in a clock similar to the one represented by the Cairo model.

A hitherto unpublished model of a prismatic inflow clock is reproduced on Plate 4, top, right, through the courtesy of the Metropolitan Museum of Art (26). It was described, in the list accompanying MASPERO's second shipment, 1886, as a " light green porcelain Nilometer." The height of this late-dynastic model is 87,5 mm. The hollow square prism rests on a base which had, no doubt, a basin in front of the cynocephalos; the knees of the cynocephalos are broken off; the draining hole is at the very bottom of the prism; the height of the prism is about

(24) Loc. cit., p. 25.
(25) Ancient Egypt, 48-49, 1924. The Journ. of Eg. Arch., 17, Pl. XXI and p. 176, 1931.
(26) Acc. No. 86.1.93.

three times its outside width; no inside graduation, of course. The square prism of the full-size clock could, possibly, be lifted from its base by means of prominences near the top of the side walls; the existence of a vertical sun dial on one of the side walls of the full-size clock is improbable, for reasons of symmetry; the prominences may be vestigial handles reminiscent of the time when the emptying of an inflow clock was accomplished by tipping the prism, not by draining it through a cynocephalos. By analogy with outflow clocks which had a graduation covering the upper two-thirds of the vessel, a square prismatic inflow clock of the proportions represented by the MASPERO model could have a diagram, of the type reproduced in Figure 1, covering the upper two-thirds only of the inside walls.

These four models prove that prismatic inflow clocks must have existed, although no fragments of full-size prismatic clocks are known. The Edfu diagram may be considered as a degenerated descendant of the diagrams which originated in tall square prismatic clocks. We know nothing of the graduation of low rectangular prismatic clocks; it is possible that the long side walls were divided into three equal parts and contained the scales of the months preceding and following the equinoxes, while the subdivision of the narrow front and back walls into three equal parts furnished the scales of the months preceding and following the solstices.

9. *Votive offerings.*

We have dealt, in the preceding section, with a class of objects which were, beyond any reasonable doubt, models of inflow clocks; they were, in all probability, used as votive offerings. The objects we are about to discuss were used as votive offerings—inscriptions prove it; it is highly probable, but not quite certain, that they were intended to represent inflow clocks.

The *šb.t* reproduced on Plate 4, bottom, is thus described by the Metropolitan Museum (27) :

" Figure of Cynocephalus. From Sakkara. Glazed faience. The figure is represented as a squatting mummy on the *heb* festival sign. There is a pillar behind, which is broken off at the top. Glaze, very thin, pale blue. Execution exquisite. Perhaps a votive offering."

(27) Acc. No. 10.176.45.

This (late-dynastic?) *šb.t* is about 4 5/8 in. high. The square pillar behind the cynocephalos had, apparently, a V-shaped notch at the top, running from the front to the back side of the pillar. We have seen that horizontal grooves on a vertical wall may represent a " flight-of-stairs " sun clock; whatever the original meaning of a notch at the top of a hieroglyph representing a prism or cylinder might have been, there is no reason why " chevron " markings on the inside of the front and back of a square prismatic inflow clock of the CEIK type should not be represented by a V-shaped notch at the top of a square prism not weakened by hollowing. The alabaster markings on the *ḥb* have, of course, nothing to do with the " chevrons " of the CEIK diagram, but their presence is very appropriate. The whole object is treated symbolically rather than realistically. The prism behind the cynocephalos is of the tall type, but the relative height of the cynocephalos and of the prism reminds us of the Leiden and the GRÉAU-MORGAN rather than of the Cairo and the MASPERO models.

Here is a partial quotation from a somewhat awkward description (28) of a similar object, PRICE No. 3796 :

" Shebt or Ushebt, an object which has been said to be the Clepsydra... it represents a cynocephalous ape seated upon the ground in human form, leaning against a column... H. 7 in. Faience, has had a green glaze."

Of the elements entering into the making of the *šb.t* group, the squatting cynocephalos gradually assumed dominating proportions; both the *ḥb* and the *nb* seem to have been used indiscriminately; the degeneration of the *ḥn*—to us, the really essential part of the *šb.t* group—from a separate square prism with a V-shaped notch at the top to a mere slab behind the back of the cynocephalos, appears to be a late-dynastic development limited to plastic—as opposed to epigraphic—*šb.t* groups.

As an example of a late-dynastic plastic *šb.t* group consisting of a cynocephalos, with a slab at his back, squatting on a *ḥb*, PRICE No. 4322 could be quoted (29), a green faience figure, 4 in. high. It is so similar to PRICE No. 3796 that the interpretation of the slab as a degenerated prism seems to be fully justified.

---

(28) A. Catalogue of the Egyptian Antiquities in the Possession of F. G. HILTON PRICE, vol. 1, p. 450, No. 3796. London, 1897.
(29) *Loc. cit.*, vol. 2, p. 38 and Pl. XII, No. 4322. London, 1908.

32

A. POGO

The Metropolitan Museum (30) has a late-dynastic miniature *šb.t* group in which the cynocephalos leans against a slab notched at the top; he squats on a *nb* showing wickerwork detail. To the modern profane eye, this miniature votive offering looks like a monkey in a rocking chair. It is of pale green faience, and is about 2 3/8 in. high.

Figure 5 represents AMENHOTEP III (31) offering to the goddess Maut a *šb.t* which might be described as a prismatic *ḥn* receptacle with a squatting cynocephalos attached to its front wall, presented on a *nb*; the emphasis seems to be on the *ḥn* receptacle rather

FIG. 5. — Votive offering. Amenhotep III. About 1400 B.C.
From : A. GAYET, Le temple de Louxor, *Mém. miss. arch. fr. au Caire*, 15, Pl. 68, fig. 195. Paris, 1894.

than on the cynocephalos; at the top of the *ḥn* prism there is a V-shaped notch. The offering of such a *šb.t* group to a goddess by AMENHOTEP III appears to have set a precedent. Although the inscriptions—which mention the *šb.t*—offer no explanation of the nature of the transaction between AMENHOTEP III and

---

(30) Acc. No. 22.2.25.

(31) A. GAYET. Le temple de Louxor. Ier fascicule. Constructions d'AMÉ-NOPHIS III. *Mémoires miss. arch. fr. au Caire*, 15, p. 109, Pl. 68, fig. 195. Paris, 1894.

the goddess, it is difficult to escape the impression that the object on the *nb* sign represents a prismatic inflow clock. If the interpretation of the notch at the top as an allusion to the " chevrons " characterizing a CEIK diagram be correct, its presence on the side walls—as opposed to the front and back walls of the plastic *šb.t* shown at the bottom of Plate 4—may be due either to the Egyptian profile conventions or to the actual construction, under AMENHOTEP III, of a prismatic inflow clock of the CEIK type with " chevrons " on the inside of the side walls and a draining hole under an equinoctial scale, as in the case of the Edfu clock.

FIG. 6. — Votive offering. Ptolemaic. About 50 B.C.
From :   A. MARIETTE, Dendérah, 3, Pl. 22a'. Paris, 1871.

The time of AMENHOTEP III is characterized by a remarkable activity of makers of time-measuring devices : in addition to the Karnak alabaster clock, several fragments of instruments bearing his cartouches and based on videly differing principles have survived; it is not impossible that ANEN (32), the " astronomer royal " of AMENHOTEP III, was partly responsible for this activity of the instrument makers. If a completely unknown object were represented on a *nb* held in the hand of AMENHOTEP III, it would be reasonable to assume that it is a time-measuring instrument;

(32) A statue of this priest-astronomer is in Turin.

if the object happens to be a square prism with a squatting cynocephalos attached to its front wall, the interpretation of the object on the *nb* as a model of an inflow clock seems to be fully justified.

Figure 6 represents a Ptolemaic (33) counterpart to the XVIIIth dynasty votive-offering scene. In 1875, A. MARIETTE (34) made the following comment on the Ptolemaic inscription :

" Le texte n'explique pas le sens de l'offrande que le roi présente à la déesse. Hathor prend le titre vague de « maîtresse des yeux ». Elle dit au roi : « J'accorde que tes yeux voient pour des millions d'années le... que tes yeux soient préservés de tout mal ». Le roi intervient dans la cérémonie comme fils de Thoth, apportant la clepsydre à sa mère."

It will be noticed that while the prism of the plastic votive offerings, discussed in the beginning of this section, gradually degenerated into a meaningless slab, the more conservative epigraphic representations preserved the vessel shape of the object behind the cynocephalos; the tapering is pronounced, and the notch at the top is present, both in the center and at the bottom of Figure 6; it is possible that the Ptolemaic offering represents an inflow clock with a circular—not with a square—cross section.

There are numerous representations, in the published epigraphic material (35), of objects which look like inflow clocks or inflow clock models; a thorough study of these inscriptions is desirable, now that the originally prismatic shape of inflow clocks may be considered as well established. The tapering of the vessel, the presence or absence of the notch at the top, of the curved (inflowing water ?) or straight (floating index ?) line at the top, of the horizontal bands (level marks ?), etc., ought to be taken into consideration, and the chronological order of their appearance established.

---

(33) A. MARIETTE, Dendérah. Texte : Paris, 1875. Planches, t. III : Paris, 1871. Our Fig. 6 is a reproduction of Pl. III.22a' (Grand temple, crypte no. 2). Concerning the empty cartouches, MARIETTE wrote, p. 48 : " Mais si les cartouches sont vides, il n'en est pas de même des noms de règne qui sont introduits pleins dans le texte courant des cryptes nos 2 et 8. Là, deux rois se révèlent par des qualifications qui ne laissent aucun doute sur la place qui leur est due dans le canon des LAGIDES. Ces deux rois sont PROLÉMÉE XI et PTOLÉMÉE XIII."

(34) *Loc. cit.*, p. 241.

(35) See, e.g., the references in GARDINER, *loc. cit.*, sign-list; ERMAN-GRAPOW's dictionary; BORCHARDT, *loc. cit.*, p. 26.

10. *Water clocks and astronomical ceilings.*

In 1897, G. DARESSY (36) published a detailed description of the astronomical ceiling of Medinet Habu, from which we quote the following passages :

" ... une salle de huit mètres de longueur sur quatre de largeur, dont le plafond était en forme de voûte surbaissée... Ces dalles [du plafond] étaient toutes brisées, heureusement on en a retrouvé dans les décombres une partie suffisante pour pouvoir rétablir les trois quarts de la toiture... La voûte est ornée de sujets astronomiques qui donnaient la copie presque textuelle d'un plafond du Rames-séum. Le tableau, encadré par la légende royale de Ramsès III, est divisé en trois registres."

In 1904, the Karnak alabaster clepsydra was discovered; its exterior decoration, " ... ces tableaux, analogues aux peintures des plafonds astronomiques du Ramesséum et de Médinet Habou " (37), did not prevent the Medinet Habu ceiling from being neglected. Plates 5 and 6 reproduce unpublished photographs of the Medinet Habu ceiling. For the sake of completeness, I have added, on Plate 7, a reduced reproduction of a composite photograph of the Ramesseum ceiling. A detailed comparative study of the exterior decoration of the Karnak alabaster clock and of the two ceilings reproduced on Plates 5 to 7 will appear elsewhere; in the present paper, I shall limit myself to a few remarks concerning the decanologues of the Karnak clepsydra and of the ceilings of SENMUT, the Ramesseum, and Medinet Habu.

In my paper dealing with the SENMUT (38) ceiling, I have shown that the Ramesseum decanologue followed the same tradition as the SENMUT decanologue, whereas the SETI decanologue followed a different tradition. Two more decanologues may now be added to the SENMUT-Ramesseum tradition—the Karnak and the Medinet Habu lists. Table III shows these four lists at a glance; since the SENMUT ceiling is older than the Karnak clepsydra, I have reproduced the SENMUT-ceiling spelling of the names of the decans; the numbering of the decans is the same as in my tabulations of the decanologues of the Middle Kingdom (39) and of the XVIIIth and XIXth dynasties (40).

---

(36) Notice explicative des ruines de Médinet Habou, pp. 154-57. Cairo, 1897.
(37) DARESSY, Deux clepsydres antiques, *loc. cit.*, p. 10.
(38) *Isis*, 14, 320, 1930.
(39) *Osiris*, 1, 507, 1936.
(40) *Isis*, 14, 317-18, 1930.

A. POGO

TABLE III

Decanologues of the XVIIIth, XIXth, and XXth dynasties

Top panel — column headers 17 … 1 (with "Decade" label at right):

17	16	15	14	13	12	11	10	9	8	7	6	5	4	3	2	1	
12	11	10	9	8	7	6	6	5	5	4	4	3	3	2	2	1	S
(12)	(11)	10	9	8	7	6	6	5	5	4	4	3	3	2	2	1	K
12	11	10	9	8	7	6	6	5	5	4	4	3	3	2	2	1	R
(12)	11	10	9	8	7	6	6	6	5	4	4	3	3	2	2	1	M

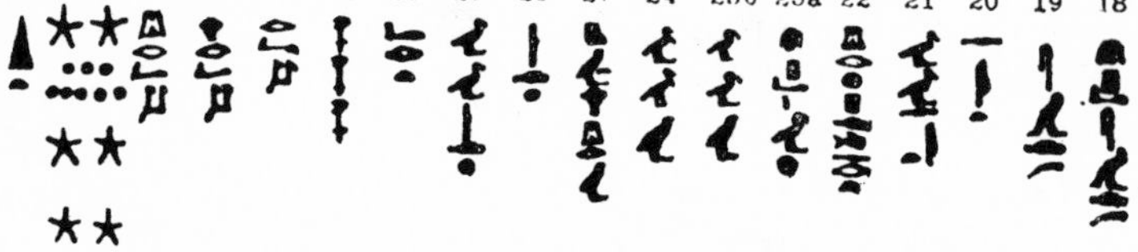

Bottom panel — column headers 37 … 18:

37	36b	34	32b	32a	31	30	29	28	27	24	23b	23a	22	21	20	19	18	
29	26	24/25	28	-	23	27	22	22	21	20	19	18	17	16	15	14	13	S
29	26	(24)/(25)	28	-	23	27	22	22	21	20	19	18	17	16	15	14	13	K
28	25	24	27	26	-	23	22	22	(21)	20	19	18	17	16	15	14	(13)	R
		24?			23	22	22	13					16	15		14	13	M

S — Senmut ceiling   XVIIIth dyn., about 1500 B.C.
K — Karnak clepsydra   XVIIIth dyn., about 1400 B.C.
R — Ramesseum ceiling   XIXth dyn., about 1250 B.C.
M — Medinet Habu ceiling   XXth dyn., about 1175 B.C.

Although the state of preservation of the Medinet Habu ceiling leaves gaps in the western half of the table, it is obvious that the Medinet Habu and the Ramesseum decanologues differed, in the Orion region, from the SENMUT and the Karnak lists.

11. *Acknowledgments.*

I hereby express my thanks to the following men and museums :

To Dr. W. D. VAN WIJNGAARDEN, for written infc. nation concerning the Leiden model reproduced in Figure 4.

To the Metropolitan Museum of Art, for the photographs reproduced on Plate 4. The MASPERO model is a hitherto unpublished item. I believe that no photograph of the votive offering from Sakkāra has been published before.

To Dr. H. H. NELSON, for the hitherto unpublished photographs of the Medinet Habu ceiling reproduced on Plates 5 and 6.

To Dr. SIEGFRIED SCHOTT, for the original positives on which Plate 7 is based. To Mr. A. C. BOECKER, of the Fogg Museum staff, for his excellent enlargements and reductions which led to the final composite positive. It was, unfortunately, impossible to preserve the beauty and legibility of this Ramesseum photograph in the reduced half-tone reproduction.

Carnegie Institution   A. POGO.
of Washington.

How Was the Tunnel of Eupalinus Aligned?

By June Goodfield and Stephen Toulmin *

HISTORIANS of philosophy, science, and engineering,[1] as well as general historians,[2] frequently allude to the Tunnel of Eupalinus on the Greek island of Samos as among the most remarkable works of civil engineering surviving from antiquity. Herodotus himself wrote of the tunnel — together with the Temple of Hera, and the mole in the harbor nearby — as "the three greatest achievements of the Hellenes."[3] The literary tradition tells us nothing about the methods by which the tunnel was constructed. By now, however, it seems to be generally assumed that this was done by applying the geometrical principles associated with the name of Pythagoras, who was a contemporary of Eupalinus and a native of Samos. The aim of this paper is to question that assumption.

The tunnel was built about 530 B. C., on the orders of the tyrant Polycrates (d. 522), in order to carry water from a spring at the site of the village now known as Agiades, through the body of the hill (Mount Castro) separating it from his city on the southeast corner of the island.[4] In the modern era, the tunnel was excavated by Prince Constantine Adosidis in 1882, after the opening at the north end had been lost for many years. In 1883, the German archaeologist Ernst Fabricius surveyed the tunnel with great care, and published a full description of it the next year.[5] We can

* Unit for the History of Ideas, Nuffield Foundation, London. In visiting, studying, and photographing the tunnel of Eupalinus, we received much help and encouragement from the Department of Antiquities of His Majesty's Government of Greece, as well as from the civil and military authorities on the island of Samos. It gives us great pleasure to acknowledge their hospitality and assistance. We have also benefited from discussions with Derek J. de Solla Price about the instrumental problems involved in the construction of the tunnel.

[1] For example, William Keith Chambers Guthrie, *A History of Greek Philosophy* (Cambridge: Cambridge University Press, 1962), Ch. 1, pp. 174, 219; Giorgio de Santilana, *The Origins of Scientific Thought; from Anaximander to Proclus, 600 B.C. to 300 A.D.* (Chicago: University of Chicago Press, 1961. London, 1961), p. 25; W. H. G. Armytage, *A*

Social History of Engineering (London: Faber & Faber, 1961), p. 23.

[2] For example, John M. Cook, *The Greeks in Ionia and the East* (London: Praeger, 1962), pp. 118–119.

[3] Cf. Herodotus, *History of the Persian War*, Ch. 3, pp. 39–60.

[4] The site of the ancient city of Samos commanded the mile-wide straits separating the island from the Asia Minor mainland at the Trogilium Promontory. It is partly occupied today by the small port of Tigani (or " frying-pan "), so called because of the shape of the harbor, which still has Polycrates' mole as its " handle." Officially, the town was rechristened Pythagorion a few years ago, to celebrate the 2,500th anniversary of the Samian mathematician and philosopher.

[5] Ernst Fabricius, " Alterthümer auf der Insel Samos," *Mittheilungen der Archäologische Institut*, Athens, 1884, 9: 165–192. The most

confirm the excellence of his general description from a firsthand inspection of the tunnel, which remains today substantially as Fabricius found it. His account has only two notable deficiencies, both of which concern the south entrance. First, he fails to mention the single " ventilation shaft," which we discuss below. Second, his diagram shows the entrance passage to the ancient door as straight, whereas in fact it curves continuously.

The construction of the tunnel poses an intriguing intellectual problem, to which Fabricius drew attention but which he did not attempt to resolve. Almost exactly halfway through the mountain — 465 yards, or to be exact 425 meters, in from the south end — he reached a point at which the line of the tunnel, hitherto almost dead straight, turned at right angles, as shown in Figure 1.[6] After close inspection of the workings in the immediate neighborhood of this point, Fabricius argued convincingly that the construction of the tunnel had begun from opposite ends.[7] The question arises, by what technique was Eupalinus of Megara able to control the direction in which the two halves of the tunnel were dug, and to do this so precisely that they met in the heart of the mountain with an error of only a few feet in a thousand yards.

The current solution to this problem appears to have been put into circulation by van der Waerden,[8] and it has recently been repeated by de Santillana.[9] This solution, which we shall quote shortly, takes as its starting point the fact that the tunnel was constructed during the lifetime of Pythagoras,[10] and analyzes its construction as an application of Pythagorean geometry. Other writers, without following van der Waerden in detail, agree at any rate that " the tunnel of Eupalinus . . . presupposes definite geometrical propositions." [11] So far as we have been able to discover, the scholars who have adopted this solution have not themselves visited Samos, let alone inspected the layout of the tunnel and its relation to the surrounding terrain. Thus, it seemed important to us accordingly not to leave a matter of this kind on a purely speculative basis, but to check *in situ* the practicability and plausibility of the solution. We have had the opportunity to pay two visits to the tunnel, in 1958 and 1961: during the second of these, we spent nine days studying the construction of the tunnel and the

recent archaeological survey of the tunnel has been made by Wolfgang Kastenbein. See his " Stollen des Eupalinus auf Samos," *Deutsches Archäologische Institut Jahrbuch*, 1960, 75: 178–198.

[6] The photograph reproduced here was taken from immediately beyond this point: looking from the northern (and slightly higher) half of the tunnel into the southern (and slightly lower) half, which leads off to the right of the picture.

[7] This may be the significance of Herodotus' epithet " double-mouthed "; though this may just possibly allude to the fact that, at each end, the water conduit entered the tunnel at a separate point from the pedestrian entrance.

[8] Bertal Leendert van der Waerden, *Science Awakening*, translated by Arnold Dresden with additions by the author (Groningen: P. Noordhoff, 1954), pp. 102–105; but cf. W. Schmidt, " Nivellierinstrument und Tunnelbau im Altertume," *Bibliotheca Mathematica*, 1903, Series 3, 4: 7 ff.

[9] De Santillana, *loc. cit.*

[10] Though it is worth pointing out that Pythagoras left Samos " in order to escape from the tyranny of Polycrates," and had reputedly arrived in Italy by 529 .B. C.; cf. John Burnet, *Early Greek Philosophy* (3rd ed. London: A. & C. Black, 1930), p. 89.

[11] Guthrie, *op. cit.*, p. 219.

layout of the surrounding countryside, with this particular problem in mind. As a result, we conclude that van der Waerden's solution, while mathematically elegant, would for practical reasons have been extremely laborious

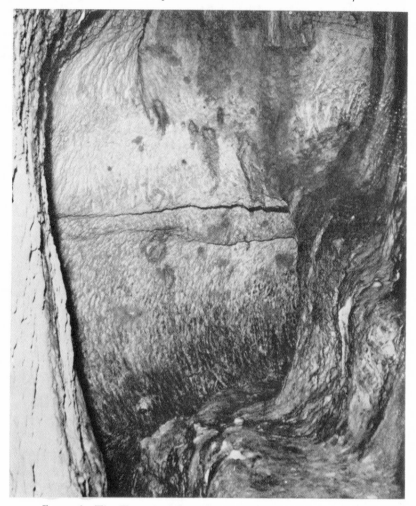

FIGURE 1. The Tunnel of Eupalinus. Junction of the two halves, looking from the northern end to the southern end.

— if not actually impossible — to carry through. Furthermore, a much more straightforward solution can be suggested, which involves no geometrical theorems, and moreover explains one fact about the siting of the tunnel that would otherwise remain a complete puzzle.

Van der Waerden's analysis of the problem reads as follows: [12]

Eupalinus did much better: his tunnel was essentially a straight line. How could this be accomplished?

The answer is found in the "Dioptra" of Heron of Alexandria (60 A. D.). Heron first describes a dioptra, i. e. a horizontal bar mounted so as to rotate, with two sights, which made it possible e. g. to sight a right angle in a

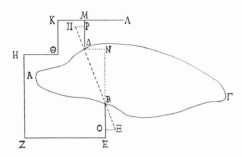

plane. Then he proposed the following problem (no. 15): "To cut through a mountain $AB\Gamma\Delta$ in a straight line, the openings B and Δ of the tunnel being given." He draws an arbitrary line BE in the plane, then, by means of the dioptra, the perpendicular EZ, next ZH perpendicular to EZ, and thus successively $H\Theta$, ΘK, $K\Lambda$. Now he moves the dioptra along the line $K\Lambda$, until the point Δ is sighted in a right angle. If this takes place at M, then $M\Delta$ will be perpendicular to $K\Lambda$.

Now drop the perpendicular ΔN from Δ on EB. Then ΔN can be determined from EZ, $H\Theta$ and KM; similarly BN can be found from BE, ZH, ΘK and $M\Delta$ by addition and subtraction. Consequently the ratio $BN : N\Delta$ is known; Heron gives for this ratio the value $5 : 1$. Now, he constructs right triangles $BO\Xi$ and $\Delta P\Pi$ whose legs have the same ratio $5 : 1$. The hypotenuses of these triangles then give the directions in which the digging must take place. "If the tunnel is dug in this manner," Heron concludes, "then the laborers will meet."

In no. 16, Heron also deals with the problem of making vertical shafts, to meet the tunnel, supposed to be rectilinear. Such shafts are indeed present on Samos.

Antique measuring instruments.

Eupalinus must also have been able to determine differences in altitude. It is quite likely that he did this like Heron and as we still do it: proceeding from point to point with vertical measuring rods and a horizontal sight. There were no telescopes; the sighting instrument must have been a dioptra. Heron obtains a level by means of communicating tubes.

The reader may think that this instrument is too clever for the era of Eupalinus; we are frequently inclined to think of the ancient Greeks as being more primitive than they actually were. We must remember that Anaximander of Milete, the pupil of Thales, had a workshop in which, among other things, wooden celestial spheres were manufactured. Anaximander also was commissioned to place a gnomon on the market place in Sparta, i. e. a vertical sundial, supplied of course with all the cleverly constructed hourlines and monthlines, which belonged there according to Vitruvius. This happened around 560, about thirty years before the construction of the tunnel on Samos.

---

[12] Van der Waerden, *op. cit.*, pp. 103–104.

This account is frankly based on a theoretical recipe formulated at least five hundred years after the actual building of the tunnel by Eupalinus. There is no internal evidence that Hero was relying on any traditional information about Eupalinus' methods; and no such information has come down to modern times. So, if he actually had the tunnel on Samos in mind, he was almost certainly in the same position as we are today: guessing how the work was done from circumstantial evidence alone. Accordingly, we cannot afford to treat Hero as an *authority* on the subject: in any case, given the likelihood that his concern with engineering problems was primarily theoretical, it is wise to reserve judgment about the merits of his recipe until its practicability has been checked on the ground.

We must ask three questions about van der Waerden's account. (*a*) Does it fit, accurately and in detail, the *actual facts* about the tunnel? (*b*) Would it have been *possible* to construct this particular tunnel according to Hero's recipe? (*c*) Would it have been *necessary* to do so?

a) On one significant point, van der Waerden's account is quite incorrect. Immediately after the main theorem, he adds: "In no. 16, Heron also deals with the problem of making vertical shafts, to meet the tunnel, supposed to be rectilinear. Such shafts are indeed present on Samos." [13] This is simply untrue: there are, in fact, no such shafts. Within the 1,100 yards of the tunnel proper, there is not one vertical shaft. Nor does Fabricius, on whose description van der Waerden relies, report finding any such shafts. At the southern end, outside the ancient doorway which guarded the entrance to the tunnel, there is a single vertical shaft (which Fabricius does not mention) whose function we discuss below; that is all. Once through the doorway, there is complete darkness, and through its entire length the square-sectioned tunnel is hewn through solid rock, far below ground (Fig. 2).

On this point, van der Waerden must have misread Fabricius. In the 1884 paper, to be sure, there is a reference to a number of vertical shafts; but this refers only to those in the ancillary surface conduits by which the water flowed, on the north side, from the reservoir to the tunnel, and, on the south side, from the tunnel to the town. These conduits are nowhere more than a few feet below ground, and no attempt was made to keep them rectilinear. Shafts were included so that the conduits could be periodically inspected and kept clear of debris carried down by the flow of water. In discussing these conduits, Fabricius makes this point quite clearly: "Zur Forderung des Schuttes waren in ungleichen Abständen [Dieselben varieren zwischen 22 und 80 Meter] Schachte angelegt, die gleichfalls entweder in den Fels gebrochen oder mit grossen Blöcken rechteckig ausgebaut sind." [14]

The fact that Hero's recipe no. 16 gives instructions for driving vertical shafts into a *rectilinear* tunnel, taken in conjunction with their complete

---

[13] *Ibid.*, p. 104.

[14] Fabricius, *op. cit.*, p. 174. " For the disposal of rubble, shafts were provided at irregular intervals (these vary between 22 and 80 meters), the shafts being either hewn into the rock or else built rectangularly from large stone blocks."

See Fabricius' map, Fig. 3. The inspection shafts on the conduits are marked by small dots.

absence from Eupalinus' tunnel, reinforces the suspicion that these recipes were put forward as *theoretical exercises*, and not as a report on the methods by which the tunnel on Samos was actually built.

FIGURE 2. The Tunnel of Eupalinus, showing square-sectioned outline. The ditch in which the water pipes were actually laid is seen in the middle foreground.

b) Would it have been possible to build the tunnel in this way? There are two parts to this question: (1) would Eupalinus have possessed instruments for taking the necessary vertical and horizontal sights with sufficient accuracy; and (2) would the nature of the surrounding terrain have permitted their use?

1) As van der Waerden recognizes, it would have been necessary to employ instruments for taking sights at right angles in a horizontal plane, and also for measuring vertical heights. In his opinion, both tasks could have been done with the *dioptra*, though for the first of these two tasks so sophisticated

an instrument would not have been strictly necessary. It is not impossible that Eupalinus had a *dioptra*, but, as we possess no description of this instrument earlier than Hero, there is no evidence or argument either way.

2) However, even given satisfactory instruments, there remains the more serious problem of the terrain. Van der Waerden's sketch map amounts to no more than an exercise in plane geometry, illustrating the theoretical basis of Hero's recipe. The moment one starts walking around on the site, the practical snags become apparent. If one is to construct the hypothetical right-angled plane triangle *inside* the mountain, one must keep on a constant horizontal contour *outside* it. This is next to impossible, as we found for ourselves. The western side of the mountain is extremely rough, being intersected with ravines. This again Fabricius confirms: " Im Westen war es aber höchst schwierig die Leitung am Berg herumzulegen, da gerade am linken Ufer des Baches in der Schlucht zwischen dem westlichen Ausläufer des Kastro und dem Kataruga senkrechte Felsen sich erheben." [15] To survey a series of similar triangles in such territory would *in practice* have been a problem in three-dimensional geometry. Eupalinus would have needed to take some hundreds of vertical sightings, in addition to the horizontal ones, before he could reproduce on the ground the proportions of Hero's similar triangles with sufficient accuracy.

c) In any case, there is, we believe, independent evidence that a more straightforward surveying technique was used to align two halves of the tunnel, involving fewer technical complications and relying on no abstract Pythagorean theorems. For there is one curious point to be noticed about the precise location of the tunnel. It was driven, not through the center, but through the western end of Mount Castro: as a result, the surface conduit on the north side doubles back for several hundred yards along the hillside after crossing the stream, before it enters the mountain. Also on the southern side the surface conduit had to be correspondingly lengthened in order to get the water to the town (see Fig. 3). If the directions for driving the two halves of the tunnel had been determined on Pythagorean principles, there is no reason why Eupalinus should not have driven through the mountain at any point he chose. By working a quarter of a mile further east, he could have shortened both the surface conduits, and brought the water out much nearer to its destination. Why did he not do so?

In the answer to this question, we suggest, lies the essential clue to Eupalinus' method. Having walked over Mount Castro several times by a variety of routes, we noticed one striking fact: the tunnel was built along one of the few lines by which one can climb easily and directly up the rugged southern hillside and then down the gentler northern slope to the valley behind. Specifically, the section of the hillside immediately behind the ancient town and harbor is far steeper and rougher than the section further west, through which the tunnel was actually driven.

---

[15] Fabricius, *op. cit.*, pp. 169–170. " To lead the aqueduct around the western side of the mountain was, however, very difficult, since there were sheer rocks rising vertically from the left bank of the brook in the gorge between the western spur of Castro and Cataruga."

The relevance of this fact to Eupalinus' practical problem is as follows: considering the problem as a straightforward matter of surveying, the most natural way to establish a line of constant direction across the mountain would have been to drive a line of posts into the ground, up one face of

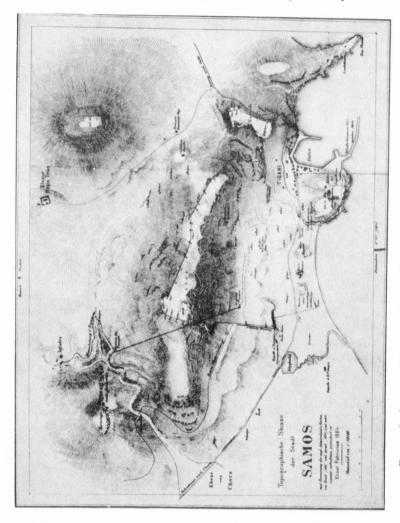

FIGURE 3. Layout of the tunnel and Tigani; from Fabricius, *op. cit.* The water conduits between Agiades and the "Eingang des Tunnels," and (at the southern end) from "Ausgang d. Tunnels," are marked ----------- .

the hill, across the top and down the other. Eupalinus was not building a Saint Gotthard: though Mount Castro presented an obstacle to the flow of water, it was not unclimbable. Along the actual line of the tunnel, there is in fact nothing to stop one aligning a series of posts by eye, to an overall accuracy of better than one degree. (This was the order of accuracy achieved by Eupalinus.) It is necessary only that a sufficient number of posts should be visible at any one time all the way across the mountain. If, on the other hand, the southern entrance had been any further east, a sufficient number of posts would not have been visible throughout, and the required accuracy could not have been achieved. The hillside immediately above the town is covered with steep scree and overhanging rocks, which would prevent one from keeping the posts visibly aligned for more than a few yards at a time. By locating the southern entrance a few hundred yards further west, these obstructions could be circumvented, and a direct line surveyed with accuracy straight over the hillside. And if this could be done, one may ask, why should Eupalinus have preferred Hero's more sophisticated and laborious recipe?

Eupalinus would, of course, have needed also to compare heights on the two sides of the hill. For this purpose, a direct traverse across the mountain would once again be less laborious than a geometrical survey round the western end. Having established the line of posts, one need only measure off the base of each post against that immediately below it, using a level; the rest is addition and subtraction.

Fundamentally, then, the problem facing Eupalinus was one of practical engineering, rather than one of geometrical theory. The undeniable fact that Pythagoras lived and taught on Samos during the same period has understandably tempted scholars to assume that, somehow or other, right-angled triangles must have entered into its construction. But local heroes often get more credit than they deserve, and Pythagoras is no exception. Near the southern entrance to the tunnel, there is a farmhouse with a mosaic floor of typical Roman Imperial workmanship: this is known locally as the *Loutra Pythagorou* (Baths of Pythagoras). Though we may never know for certain exactly how Eupalinus constructed the tunnel, it is certainly unwise to assume, without more positive evidence, that Pythagoras had anything to do with it.

We may end with another question. Once one has established the line of the tunnel *outside* the mountain, there remains the further practical problem of keeping to the same line *inside* the tunnel. From our inspection, it is not absolutely clear to us just how this was done; but it is possible that a pair of lights was used, like the leading lights in a harbor. If this is so, one of them can almost certainly be identified. We mentioned earlier the vertical shaft just outside the ancient entrance door at the southern end of the tunnel. This shaft illuminates the entrance passage, and the little patch of light so produced remains visible throughout the whole undamaged length of the southern half of the tunnel. Once the tunneling was well started, the direction could have been maintained simply by looking back along the stretch already dug, and keeping this spot of light properly centered. During the early stages, however, one light alone would be insufficient to fix the direction inside the mountain. On this point, Fabricius' detailed sketch plan of the tunnel is misleading.[16] It suggests that the entrance passage at the southern end of the tunnel (labeled *Ausgang*) is perfectly straight, so that one might line up the light from the vertical shaft against that coming down the entrance steps. In fact, it is slightly curved, so that this would have been impossible. How, then, was the interior line of work established? Was there a second vertical shaft? If so, we found no sign of it. Perhaps a sharp stake was driven through the shallow topsoil into the entrance chamber of the workings, either to occult the light from the surviving shaft or to mark the position for a second, artificial leading light. This, however, is a question which cannot be answered by guesswork alone.

[16] *Ibid.*, Tafel VIII.

EUPALINOS AND HIS TUNNEL

By B. L. van der Waerden[*]

In my book *Science Awakening*[1] I described the tunnel constructed about 530 B.C. by Eupalinos on the island of Samos. This tunnel was dug from both ends, and the working men met in the center. On page 103 I raised the question: "How could this be accomplished?" and answered it, following J. Bidez, by quoting a passage from the *Dioptra* of Heron of Alexandria. In an article in *Isis*[2] June Goodfield and Stephen Toulmin criticized my analysis of the tunnel alignment problem.

Let me first state that in the main point Goodfield and Toulmin are right. The tunnel of Eupalinos was probably not constructed by the method indicated by Heron. Also, I admit that I have misread Fabricius, and that his mention of vertical shafts does not refer to the tunnel itself but to the ancillary surface conducts north and south of the tunnel.

On the other hand, I want to point out that Goodfield and Toulmin are wrong on two other points. In the first place, they state that my proposed solution "takes as its starting point the fact that the tunnel was constructed during the lifetime of Pythagoras and analyzes its construction as an application of Pythagorean geometry."[3] I can assure that I never connected the construction of the tunnel with Pythagoras or "Pythagorean geometry." My starting point was quite different. My attention to the fact that the tunnel was dug from two sides and that the working men met at the center was drawn by Bidez, whose book *Eos; ou, Platon et l'orient* I have quoted in a footnote.[4] Bidez had already indicated a possible connection between the project of Eupalinos and the *Dioptra* of Heron. I studied Fabricius and Heron and worked out the idea of Bidez. I never dreamt of connecting it with the reputed stay of Pythagoras at Samos during the tyranny of Polykrates.

The expression "Pythagorean geometry" may mean either "the geometry

* Universität Zürich.

1 B. L. van der Waerden, *Science Awakening* (Groningen: Noordhoff, 1954; 2nd ed., 1961).

2 June Goodfield and Stephen Toulmin, "How Was the Tunnel of Eupalinus Aligned?" *Isis*, 1965, *56*:46–55.

3 *Ibid.*, p. 47.

4 (Brussels: M. Hayez, 1945) quoted in *Science Awakening*, p. 103.

of Pythagoras" or "the geometry of the Pythagoreans." The *mathematikoi* among the Pythagoreans lived after Hippasos, hence after 500 B.C. Therefore I shall assume, for the sake of argument, that Goodfield and Toulmin meant the geometry of Pythagoras. Now on page 103 of my book, just before the section on the tunnel, I expressly said that we know "nothing at all about his geometry." So it would be absurd to use this geoemtry to explain the project of Eupalinos. My book may contain errors and uncertain hypotheses, but not such absurdities.

If there is any historical connection between the mathematics Eupalinos used and the mathematics of Pythagoras and his followers, it would be, in my opinion, just the other way around. In the same book I have written:

Surveyors and architects, such as Eupalinos, had to know something of geometry, and the training of instrument makers in the workshop of Anaximander undoubtedly involved astronomy. But (according to the Proclos tradition) Pythagoras freed mathematics from these practical applications. The Pythagoreans pursued mathematics as a kind of religious contemplation, as a way to approach the eternal Truth.[5]

The second point in which Goodfield and Toulmin are wrong is their statement concerning Heron of Alexandria: "So, if he actually had the tunnel of Samos in mind, he was almost certainly in the same position as we are today: guessing how the work was done from circumstantial evidence alone."[6]

Bidez supposed (and I think he is right) that Eupalinos must have submitted a project to Polykrates; he must have persuaded Polykrates that it could be done and that the cost would not be too high. The project might have existed in several copies, one of which perhaps found its way into the library of Alexandria. So it is not true that Heron was "almost certainly in the same position

as we are today." Heron was not a historian of science, but a professor of engineering and applied mathematics. In his works he gives a sober account of existing instruments and known methods; guesswork was not much in his line.

Bidez' own words are:

Eupalinos travailla à Samos, vers l'an 530, au service du tyran Polycrate. Les hommes compétents que le tyran ne manqua pas de consulter avant de tenter la coûteuse entreprise méditée par l'ingénieur de Mégare se seraient montrés fort réservés sans doute, à l'appui du projet, ils n'avaient pas vu des calculs de nature à les rassurer. Le milieu dont Eupalinos avait à gagner la confiance était trop accoutumé aux opérations d'une géométrie assez avancée déjà, pour que nous puissions lui dénier une connaissance plus ou moins rudimentaire de méthodes et d'instruments de travail analogues aux pratiques et à l'outillage décrits chez Héron.[7]

I still feel that Bidez' point of view is perfectly reasonable. Eupalinos must have made a project, and in order to persuade Polykrates he must have given some publicity to it. It is not likely that Heron, living as he did in Alexandria, in completely flat country, would figure out a project for a tunnel; but it is perfectly possible that Eupalinos, living in Megara and making a project for a tunnel on the island of Samos, invented a method for determining the direction of the tunnel. He might have sent copies of the project to people in positions to influence Polykrates. Later on, when Eupalinos came to Samos to build the tunnel, he might have seen that there was a better method to determine the direction.

This note is not written to renew the argument about the tunnel (for I feel it has been decided by the investigations of the Toulmins), but to give due credit to the idea of Bidez and to show that a connection between Eupalinos and Heron is not at all impossible.

5 *Science Awakening,* p. 105.
6 *Op. cit.,* p. 50.
7 *Eos* . . . , p. 13.

The Tunnel of Eupalinus and the Tunnel Problem of Hero of Alexandria

By Alfred Burns*

I

THE FOLLOWING DISCUSSION of the Tunnel of Eupalinus on the Greek island of Samos relies heavily on Ernst Fabricius' original description,[1] the excellent photographs and descriptions by June Goodfield and Stephen Toulmin,[2] Wolfgang Kastenbein's meticulous survey,[3] and to some extent on my own investigations on the site. In addition to the modern descriptions, it is also important to keep Herodotus' account in mind:

> I have dwelt rather long on the history of the Samians because theirs are the three greatest works (*ergasmata*) of all the Greeks. One is a tunnel (*orygma amphistomon*) through the base of a nine hundred foot high mountain. The tunnel's length is seven stades, its height and length both eight feet. Throughout its length another cutting (*orygma*) has been dug (*orōryktai*) three feet wide and three feet deep, through which the water flowing in pipes is led into the city from an abundant spring. The builder (*architektōn*) of the tunnel was the Megarian Eupalinus, son of Naustrophus. This is one of the three, the second is a jetty around the harbor in twenty fathoms of water more than two stades long. Their third work is the largest of all temples we have seen. Its original architect was Rhoecus son of Phileus. Because of these accomplishments I have carried my account of the Samians to greater length.[4]

The admiration expressed by Herodotus, the good preservation of the tunnel, the exact confirmation of Herodotus' description, and, perhaps most of all, the surprise discovery of the tunnel's two-way construction have made it a fascinating subject of

* Department of European Languages, University of Hawaii, Honolulu, Hawaii 96822.

I want to express my deep appreciation to Dr. A. G. Drachmann for his invaluable advice and suggestions. I also want to thank Professors Anthony Raubitschek of Stanford University, B. L. van der Waerden of Zürich University, and Ulf Jantzen of the German Archaeological Institute in Athens for their kind assistance, and the Bibliothèque Nationale in Paris for permission to use the illustration in the Mynas Codex. Continued study of ancient engineering structures has been made possible through a grant

by the National Science Foundation.

[1] Ernst Fabricius, "Altertümer auf der Insel Samos," *Mitteilungen des Deutschen Archäologischen Institutes in Athen*, 1884, 9:165–192.

[2] June Goodfield and Stephen Toulmin, "How Was the Tunnel of Eupalinus Aligned?" *Isis*, 1965, 56:45–56.

[3] Wolfgang Kastenbein, "Untersuchungen am Stollen des Eupalinos," *Archäologischer Anzeiger*, 1960, 75:178–198.

[4] Herodotus, *Histories* 3.60 (the translation is mine).

speculation in the ninety years since its rediscovery. Most of the tunnel's problems remain unsolved:

1. What mathematical methods were used to plan direction and slope?
2. Once determined, how was the plan executed?
3. Why were the pipes laid in a special secondary tunnel rather than simply on the main tunnel's floor?
4. Does construction of the tunnel shed any light on the status of mathematics in Samos during the late sixth century B.C., and thus possibly on Pythagoras' connection with mathematics?
5. Hero of Alexandria, writing about six hundred years later on practical mathematical problems, offers a solution to the problem of how "to dig through a mountain in a straight line when the mouths of the tunnel on the mountain are given."[5] Does Hero's problem refer to our tunnel?

II

Herodotus tells us nothing about how the tunnel was built and no other specific mention of the tunnel has come down to us from antiquity. Fabricius, the first modern investigator to measure the tunnel, gave us an accurate description in 1884. Kastenbein in 1960, having used up-to-date surveying methods, made only minor corrections to Fabricius' measurements and added the important data of elevation which Fabricius had been unable to obtain.[6] The apparently unique and most intriguing feature of the tunnel—the fact that it was constructed from both sides according to an accurately calculated and precisely executed plan—had already been noted by Fabricius.

Tunnels and underground water-supply systems were nothing new to the sixth century B.C. A four-mile underground drainage channel from Lake Copais in Greece to the sea dates back to Mycenaean times. In Jerusalem, the spring of Siloam was diverted into the city underground when it was threatened by Senacherib, the Assyrian, in the eighth century B.C. That tunnel too was built from both sides to a meeting, as is attested by the oldest known Hebrew inscription, but it was a crude trial-and-error affair with many false starts in wrong directions and took 1,500 feet to cover a distance of 1,000 feet. An underground conduit system was built in Megara under the tyrant Theagenes late in the seventh century. It has been conjectured that Eupalinus, a native of Megara, was brought to Samos because of his experience with this type of construction in his hometown; we know nothing, however, about the tunnel in Megara. A tunnel in Athens, of similar construction and contemporary with the one on Samos, has not been explored far enough to learn much about the way it was planned, and there is no evidence to indicate that it was built from two sides.

The proof for the simultaneous construction from both ends of the Tunnel of Eupalinus is found in its greatest irregularity, which is the place of juncture near the center. Actually, the part of the tunnel dug from the south, after turning slightly to the right (east), comes to a dead end; the pick marks can still be seen on the blind headwall that terminates it. Short of this wall the tunnel coming from the north, which has also turned east, breaks into the south tunnel through its western sidewall. In other

[5] Hero, *Dioptra*, Ch. 15. Throughout I will be referring to the edition by Hermann Schöne, *Herons Dioptra: Herons von Alexandria Ver-* *messungslehre und Dioptra* (Leipzig:Teubner, 1902–1903).

[6] Kastenbein, "Eupalinos," p. 182.

words, a few feet before meeting, both tunnel halves turn somewhat to the east and thus meet almost at a right angle. In addition, at the meeting place, the floor of the north tunnel is about even with the ceiling of the south tunnel. Besides this difference in elevation, according to Kastenbein's calculations the two tunnels would have met head-on in a straight line had they not turned east just short of their meeting.

Kastenbein offers two possible explanations for this irregularity. In mining it is a common occurrence that sounds underground are distorted by the configuration of the rock formation so that they seem to come from a different location than their actual place of origin. Thus, the diggers might have heard each other, but could have been deceived into believing that the sounds were coming from the east. The second possibility is that because of an error in the builder's calculations it appeared that the tunnels should have met already, and consequently the two groups started looking for each other. A third possibility occurs to me: realizing that with the slightest directional error the two tunnels would bypass each other, the builder made the two work parties turn obliquely to the same side; then they would *have to meet* provided they were in the same plane. In any event, the error, intentional or not, is very minor: essentially, through almost their entire length, the two halves of the tunnel are perfectly in line, attesting to the accuracy of the builder's calculations. It should also be mentioned that according to Kastenbein's survey the elevation of the north entrance is 6 feet higher than that of the south exit.

The water pipes were laid in a channel along the east wall of the tunnel. Where the water channel enters the tunnel close to the north entrance, it was dug as a trench about 4 feet deep, but as its depth increases progressively to 25 feet at the south exit, it becomes a second tunnel driven through bedrock under the first, connected with the main tunnel by shafts at regular intervals and in places where its roof has collapsed. Fabricius was the first to raise the question of the need for this second tunnel and suggested that it had become necessary because an error in planning had provided insufficient slope for good flow within the tunnel. Fabricius was quite reluctant to impute such an error to an engineer who had been skillful enough to accomplish the successful junction under the mountain. Accordingly, he offers several explanations for the error: (a) construction of the underground reservoir might have been an after-thought when work on the tunnel had already started and could have lowered the source of the flow; (b) the wish to provide the highest possible terminal above the city, to facilitate the distribution of the water to all parts of town, might have induced the error. Fabricius also noticed that most of the covered water channels were about 6 feet high, just sufficient to allow passage of a man, but that at the south exit the channel was 9 feet deep. He considered this an indication that the channel was deepened later to improve the flow and also further evidence that the channel was dug afterward by trial and error, to correct the original underestimate of the degree of slope required.

Kastenbein, as well as Goodfield and Toulmin, quote and accept Fabricius' explanation. In doing so, however, they ignore the fact pointed out by Fabricius him-self in a later article: that similar underground conduit systems in Syracuse, Acragas, and Athens show the same double-tunnel construction.[7] Doerpfeld, in 1894, called

---

[7] E. Fabricius, "Eupalinos," in Pauly-Wissova,   Vol. VI (Stuttgart:J. B. Metzler, 1894–1963),
Realencyclopädie der Altertumswissenschaften,   Col. 1159.

attention to the similarity of the water system for the Enneacrounos in Athens, dating from the same period, to the one on Samos.[8] There, too, two tunnels were found, one above the other with the lower one containing the identical type of pipes as found in the Tunnel of Eupalinus; both tunnels were connected by vertical shafts. Thus, it becomes difficult to ascribe this building method to an error, and we rather must assume that it was intentional and customary. Indeed, Carl Curtius conjectured that ventilation was the reason for this type of construction. All Greek and Roman aqueduct systems have airshafts at regular intervals, This is true even as early as the Mycenaean system for Lake Copais, which had at least twenty airshafts to the surface.[9] It also should be noted that the covered trench-type channels to and from the Tunnel of Eupalinus were provided with regularly placed access shafts. Even Roman aboveground aqueducts had such shafts, and Vitruvius prescribes an opening every 120 feet.[10] Accordingly, it is Curtius' opinion that in places where it was impossible to reach the surface with airshafts (such as under a mountain) the upper tunnel was built to assure ventilation.

Curtius may be right and the need for ventilation may have played a part, but the primary reason for the shafts was certainly more basic. The original way to build an underground passage was to sink shafts and then connect them. In Asia Minor and Iran this is the method by which tunnels, the so-called *qanats*, are driven into the mountains to tap the groundwater trapped in the rock strata for irrigation purposes. It is a technique that has been continuously in use, possibly since the second millennium B.C.[11] The Mycenaean drainage tunnels for Lake Copais similarly connected shafts that were needed not only to bring the excavated material to the surface, but also subsequently for access to keep the passages free from obstructions. Where pipes or conduits were used, they had to be periodically maintained and replaced. Therefore, shafts probably came before the need for ventilation was recognized through experience in mining. Thus, it may well be that in the sixth century, when Pisistratus and Polycrates had their tunnels built, ventilation was considered, but the primary reason for the double construction was probably the difficulty of holding a constant slope of less than 1% in the depth of a mountain with primitive instruments. (Vitruvius[12] prescribes a minimum slope of 0.5%, but even in his time—the late first century B.C.— contemporary aqueducts show inexplicable error margins in slopes varying from 0.001% to 24.7% not caused by terrain factors.[13]) Various types of levels, however, were an effective aid in maintaining the horizontal. It was necessary to get through the mountain first in level tunneling; then, from this base, one could dig a sloping trench or second tunnel with the customary shafts by trial and error or by increasing the depth by a certain increment over each unit of distance.

Fabricius had no means of measuring elevation and assumed that the main tunnel had a slope. When Kastenbein's first professional triangulations showed that the north entrance is 6 feet higher in elevation than the south exit, Goodfield and Toulmin, who

[8] Wilhelm Doerpfeld, "Die Ausgrabungen an der Enneakrunos," *Athenische Mitteilungen*, 1894, *19*:144–146.

[9] As quoted by Augustus C. Merriam, "A Greek Tunnel of the 6th Century B.C.," *The School of Mines Quarterly* (New York), 1885, 4:272.

[10] Vitruvius, *On Architecture* 8. 6. 7.

[11] R. J. Forbes, *Studies in Ancient Technology*, Vol. II (Leiden:Brill, 1965), p. 11.

[12] Vitruvius, *On Architecture* 8. 6. 1.

[13] Abbott Payson Usher, *A History of Mechanical Inventions* (Harvard:Harvard Univ. Press, 1966), p. 148.

made no measurements of their own, assumed that a slope must have been planned. But this 6-foot difference in elevation at the exits is the same difference as at the point of juncture at the center, where the floor of the north tunnel is level with the 6-foot-high ceiling of the south tunnel. Consequently, it is quite clear that the two tunnel halves are almost horizontal (actually they sag very slightly toward the center) and were meant to be horizontal.

III

The only clue from antiquity about how the tunnel might have been designed comes from Hero of Alexandria, in the first century A.D. In his *Dioptra*, Chapter 15, Hero poses the problem of digging through a mountain in a straight line when the mouths of the tunnel on the mountain are given. Later he indicates that the digging can be done from either side or from both. His last sentence in the chapter, however, indicates that he had construction from both ends especially in mind: if the digging is done in this manner, the workers will meet.[14] He solves the problem by means of the instrument which gives the book its name—the dioptra, which is a surveyor's instrument combining a theodolite with a water-level.[15] The instrument is highly sophisticated, probably invented by Hero himself, but seems never to have been used in antiquity.[16] Hero's proposed solution consists essentially in a series of right-angle offset horizontal sightings and measurements around the mountain. The angle of attack from both sides is determined by laying out on the ground, at the tunnel endpoints, two triangles similar to each other and to an imaginary triangle formed within the mountain by the actual line of the tunnel and an arbitrarily assumed base line.[17]

Hero mentions no specific tunnel, and no evidence exists in his writings that he had the Tunnel of Eupalinus in mind or that he even knew the tunnel. The temptation, nevertheless, is great to connect Hero's problem with our tunnel since Herodotus had made it the best known tunnel in the Greek world.[18] Relationships between Samos and Egypt had always been close, as we shall show later. Wilhelm Schmidt, in 1903, therefore suggested that the tunnel was designed as described by Hero,[19] and his suggestion was accepted by Bidez, van der Waerden, and others[20] and remained undisputed until recently. When Kastenbein and Goodfield and Toulmin, however, visited the tunnel, they raised serious doubts about this assumption.

Kastenbein made his survey in 1958 and published his findings in 1960. As a professional mining engineer, he made no pretenses of being a classicist or an historian of

---

[14] *Dioptra*, ed. Schöne, Vol. III (1903), pp. 238–241.

[15] This instrument has been described by A. G. Drachmann in "Dioptra" in Pauly-Wissova, *Realencyclopädie*, Suppl. Vol. VI, 1287–1290, and in his "Heron's Dioptra and Levelling-Instrument" in *A History of Technology*, Vol. III (Oxford: Clarendon Press, 1957), pp. 609–612.

[16] See A. G. Drachmann, *The Mechanical Technology of Greek and Roman Antiquity* (Copenhagen: Munksgaard, 1963), p. 198, and A. G. Drachmann, "A Detail of Heron's Dioptra," *Centaurus*, 1969, *13*: 243.

[17] B. L. van der Waerden, *Science Awakening*,

trans. Arnold Dresden (Oxford: Oxford Univ. Press, 1961), pp. 103–104; also quoted in Goodfield and Toulmin, "How Was the Tunnel Aligned?" p. 49.

[18] *Cf.* Aristotle, *Politics* 5. 11, referring to the building activity of Polycrates on Samos.

[19] Wilhelm Schmidt, "Nivellierinstrument und Tunnelbau im Altertume," *Bibliotheca Mathematica*, 1903, Ser. *3–4*: 7–11.

[20] J. Bidez, *Eos, Platon et l'Orient* (Brussels: M. Hayez, 1945), p. 12; van der Waerden, *Science Awakening*, p. 103; Giorgio de Santillana, *The Origins of Scientific Thought, from Anaximander to Proclus, 600 B.C. to 300 A.D.* (Chicago: Univ. Chicago Press, 1961), p. 25.

science. He made a highly competent survey and judged from an engineering point of view how the layout of the tunnel could have been accomplished in the easiest fashion. If he was familiar with Hero's problem 15, he gave no indication in his first article. Kastenbein came to the conclusion that the easiest method of establishing the direction of the tunnel would have been to plant a row of poles over the mountain. The elevation of the endpoints could have been found by measuring up from a base line established by surveying around the western end of Mt. Kastro. This would have involved sighting along the south slope of the mountain toward the west at the edge of the coastal plain, then north through the streambed which separates Mt. Kastro from Mt. Kataruga— quite a tricky procedure, as Kastenbein says. In a second article, in 1966, however, Kastenbein acknowledges the feasibility of Hero's method and states that a decision as to which method was actually used is impossible.[21]

June Goodfield, writing in 1964, flatly denies that the tunnel could have been planned in the manner described by Hero.[22] Her conclusions are based on the following considerations:

• Hero's construction would not have solved the problem of slope.

• The roughness of the terrain would have made surveying around the west end of the mountain impossible.

• The site of the tunnel, far toward the western end of the city rather than above the city center, indicates that the location must have been chosen for a special reason. The reason for the choice, she believes, was the fact that this was the only place on the mountain where it was easy to run a straight line of poles over the ridge between the endpoints of the tunnel (as described by Kastenbein). To determine elevation one could sight horizontally from the foot of one pole to the next pole and measure the height intercepted. Thus the problem of distance and elevation would become simply one of addition and subtraction, without any need for more sophisticated mathematics:

> It has been suggested that his theory of similar triangles was applied to the building of the tunnel. The only evidence for this comes from Hero of Alexandria, who lived 600 years later. Hero was noted for thinking up charming theoretical solutions for difficult practical problems, and he gives as a theoretical exercise a method for aligning a tunnel.[23]

A year later in the *Isis* article written jointly by June Goodfield and her husband, Stephen Toulmin, they repeat essentially the same arguments, taking specific issue with van der Waerden's presentation of the view that the tunnel might have been built by use of the principles described by Hero, and also with the implication that "Pythagorean" mathematics might have played a part.[24]

Most recent scholars consider Hero not an elegant theorist but a practical engineer,[25] and his works handbooks for the working engineer and architect.[26] This is why Hero's

[21] W. Kastenbein, "Markscheiderische Messungen im Dienste der Archäologischen Forschung," *Mitteilungen aus dem Markscheidewesen*, 1966, *73*:26–36.

[22] June Goodfield, "The Tunnel of Eupalinus," *Scientific American*, 1964, *210* (No. 6):104–112.

[23] *Ibid.*, p. 112.

[24] Goodfield and Toulmin, "How Was the Tunnel Aligned?" p. 52.

[25] E.g., Edmond R. Kiely, *Surveying Instruments, Their History* (New York:Columbia Univ. Teachers College, Bureau of Publications, 1947), p. 19.

[26] Thomas Heath, *A History of Greek Mathematics*, Vol. II (Oxford:Clarendon Press, 1921), p. 307.

writings enjoyed popularity and influence into Roman times and the Middle Ages while the abstract mathematics of Archimedes was all but forgotten.[27] Giorgio de Santillana sees Hero expressing contempt for pure theory,[28] and Otto Neugebauer considers Hero a typical practitioner of the Egyptian-Mesopotamian mainstream of cooking-recipe mathematics which continued into the Arabic and Indian tradition, only superficially influenced by the axiomatic mathematics of the Hellenistic school.[29] It is for this reason that the objection of the six-hundred-year interval between the construction of the tunnel and Hero's writings loses much of its validity. The surveying methods that Hero described were the same that had been in use for many centuries.[30] In his *Dioptra* he only shows that all the ordinary problems, for which the *groma* and the leveling instruments with line and plummet were used, could be better solved by application of his instrument.[31] The *groma*, of Egyptian origin, and the *chorobates* both seem to predate the construction of the tunnel.[32] Thus it would appear that Hero is very much part of an engineering tradition that had not changed much in the intervening time.[33]

The view that the site was chosen because of its relative suitability for aligning a row of poles over the mountain is not fully convincing. The purpose of the tunnel was to bring a safe water supply within the city walls. So long as the tunnel exit was within the fortification, this purpose was achieved. From the tunnel's mouth a conduit had to be laid along the slope in an east-westerly direction, paralleling the length of the city, so that branch lines could be run downhill to feed all parts of the city. It would not have made any difference whether the tunnel ended above the city center and conduits had to be laid from there, both to the east and to the west, or if the tunnel came out in the west and a single longer conduit had to be run from there toward the eastern end. Essentially, the tunnel follows the straight and shortest line from the spring in Agiades to the closest point within the city walls. The only notable exception is the detour around the streambed below the north entrance. A move of the tunnel exit to the east would have lengthened the tunnel. The obvious objective was to keep the length of the tunnel to a minimum. The labor of digging a trench-type channel outside of the mountain was insignificant in comparison with tunnelling through solid rock. Consequently it would seem that the only determining factor in site selection was the required length of the tunnel.

Although the slope is quite steep and rocky, there is no doubt that the method of measuring *over* the mountain, proposed by Kastenbein and Goodfield and Toulmin, is quite possible. Is the other method of measuring *around* the mountain, as suggested by Hero, also feasible? In his second article Kastenbein did not rule out the possibility, and he refrained from making a judgment which would favor one method over the

[27] Otto Neugebauer, *The Exact Sciences in Antiquity* (Providence, R. I.: Brown Univ. Press, 1957), p. 146.
[28] De Santillana, *Origins of Scientific Thought*, p. 276. *Cf. Herons Belopoiica*, ed. H. Diels and E. Schramm (Abhandlungen der preussischen Akademie der Wissenschaften) (Berlin, 1918), Ch. 1.
[29] Neugebauer, *Exact Sciences*, p. 80.
[30] *Ibid.*
[31] Kiely, *Surveying Instruments*, p. 28.

[32] *Ibid.*, p. 14. The *groma* consists of a rectangular cross suspended horizontally at its fulcrum, with plumblines hanging down from the four endpoints, and serves to lay out directions at right angles to each other in the field. *chorobates* is a levelling instrument shaped like a four-legged wooden bench; it may be levelled either by aid of plumblines suspended from it or by observance of the level of water in an appropriate depression in its upper surface.
[33] Usher, *Mechanical Inventions*, pp. 98-99.

other.[34] I believe the difficulties of the terrain on the west slope have been overstated. There is a considerable difference between difficult and impossible, and it is hard to tell where the line should be drawn. I was able to walk on a fairly horizontal traverse around the western end of Mt. Kastro in less than a hour. There are no overhanging rocks on the west slope, and whatever rocky outcroppings there are offered no serious obstacles to anyone willing to scramble over them. I also think it is a mistake to assume that the terrain has always been as we find it today. In 2,500 years erosion has taken its toll. In antiquity, before the hillsides were denuded of vegetation, they may have been covered with a thick layer of topsoil. A portion of the ancient bay has been filled by silt, and the modern town of Pythagorion is built on alluvial land that used to be part of the ancient harbor.[35] All this material can have come only from the mountain above the city whose slopes once stretched to the sea. Thus, we have no assurance that the terrain features in antiquity were the same we see today, but even if they were similar, they would not have offered any insurmountable obstacles. For instance, in plotting the similar triangles at the tunnel exits, it would have been possible to erect poles or rough wooden scaffolds to compensate for the differences in elevation and thus to obtain level measurements without resorting to "hundreds of vertical measurements."[36]

I also believe that much confusion has been created by drawings that have been reconstructed by modern editors to illustrate Hero's problem 15. Figure 1 shows Fabricius' map, whereas Figure 2 is a drawing by van der Waerden for his English version of *Science Awakening*, which was subsequently used by Santillana and then by Goodfield and Toulmin in their *Isis* article.[37] A comparison of Figures 1 and 2 shows instantly the influence of Fabricius' map. The outline of the mountain and the angle of the tunnel are the same. The important feature to note is that van der Waerden's drawing shows sightings around the *west* side of the mountain. (The author has apparently not seen the drawing in the codex.) Figure 3 is taken from Hermann Schöne's *Herons Dioptra*, which has been the standard edition ever since its publication in 1902. From this drawing the following is evident: Schöne either was not familiar with the tunnel on Samos or, more likely, he chose not to refer Hero's problem to any specific tunnel (he never mentions the Tunnel of Eupalinus). We know, however, that Schöne was familiar with the sketch in the codex (Fig. 4), and this is clearly reflected in his own drawing, which shows the sightings around the *eastern* end of the mountain. We also can see that the similar right triangles are constructed as they are in the codex, while van der Waerden's are reversed. Figure 4 is a reproduction of the actual drawing in the Mynas Codex (Paris, Bibliothèque Nationale, Supl. Grec No. 607), dating from the eleventh or twelfth century.[38] This is the primary manuscript from which all other existing ones are derived.[39] The drawing shows measurements around the *east* side of the mountain. Now, if one concedes any significance to

[34] Kastenbein, "Markscheiderische Messungen," *loc. cit.*

[35] Ulf Jantzen, "Samos 1966," *Archäologischer Anzeiger*, 1967, *82*:278.

[36] Goodfield and Toulmin, "How Was the Tunnel Aligned?" p. 52.

[37] Van der Waerden, *Science Awakening*, p. 103; de Santillana, *Origins of Scientific Thought*, p. 25; Goodfield and Toulmin, "How Was the Tunnel Aligned?" p. 49.

[38] Drachmann, *Mechanical Technology of Antiquity*, p. 163.

[39] Drachmann, "A Detail," p. 241.

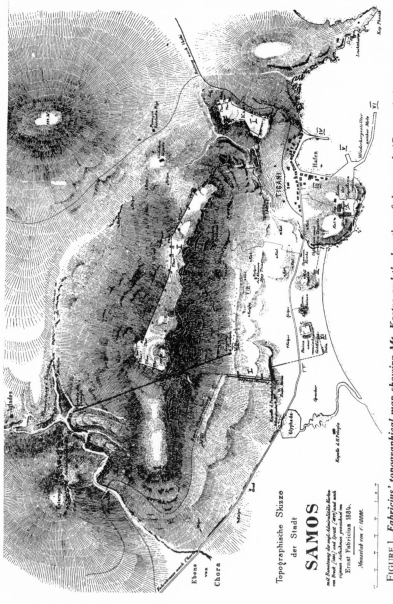

Topographische Skizze
der Stadt

SAMOS

mit Benutzung der engl. Admiralitäts-Karten
von Brock (1861) und Spratt (1857) und nach
eigenen Aufnahmen gezeichnet von
Ernst Fabricius 1884.

Maasstab von 1:10000.

FIGURE 1. Fabricius' topographical map showing Mt. Kastro and the location of the tunnel. (By permission of the German Archaeological Institute in Athens.)

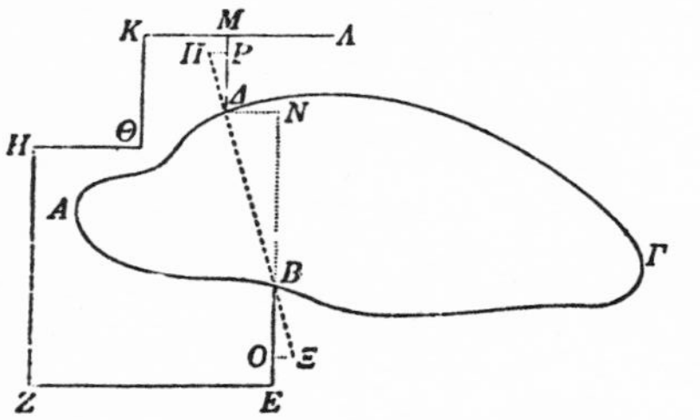

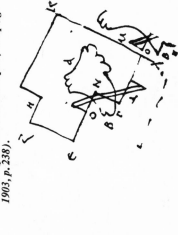

FIGURE 3. Schöne's drawing of the layout of the tunnel (from Herons Dioptra, Leipzig: Teubner, 1903, p.238).

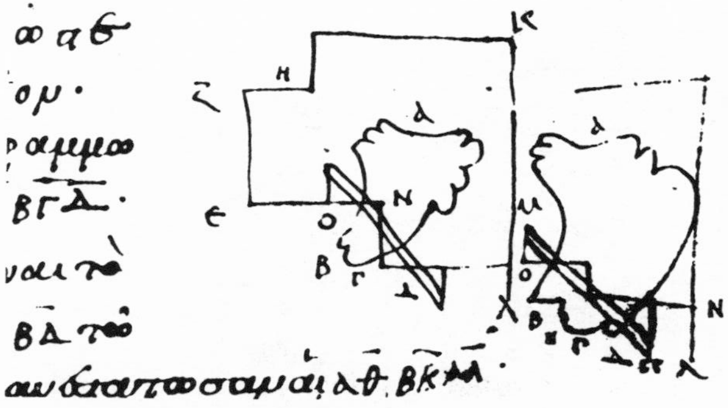

FIGURE 4a

FIGURE 4. Photographic reproduction of the drawing in the Mynas Codex, Dioptra, Ch. 15; 4a is the drawing oriented with Fabricius' map. (By permission of the Bibliotheque Nationale, Paris.)

FIGURE 2. Van der Waerden's drawing of the layout of the tunnel (from Science Awakening, Oxford: Oxford Univ. Press, 1961, p. 103).

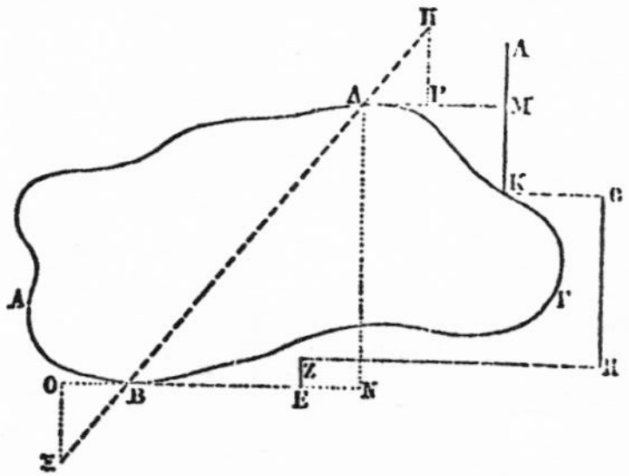

FIGURE 4

the drawing in the codex, the argument—which is based on the difficulty of the terrain on the west slope of the mountain—collapses. The eastern circuit is somewhat longer but, I believe, a much easier route. A wide plain stretches from Agiades toward the east, where a relatively gentle saddle leads toward the south side of Mt. Kastro. From there, I believe, the traverse west to the exit of the tunnel is quite straight. I have to admit, however, that at the time of my visit I had not seen the codex drawing and was only familiar with van der Waerden's sketch. Consequently, like everyone else, I never investigated the eastern circuit around the mountain. An experimental survey over this route would be definitely required before any conclusions are drawn.

This brings us to the crucial question: can any weight as evidence be given to the manuscript drawing for or against the conjecture that Hero's problem refers to the Tunnel of Eupalinus? First we must ask the question whether there is any resemblance between the drawing and the actual situation on Samos. I believe that, allowing for a certain amount of distortion, sufficient similarities exist when we compare the codex drawing with Fabricius' map to conclude that the author of the sketch, or the author of the source from which this drawing was copied, appears to have been aware of the topography and the layout of the tunnel on Samos. The following resemblances seem too numerous to be ascribed to coincidence:

1. The direction of the tunnel in relation to the mountain is quite correct.
2. The location of the tunnel near the west end of the mountain is fairly correct.
3. The three fingerlike ridges jutting from the mountain toward the northwest can be clearly recognized on both the drawing and the map.
4. To a lesser degree this holds true for the cliffs at the southwest and east ends of the mountain.
5. The angles of the sightings around the east side of the mountain would be approximately correct.

The foreshortening of the east-west dimension and the exaggerated bulge of the mountain toward the north, as well as the shifting of the tunnel entrance to the south-west of the three finger ridges, would have to be ascribed to the distortion that is to be expected in repeated copyings by scribes, unfamiliar with the true situation and most likely unable to understand the subject matter. Some of the distortions, as A. G. Drachmann has pointed out to me, are readily explainable by the way the drawing was made. It seems the draftsman drew the straight lines first and then tried to fit the out-line of the mountain onto them. But since he missed the important point of intersection between the tunnel line and the outline of the mountain at Delta, he tried a second time (in the drawing at the right), but failed this time to have his two similar right triangles originate at the Delta intersection. Because the angles are approximately 45°, Dr. Drachmann believes that the original from which the freehand sketch was copied must have been drawn with the help of a triangle: he considers that an indication that the drawing might have been a purely theoretical illustration. It seems to me, however, that the identifiable resemblances are too numerous to be all ascribed to coincidence, and it might have been the very use of a 45° triangle by one of the scribes that contri-buted to the distortion. I admit that all this is very much a matter of opinion, but so are all previous speculations concerning the tunnel, and the codex drawing may come closest to offering a tangible clue.

We may then sum up our findings so far:

(1) The identical difference of 6 feet between the elevation of the tunnel halves at

their endpoints as well as at the junction point indicates that the main tunnel was planned to be level. Because previous observers interpreted this difference in altitude as an attempt to provide a slope, they were prone to reject Hero's solution because it failed to provide an answer to the problem of slope.

(2) The second (lower) tunnel was dug to provide the slope. This double construction was intentional and customary (it is also found in other tunnels of the same period). The reason for the construction is probably the fact that no adequate instrument existed to hold a slope of less than 1 %, while tools such as the *chorobates* were effective in holding the horizontal. Ventilation may have been a factor; easy access certainly was.

(3) The tunnel could have been laid out by measuring over the mountain or around the east as well as the west slope.

(4) The argument that site selection offers a clue to the method of alignment is not convincing. If one accepts the drawing in the Mynas Codex as evidence that Hero had information about the tunnel, it seems that the surveying was done around the east end.

IV

Lastly, I would like to discuss the possibility of a connection between the tunnel and Pythagorean mathematics. Pythagoras' role in this field is a much-debated question and in fact is one of the reasons for the interest in the tunnel. Many scholars have considered Pythagoras a legendary sage, no more than a glorified medicineman,[40] while others believe that the early Ionion thinkers such as Pythagoras and Thales might have played the initial part in the development of Greek mathematics with which they are credited by the ancient tradition.[41] The purpose of the speculations concerning the tunnel is not to ascribe to Pythagoras an active part in the calculations, but rather to ascertain the state of mathematics in his age and area in order to determine the likelihood of his having discovered some of the theorems which antiquity connected with his name. After all, there is nothing in the mathematics ascribed to Pythagoras that was not part of the empirical knowledge of the Mesopotamians for the previous eight hundred years and subsequently of the Egyptians.[42] The question remains unanswered whether scientific mathematics (i.e., the system whereby each successive theorem requires rigid proof on the basis of previously recognized axioms or proven theorems) burst forth fully developed at the dawn of the fourth century or if it was the endproduct of an evolution that had begun when Greek thinkers first became acquainted with the handed-down mathematical procedures of the Near East. If we review Samos' relationship with Egypt, we shall find that the island was a most likely spot for early penetration by Egyptian mathematical knowledge.

Samos had become an important maritime power during the sixth century B.C. and had conquered many islands and mainland cities.[43] The Samians developed an effi-

---

[40] E.g., Walter Burkert, *Weisheit und Wissenschaft. Studien zu Pythagoras, Philolaos und Platon* (Nuremberg: Verlag Hans Carl, 1962), pp. 443–445, 141–142, 409.
[41] W. K. C. Guthrie, *The Greek Philosophers from Thales to Aristotle* (New York: Philosophical Library, 1950), p. 88; G. S. Kirk and J. E. Raven, *The Presocratic Philosophers* (Cambridge: Cambridge Univ. Press, 1957), pp. 229–230; James A. Philip, *Pythagoras and Early Pythagoreanism* (Toronto: Univ. Toronto Press, 1966), pp. 174 f.
[42] Neugebauer, *The Exact Sciences*, p. 36.
[43] Herodotus, *Histories* 3. 39.

cient type of vessel for their far-flung trade, the so-called Samaena, "more capacious and paunchlike, so that it is a good deepsea traveler and swift sailor too."[44] The Samians remained an important seapower into the fourth century, despite their defeat by Pericles; Thucydides could put the words into their mouths that "they had come within an inch of defeating the Athenians."[45]

Ample archaeological evidence for intensive interchange with Egypt has been found on Samos. A glance at the early Samian works of "orientalizing" art in the museum of Vathi immediately drives home the Egyptian influence: statuary, bronzes, and pottery of Samian make reflect their Egyptian models; sphynx and griffin motifs abound. In addition, numerous imported Egyptian artifacts dating from all periods have been found, especially in the Hera sanctuary.[46] Herodotus, of course, tells us of the close friendship between Polycrates and the "Egyptian king Amasis."[47] Bearing more directly on the subject of mathematics, Hultsch has shown that the unit of measurement employed in building the Hera temple on Samos was the royal Egyptian cubit.[48] The temple (about two miles from the tunnel exit), the breakwater of the port of Samos, and the tunnel are the three structures that elicited Herodotus' admiration because of their colossal scale ("the greatest works of all the Greeks"), which alone might indicate the Egyptian influence.

Now we have previously pointed out that the procedures described by Hero are the ones that had been in use for hundreds of years in connection with traditional instruments such as the *groma* and the *chorobates*, or its predecessor the plumbline level.[49] All these instruments have been shown to be of Egyptian origin. (The dioptra seems to be Hero's own invention and was apparently never used, as mentioned earlier.[50]) Such instruments were a necessity for construction of the temple as well as the tunnel. In this connection it is interesting that Pliny the Elder tells us that Theodorus was co-architect of the Hera temple, and, in a different context, he mentions the same Theodorus as the inventor of the *norma* and the *libella*.[51] The *norma* was the tool (essentially a carpenter's square) commonly used by the Romans to lay out right angles in the field; the *libella* was a plumbline, probably connected with a leveling instrument. The story is significant because it points to a tradition that the basic survey tools were "invented" on Samos in the sixth century B.C. We know, of course, that they had been in use in Egypt for a long time.[52] Since Hultsch has shown the use of the Egyptian measurement system, it is not unreasonable to assume that the implements to apply the measurements found their way to Samos at the same time.

In any event, from the close commercial and political relations between Egypt and Samos, and from evidence of some technological interchange, it would appear that Samos (like Miletus) was one of the crossroads where the Greeks had early access to the accumulated store of practical mathematical knowledge that was to an extent common to Mesopotamia and Egypt. This consideration, I believe, will shed some light on the interrelationship of "Pythagorean mathematics," the construction of the

[44] Plutarch, *Pericles* 26. 3.

[45] Thucydides, *History of the Peloponnesian War* 8. 76. 4.

[46] Ulf Jantzen, "Archäologische Forschungen auf Samos," *Bild der Wissenschaft*, 1967, *1*:49.

[47] Herodotus, *Histories* 3. 39–41.

[48] Friedrich Hultsch, *Griechische und Römische Metrologie* (Berlin: Weidmann, 1882), p. 551.

[49] Kiely, *Surveying Instruments*, pp. 10, 14, 19; also Usher, *Mechanical Inventions*, pp. 98–99, 147.

[50] See Drachmann, "A Detail," p. 243; also Kiely, *Surveying Instruments*, pp. 24–25.

[51] Pliny, *Natural History* 34. 83 and 7. 198.

[52] Kiely, *Surveying Instruments*, p. 10.

tunnel, and Hero's problems, even if we come to the reluctant conclusion that none of our findings in investigation of the tunnel is sufficient evidence to decide any of the more specific questions.

There is no clear evidence whether the tunnel was planned by measuring over the mountain or around the mountain. Both methods are possible, and Hero offers procedures for both; whether he knew which one was used is a moot question. Goodfield and Toulmin argue that Hero was "almost certainly in the same position as we are today: guessing how the work was done from circumstantial evidence alone."[53] To this van der Waerden replied that the plans and calculations for the tunnel would have been put into writing and that it is entirely possible that the original plan or a copy might have found its way into the library of Alexandria.[54] Both opinions are pure conjecture, and, I believe, beside the point.

If we can draw any positive conclusion at all, it might be this: during the sixth century Samos became familiar with the Egyptian mathematical tradition and, possibly through the Ionian mainland cities, with the Babylonian. The procedures used in laying out the tunnel are an integral part of the Near Eastern mathematical tradition, and so are the procedures described by Hero. The so-called Pythagorean mathematics is an offshoot of that same tradition. Even if no tangible piece of evidence from Eupalinus ever reached Hero, he was more than guessing; he knew and described the practical methods of a craft that had changed little in the intervening period and that was to continue with little change for centuries after. These traditional methods had become the basis of scientific mathematics when the Greek thinkers began to ask the question "why?"; but the traditional way of doing things remained unaffected by the abstract speculations that went on side by side with them.[55] That both branches of mathematics—the practical and the theoretical—gained a foothold in Samos is evidenced by an elaborate water clock on the agora of Samos described in a commemorative inscription,[56] and by the work of Aristarchos of Samos, who 200 years later developed the model of a heliocentric universe which was essentially the same as Copernicus' 1,750 years later.

[53] Goodfield and Toulmin, "How Was the Tunnel Aligned?" p. 52.
[54] B. L. van der Waerden, "Eupalinos and His Tunnel," Isis, 1968, 59:82–83.
[55] Van der Waerden, Science Awakening, pp. 83–94. See also my article "The Fragments of Philolaos and Aristotle's Account of Pythagorean Theories in Metaphysics A," Classica et Mediaevalia, 1966, 25:93–128, and Neugebauer, The Exact Sciences, p. 146.
[56] Renate Tölle, "Uhren auf Samos," Opus Nobile. Festschrift für Ulf Janzten (Wiesbaden: Franz Steiner, 1969), pp. 169–170.

The Arsenal in Piraeus and the Ancient Building Rules

The modern world has not succeeded in reaching the grandeur and noble monumentality, which characterized the buildings of Greek and Roman antiquity, qualities that were based on certain building rules, handed down as precious secrets from generation to generation. The rules were at once practical and theoretical or esthetic, but first of all practical. They aimed primarily at the adoption of simple functions of particular dimensions or measures chosen as units, the functions being generally simple multiples leading to certain integer relations between the various principal dimensions. Thus in the temples, the diameter of the columns or the dimensions of the triglyphs served as units. The Pythagorean theory of numbers and the division of a line in extreme and mean ratio seemed to play an important part in sacral architecture throughout antiquity and the middle ages.

None of the inscriptions preserved from antiquity gives so complete information concerning the details of construction as the so-called Arsenal Inscription found in 1882 in Piraeus. It is cut in a slab of blue-grey Hymettos marble and is uncommonly well preserved; in fact, only 24 out of the 5161 letters are illegible and they can be interpolated with certainty. The inscription dates from about 347 B. C. and gives a complete specification of the famous Skeuothek or Naval Arsenal in Piraeus, which was one of the most admired buildings of antiquity. The inscription was found near the south-east harbour of Piraeus, the ancient Zea, which at the time of the Arsenal was the most important of the Athenian Navy Yards. KOEHLER gives an excellent transcription of the Greek text in *Inscriptiones Graecae* (I. G., II, 1054) and a translation in the English language is given by THOMAS W. LUDLOW in the *American Journal of Philology*, 1882 : « The Athenian Naval Arsenal of PHILON ». Recently the Danish architect VILHELM MARSTRAND has made a profound study of the inscription and published the result

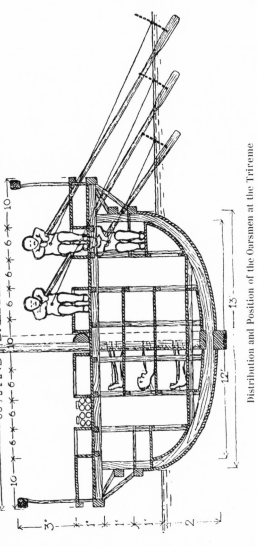

Distribution and Position of the Oarsmen at the Trireme

Part of the Arsenal Inscription (c. 347 B. C.).

Isis, VIII, pl. 2.

W. HOVGAARD.

Marstrand's Reconstruction of the Arsenal in Piraeus

W. Hovgaard.

of his investigation in a book entitled : « Arsenalet i Piraeus og Oldtidens Byggeregler », Copenhagen, 1922 (288 pages with numerous illustrations and plates). It is the principal object of this article to draw the attention of the international public to this valuable work, which gives what is believed to be the most exhaustive discussion of that document.

As indicated by the title of the book, it was MARSTRAND's first object to determine definitely the secret building rules of the ancient architects, about which rules there is so much difference of opinion, but actually the work covers a much larger field. A critical analysis is made of other correlated inscriptions, and the writings of VITRUVIUS and other authors bearing on the same subject are discussed. A most interesting study is made of the design of the Greek trieres and MARSTRAND points out the intimate connection which in his opinion existed between the building rules of the ships and those of the temples. MARSTRAND has rare qualifications for dealing with these questions, being both a scholar and a scientifically trained architect. His thorough study of the work of the philologists in this field as well as his intimate knowledge of Greek and Latin and the ancient literature concerning this matter has enabled him to do full justice to the philological aspect of the analysis. As an experienced architect he is in a better position than most philologists to interpret obscure technical words and phrases that may occur in the inscriptions. Finally, MARSTRAND's work deserves the appreciation of all students of Greek inscriptions and of problems connected with the construction of ancient buildings and ships on account of his enthusiasm and his painstaking efforts to disentangle the many difficult and obscure questions involved in this study.

The Inscription. — MARSTRAND gives the complete text of the inscription with an excellent translation in Danish. As in the original text the figured dimensions are written out in full, given in Greek or Egyptian measures : feet, palms, and fingerbreadths, but in the book the corresponding metric measures are everywhere added in ordinary numerals.

The inscription excels in conciseness, there is not one contradiction or ambiguity. The text was in all probability prepared by the architect himself, the famous PHILON, whose name is well known not only as the designer of the Arsenal but also of other structures and as the author of several works on architecture. VITRUVIUS refers to him as one of the greatest of Greek architects, and gives the title of two of his books : « On the harmonious construction of the sacred temples » and « On the Arsenal ». These works are unfortunately lost. It is clear from the inscription that P<small>HILON</small> wanted to give all information necessary for constructing the building, but he did not directly reveal the rules according to which the design was carried out. No one who is unfamiliar with those rules can see how he arrived at the results, but as shown by M<small>ARSTRAND</small>, a scrutiny of the inscription and a graphical reconstruction of the building, throws new light on this difficult question.

Figure 1 gives a photographic reproduction of a part of the inscription comprising a fragment of the last five lines. The rectangular network of lines is drawn in to exhibit the regularity with which on the whole the letters are placed. One irregularity is found in the upper line to the left (line 93), and is believed to be due to an error of the stone-cutter. Probably one Σ had been cut instead of two, whence it became necessary to erase this Σ and the following K and to replace them by ΣΣK in two squares.

The inscription is an official document, authorizing the expenditure and containing a complete detailed specification of the building, the materials to be employed, the principal dimensions, the mode of construction and all the scantlings of blocks and timbers. It also states the names of the contractors, E<small>UTHYDEMOS</small>, who was probably the financial manager, and P<small>HILON</small>, the architect, and prescribes that the work shall be carried out by paid artisans in accordance with the specifications and the patterns provided by the architect. In the last sentence it is stated that workmen shall deliver (or complete) the work on the date to which they have received payment for each job (KAI EN TOIΣ XPONOIΣ AΠOΔΩΣ-OYΣIN OIΣ AN MIΣΘΩΣΩNTAI EKAΣTA TΩN EPΓΩN). It is clear from this that the work was not carried out by slaves and it appears that the men did not receive fixed wages, but that they were employed on contract or at piecework.

The term « Arsenal » (a place where arms and munitions are stored and manufactured) employed by M<small>ARSTRAND</small> and by several French and English writers as a translation of the word Skeuothek (ΣKEYOΘHK), i. e. a ship magazine or ship store house, is a misnomer, as the building was actually a store house for the riggings and sails (skeue kremasta) of the fleet, and was not used for storage of arms of any kind. It is difficult to find a satisfactory English translation and it would seem that the word Skeuothek used by several German writers is preferable to Arsenal, but as the latter term was adopted by MARSTRAND it will be here used. All the weapons and war engines were stored in separate buildings located elsewhere in the Navy Yards and the ships were housed in « ship-houses » provided with hauling slips. In these houses were also stored all outfit of wood, such as masts, yards, oars, etc. Previous arsenals were generally constructed of wood as known from the so-called Naval-Inscriptions, found in Piraeus in 1834 (KOEHLER's I. G., II).

The Rules of Construction. — The construction of the Arsenal was commenced in the year 346 B. C. but was interrupted in 339 on account of the war with PHILIP of Macedonia. In 338 the work was resumed and the Arsenal was placed in use in 329. In 86 B. C. SULLA destroyed all the fortifications and Navy Yards, including the ship-houses and the arsenal.

MARSTRAND'S reconstruction of the arsenal, shown in plate 3, is based on a careful study of the inscription and on an analysis of previous attempts in this direction, together with what is known from VITRUVIUS and other writers. He also makes comparisons with temples and other buildings, ancient and medieval, and finally presents what he believes to be the building rules. These rules seem to have been lost in the middle ages, and it has been asserted by some that no rules ever existed beyond certain practical pre-scriptions, but MARSTRAND maintains that this is unthinkable since in that case there could be no such definite architectural style as was manifestly exibited in the Greek temples. He says that too much weight has been assigned to the theoretical and esthetic origin of the rules; it has been overlooked that the rules must first of all be practical. The entire structure as well as its component members must possess sufficient strength, and a building must fulfil certain requirements determined by its purpose. It has been shown by THIERSCH and THEUER that certain numerical relations are repeated over and over again in the same temple groups as for instance 2 : 5 in the Apollo-temples, 3 : 8 in the Hera-temples, 5 : 11 in the Zeus-temples and so on. It seems almost certain that there was a connection between the Pythagorean philosophy and the dimen-sional proportions of the temples. The central idea of the Pytha-goreans was that numbers are the essence of all things and the principle of rational order in the universe. This mystic concep-tion is difficult to grasp, and probably had its root in the much older speculations on numbers by the Babylonians and Egyptians. PYTHAGORAS took the pentagon as a symbol of the relation between the various building rules and according to MARSTRAND the extreme and mean ratio, which is intimately connected with the pentagon, played an important part in those rules. The connection between that ratio and the pentagon is shown in the thirtheenth book of EUCLID. The ratio between the *minor* and the *major* of a line cut in the extreme and mean ratio can be expressed as a continued fraction, from which the following series of convergents is obtained, the successive members of which deviate less and less from the true irrational value of that ratio :

$$\frac{1}{1}, \quad \frac{1}{2}, \quad \frac{2}{3}, \quad \frac{3}{5}, \quad \frac{5}{8}, \quad \frac{8}{13}, \quad \frac{13}{21}, \ldots..$$

In this series, which was well known in antiquity, each new member may be formed by the addition of the numerators and denominators of the two previous members. The ratios indicated by the terms are according to MARSTRAND those most commonly met with in all buildings. The first three terms are regarded as simple numerical relations, but the last terms, beginning with 3 : 5 are referred to as extreme and mean ratios, being approximations of increasing accuracy. These relations were used mostly in the vertical dimensions, but in the horizontal directions the division was *minor : major : minor* for the sake of symmetry :

$$\frac{1:1:1}{3}, \quad \frac{1:2:1}{4}, \quad \frac{2:3:2}{7}, \quad \frac{3:5:3}{11}, \quad \frac{5:8:5}{18}, \quad \frac{8:13:8}{29}$$

MARSTRAND discusses the design and construction of the Arsenal in the smallest detail and shows that the dimensions of this building were actually governed throughout by the proportions indicated in those series. This was verified by drawing rectangular networks of straight lines over the plans.

VITRUVIUS (Book III, chap. I) states very clearly the principle of simple numerical relations or commensurability. Describing first how this principle is followed in the human body he says that consequently, as found by the ancients (the Greeks), in all buildings, but especially in the temples of the Gods, these rules should be followed : « Cum causa constituisse videntur antiqui ut, etiam in operum perfectionibus : Singulorum membrorum, ad universam figurae speciem, habeant commensus exactionem. »

It appears that in general the Greeks based their designs on similarity of proportions. In all temples, from the smallest to the largest, there is very approximately the same relations between breadth, length and height; the number of columns does not increase with breadth and length but individual columns are made of correspondingly greater diameter and height. The rule of similarity, however, has its limitations in the scantlings of beams, dependent on the increase in load, and failed in the construction of Erechtheum (409 B. C.). As known from the preserved record of the accounts from that temple, the beams under the ceiling took a dangerous deflection and an extra beam of very great dimensions had to be fitted under the ceiling of the Poseidon-Erechtheus cella, detracting much from the beauty and harmony of the temple. Fifty years later, when the Arsenal was designed, it seems that the problem of calculating the strength of beams had been solved, probably by EUDOXOS, who may have been the teacher of PHILON. It appears to be then realized that the weight of the beams themselves had to be taken into account, especially in structures of stone. MARSTRAND, through a careful analysis of the load distribution and strength of the beams in the Arsenal, arrives at the conclusion that the scantlings of the beams were unmistakably determined by a method which differed only in form from that applied by modern engineers. In fact, beams of entirely different cross-section, both in the roof and the floors, were found, within each group, to be subject to the same maximum stress when calculated by modern methods. Probably the rule used by PHILON was geometric, but equivalent to the ordinary modern formula for bending.

The imposing and costly Arsenal was closely bound up with economic and political conditions of Athens and was of the greatest importance in case of quick mobilization of the fleet. About 400 years later VALERIUS MAXIMUS wrote : « The Athenians were exceedingly proud of their Arsenal and not without reason, for it gave an impression of grandeur and beauty. It is told that the architect PHILON in the theatre gave such a good account of his calculations before the Popular Assembly, that this pampered people praised him no less for his eloquence than for his art. »

The Trieres. — At that time the trieres or trireme, as it was termed in Latin, was the standard fighting unit in the Athenian fleet and the Arsenal was built to accommodate the sails and riggings of 400 vessels of this type. Larger ships with four and five banks of oars had indeed been developed by the Carthaginians, and also the Greeks soon found it necessary to commence building such vessels, but they were loath to abandon the well-tried trieres, the construction of which was perfected and standardized. The trieres, moreover, excelled in speed and handiness and the entire plant of the Navy Yards, especially the ship-houses, were built to accommodate this type.

The ship was for the Greeks something sacred and was regarded as the gift of the Olympian Gods. The economic life of the population around the Aegean Sea was based on shipping. It was no mere accident that the inner shrine of the Greek temples was given the same name as the ship, *naos*. The word *nave* used in the Christian churches to this day is probably derived from the Latin word *navis* and handed down from the days of the temples, and it is known that in the early Christian Church the ship stood as a sacred symbol.

The trieres was perfect in design; it was an expression of the same rhythm and harmony that characterized the temples, and which by the Greeks were admired in everything. In the ships as in the temples MARSTRAND found that the principal dimensions were multiples of a certain basic measure, in this case the distance between the oarholes. There was the same proportion between the length and beam of the trieres as between the length and breadth of the Arsenal and also several other dimensions were similar. MARSTRAND placed a rectangular network of straight lines over the transverse section of the ship and was thus able to analyze the proportions very readily.

The distribution and position of the oarsmen is a question which has given rise to much controversy. MARSTRAND based his study of this problem chiefly on the Akropolis relief of a trieres and arrived at the solution illustrated in figure 3. He placed the thranites, or oarsmen of the highest bank, and the zygites, or oarsmen of the second bank, on the same level, while the thalamites, or oarsmen of the lowest bank, were placed vertically below the thranites. This arrangement was made possible by the overhang of the deck, which permitted the oarlocks of the second bank to be placed further inboard and thus prevented the length of these oars to become excessive. All three banks of oars were parallel and equidistant; the oars of the two upper banks were of the same length but those of the lower were shorter. This solution is in good accord with the descriptions handed down in writings, inscrip-

tions and works of art and is similar to that proposed by TENNE (1),
except that TENNE places the thranites and zygites directly on the
deck beams, while MARSTRAND places them on benches. On the whole
MARSTRAND's solution seems to satisfy all technical and nautical
conditions.

The hypozomata mentioned in the Arsenal Inscription as well as
in the Naval Inscriptions were heavy cables, used for girding the
ships and may properly be called rope-girdles. There has been
much discussion as to how they were applied, but it is certain that
the purpose was to strengthen the ship by holding the frames in
place when in a seaway and when exposed to ramming. According
to MARSTRAND, these ropes were carried along the sides entirely
around the ship and *inside* the frames, but he does not offer any
explanation as to how they were attached to the frames. Some other
writers maintain that the ropes were laid externally, which indeed
seems more natural. These rope-girdles must not be confounded
with the hogging ropes used in Egyptian ships and found even in
our times in shallow boats on the Mississipi River. Such hogging-
ropes are carried from the stem to the stern in the vertical central
plane of the ship or parallel with this plane, and rest on vertical
posts or crutches forming a truss which resists the hogging strains.

General Remarks. — According to MARSTRAND no sharp distinction
should be made between the technical and the esthetic requirements
in construction. That which is perfectly beautiful must strive
towards the same goal as that which is perfect technically; the two
requirements must be made to coalesce. Art is the most perfect
application of all our technical science and not something apart.
This the Greeks and Romans understood, as clearly expounded by
VITRUVIUS.

The building rules as formulated by MARSTRAND are based
primarily on the Arsenal Inscription and were tested on the Erechtheum and other temples as well as on the trieres. Although they
cannot be said to be established with certainty and require to be
further tested by application to a greater number of buildings, the
solution offered seems logical and is well supported by the known
facts. MARSTRAND's conception of the trieres as being derived from
the same building rules as the temples is of great interest. His
study of the strength calculations of the beams in the Arsenal, of

(1) « Kriegsschiffe zu den Zeiten der alten Griechen und Römer », Olden-
burg, 1915.

the position of the oarsmen in the trieres, and of numerous other questions which cannot be discussed in a brief article, bring fresh points of view and constitute valuable contributions to our knowledge of ancient engineering. It is refreshing to read a book which is written with so much enthusiasm and love of the subject, but it is to be regretted that it is written in a language which is accessible only to a relatively small number of readers.

(Massachusetts Institute of Technology,   WILLIAM HOVGAARD.
Cambridge, Mass.).

La meunerie de Barbegal (France) et les roues hydrauliques chez les anciens et au moyen âge

PAR C. L. SAGUI

D ANS un mémoire de 1940 F. Benoit [1] nous parle de l'importante meunerie hydraulique de Barbegal, dont les restes imposants témoignent aujourd'hui encore de l'importance industrielle de cette usine gallo-romaine. En cette étude je ne ferai qu'une courte analyse technique de la meunerie en ques-

---

Benoit, F.: L'usine de meunerie hydraulique de Barbegal: *Rev. Arch.*, pp. 19–80, Paris, 1940.

Meunerie gallo-romaine de Barbegal, prés d'Arles, avec deux séries de roues hydrauliques de huit roues chacune et actionnant globalement 32 moulins avec une production de 28 tonnes de farine en 24 heures

tion, en y ajoutant quelques détails sur l'emploi des roues hydrauliques chez les anciens et au Moyen âge.

L'eau, come force motrice, fut largement utilisée au Moyen âge, ainsi qu'elle le fut aux temps des Grecs et des Romains. De ces derniers il nous restent quelques débris archéologiques, parfois très importants, comme c'est le cas pour la meunerie gallo-romaine de Barbegal, près d'Arles. L'eau qui l'actionnait arrivait par un aqueduc qui, d'après Benoit, captait les sources de Mausane et des Baux, au sud des Alpilles. A la vérité il paraît bien qu'on utilisait par contre l'eau de la Durance puisqu'à l'époque romaine ce fleuve, suivant Barral,[2] passait au Sud des Alpilles en continuant vers Barbegal. En effet les cailloux de la Grau sont identiques à ceux du lit actuel de la Durance.

On utilisait pour la meunerie la pente d'une colline inclinée d'environ 30°, donnant une différence de niveau de 20 mètres entre le canal d'arrivée et le canal de fuite. L'aqueduc aboutissait à un bassin de répartition alimentant deux séries de chute, de m.2,5 chacune, ce qui permettait le fonctionnement simultané de 16 roues hydrauliques à augets de m.2,10 de diamètre et larges d'environ m.0,70. L'aqueduc à l'arrivée au bassin de répartition avait une largeur de m. 80 et, d'après des traces laissées, l'eau y avait une hauteur de m.0,50.

La portée de cet aqueduc était, d'après mes calculs, d'environ un mètre cube d'eau par seconde, ce qui donnait une puissance d'environ 260 HP. La puissance utile de chaque roue hydraulique à augets n'était cependant que de onze chevaux-vapeur, car le rendement de ces roues n'est que de 65% au maximum. Les meules en basalte de cette usine avaient un diamètre de m.0,90 et pesaient 1050 Kg. le mètre carré. Une meule pareille de nos jours, avec ventilateur, du poids de 850 Kg/m², peut moudre environ 40 Kg. de blé par heure.[3] Les meules de Barbegal par conséquent devaient moudre 45 Kg. de blé par heure, en faisant environ un tour par seconde.

Bélidor [4] nous dit qu'une meule pesant 2170 Kg., ayant un diamètre de m.1.90 et

---

[2] Barral: *Vues Générales d'un projet de canal d'encaissement pour la Durance, du Cante-Perdrix, au Bac de Mirabeau*, Marseille, 1792.

[3] Mazzocchi, B.: *Memoriale tecnico*, p. 514.
[4] Belidor, *Arch. Hydr.*, vol. 1, L. II, p. 283, Paris, 1737.

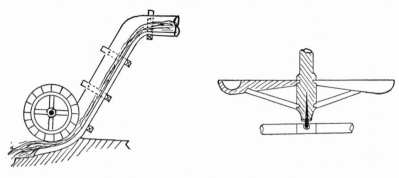

FIG. 1   FIG. 2

une vitesse de 53 tours par minute, peut moudre en 24 heures 120 septiers de 75 livres chacun. Cela nous fait environ 200 Kg. par heure. La surface d'une pareille meule étant de m²2,75 le poids du mètre carré est de Kg. 862, ce qui nous donne pour une meule de m.o.90 de diamètre du même poids par unité de surface, Kg. 44 de blé moulu en une heure.

L'usine de Barbegal avec deux séries de roues de 8 roues chacune, pouvait faire marcher 32 meules à la fois puisque la puissance absorbée par chaque meule n'est que de 5 ch.v. La production totale en farine, lorsque toute la meunerie marchait, était donc d'environ 28 tonnes en 24 heures. Il restait encore 16 ch.v. disponibles qu'on utilisait pour les appareils de lavage du blé. La ville d'Arles comptait au IIIᵉ siècle environ 10,000 habitants tandis que la farine ainsi produite en pouvait nourrir 80,000. Sans compter la production de petits moulins des campagnes environnantes qui eux-aussi travaillaient certes à plein rendement en fournissant la farine aux villageois des alentours et même aux habitants d'Arles. Il faut donc croire que l'importante meunerie de Barbegal travaillait surtout pour l'exportation, ainsi que Benoit nous le fait bien remarquer. En effet le blé de la Gaule approvisionnait en partie Rome et ses armées, et Arles, port important sur le Rhône, pouvait servir à l'exportation des céréales moulues à Barbegal. Au reste Arles au IIᵉ siècle était la résidence du *Procurateur* pour le service de l'Annone en Narbonnais et même en Ligurie sous Marc-Aurèle.[5] Cela nous fait croire que la meunerie de Barbegal soit du IIᵉ siècle.

Ces grandes usines à blé n'étaient d'ailleurs pas rares. À Tournus, en Bourgogne, il y avait aussi un port important pour les céréales de la Saône que l'armée romaine utilisait.[6] Sur les coteaux de cette vallée on a découvert en effet un grand nombre de meules, près du village de Préty (*Pistriacum*) et non loin de la source Bouat. Cela fait croire qu'une importante usine à blé et une boulangerie étaient ici utilisées par les Romains. Du reste sous le Bas-Empire [7] ces usines étaient nombreuses. Du temps de Vitruve même d'ailleurs des meuneries actionnées par l'eau existaient dans toutes les régions d'Italie, productices surtout de farine de blé, et c'est en Pouille et en Sicile qu'elles étaient plus nombreuses. En Afrique du Nord aussi les moulins à blé et à huile actionnés par l'eau se trouvaient en grand nombre.

Le moulin du Vᵉ siècle découvert a l'Agora d'Athènes fonctionnait quand cette ville n'était plus qu'un bourg.[8] Cela signifie que même pendant une époque bien triste pour cette ville autrefois si fameuse, le moulin hydraulique à blé n'avait point disparu avec la civilisation grecque, comme il n'a pas disparu au Moyen âge. Il n'y avait aucune

[5] Benoit, F.: *op. cit.*
[6] Jeanton, G. L'ancienne ville romaine de Tournus, *Bull. Arch. du Comité*, p. 158, 1920.
[7] Rostovzeff. *The Soc. and Econ. Hist. of the Roman Empire*, pp. 166 et 539, Oxford. 1926.
[8] Parson, A. W., A Roman water-mill in the Athenian Agora. *Hesperia*, Vol. 1, p. 90, 1936.

FIG. 3   FIG. 4, Moulin du moyen âge

raison d'ailleurs, puisque la mouture ne pouvait cesser, même si la civilisation sombrait: Athènes, devenue un village avait en effet toujours besoin de farine par conséquent l'art de la produire se perpétuait sans interruption. C'est pourquoi certaines inventions anciennes ont pu traverser les ténèbres du Moyen âge sans disparaître.

La roue du moulin de l'Agora aurait tourné contre le courant [9] et avait un diamètre de m.3.24 sur une largeur de m.0.54. Parson croit que le rouet (*tympanum dentatum*) fixé à l'axe de la roue hydraulique et actionnant la lanterne, roue horizontale de transmission, était d'un diamètre supérieur à celui de cette dernière dans le moulin de l'Agora. Cela était possible si la roue en question était du type des roues de poitrine avec vanne à coulisse, puisque la hauteur de chute du bief athénien mesurait 5 mètres environ, ce que donnait à l'eau une vitesse d'environ 10 mètres par seconde en faisant faire à la roue un peu plus d'un tour par seconde. Cette roue cependant devait avoir un diamètre un peu inférieur à celui calculé par Parson.

On a toutefois comme règle que la lanterne fait 5 tours tandis que le rouet en fait un. On a cru de bien faire en corrigeant sur cette donnée le texte de Vitruve [10] où il est dit que la lanterne devait être d'un diamètre supérieur à celui du rouet: *secundum id tympanum maius* (correction minus) *item dentatum planum est colocatum, quo continetur.* Cette correction est, croyons-nous, arbitraire, ainsi qu'il a été indiqué plus haut. Du reste le texte de Vitruve s'adapterait encore mieux pour des roues hydrauliques d'environ un mètre de diamètre et de m. 2 de large, fig. 1. L'eau conduite par une auge très inclinée, de la largeur de la roue, descend avec une grande vitesse en frappant les aubes étroites de cette roue, car l'épaisseur de l'eau sur le plan incliné de l'auge n'est que de quelques centimètres. C'est une véritable lame d'eau qui se précipite de la hauteur d'environ 6 à 7 mètres, et même plus, sur les aubes de la roue hydraulique, laquelle acquière ainsi une grande vitesse circonférencielle qu'il faut réduire à l'intérieur du moulin pour avoir la vitesse de régime des meules. Le texte de Vitruve ne semble donc point erroné; il prouverait par contre que des roues hydrauliques de ce modèle existaient de son temps.

Bélidor [11] nous décrit une pareille roue, utilisant cependant des chutes de 2 à 3 mètres seulement, quand l'eau est abondante. De ces roues font depuis plusieurs siècles

---

[9] Parson: *op. cit.*, p. 80.   [10] Vitruve: x, 5.   [11] Bélidor, *op. cit.*, vol. 50, p. 284, fig. 8.

marcher des scieries dans les Alpes Cadoriques où, même de nos jours, ces scieries débitent en planches de grandes quantités de sapin. Des usines semblables sont du reste signalées en France même par Bélidor.[12] Les anciens nous ont certes transmis la technique de ces scieries hydrauliques lesquelles, même a l'époque de grandes invasions, continuaient à fonctionner dans les profondes vallées des Alpes, éloignées des routes romaines par où arrivaient les barbares venant du Nord.

De même la turbine nous vient des anciens, puisqu'on trouve dans le haut moyen âge des moulins actionnées par elle. C'est une sorte de roue Pelton à axe vertical d'un diamètre d'environ 2 mètres dont les aubes sont faites en cuillière et reçoivent le choc de l'eau d'une auge, fig. 2. Ces moulins, d'une grande simplicité, où la roue hydraulique communique directement le mouvement à la meule, utilisaient de fortes chutes d'eau à débit limité. De même les roues Pelton utilisent un rapport $H/Q = \sim 150$, ou H est la hauteur de la chute en mètres et Q le débit d'eau en mètres cubes. En Provence, et dans beaucoup d'endroits en Dauphiné ces roues étaient d'usage courant au XVIIe siècle.[13] Des roues semblables étaient utilisées aussi en Italie dès le Moyen âge. J'ai vu en effet les restes pourrir d'une pareille roue à Gualdo Tadino, Ombrie; ils étaient ensevelis sous les ramblais d'une très vieille mine abandonnée.

Très anciennes aussi sont les roues à tambour, ayant la figure d'un cône tronqué, que Bélidor nous signale sur la Garonne. Ces roues tournaient avec une grande vitesse dans une cuve en maçonnerie, et avaient des aubes formées par des portions de spirale, fig. 3. Au Basacle, à Toulouse, 16 meules de front, dans un même bâtiment en travers de la rivière, étaient encore actionnées au XVIIIe siècle par des roues de ce modèle.

La force hydraulique était donc très adroitement utilisée au Moyen âge, et ses diverses applications venaient des civilisations disparues. Les grandes usines à blé devaient surtout fonctionner avant Dioclétien, qui régna de 284 à 305, puisqu'à son époque une crise économique effroyable sévissait sur l'Empire, ce qui réduisait l'activité sociale d'une façon considérable. Les temps de la grande industrie étant revolus, et le libéralisme économique ne répondant plus aux nécessités de l'heure, Dioclétien crut trouver un remède à cet état de choses dans une discipline aussi sévère qu' inutile, en developpant un étatisme myope qui devait finalement entrainer l'Empire dans le désastre. Il ne parait pas en conséquence impossible que la meunerie de Barbegal puisse avoir été construite au IIIe ou IVe siècle, dans une atmosphère économique de catastrophe. Pour cela Q. Candidius Benignus, ingénieur de grande valeur du Bas-Empire n'a pu être, croyons-nous, le constructeur de cette usine à blé.[14] Il est intéressant cependant de remarquer les signes lapidaires du métier sur le sarcophage de cet ingénieur, c'est-à-dire l' *ascia* et le niveau à fil à plomb. Les maîtres lombards (*i maestri comacini*) n'ont fait donc que continuer une pratique fort ancienne en laissant sur les monuments qu'ils construisaient, en guise de signature des symboles représentant le plus souvent leurs outils.[15] Ces mêmes signes lapidaires étaient employés aussi du temps d'Athènes.[16]

L'usine de Barbegal se rattache par ses details à celle du Janicule à Rome.[17] En effet à Barbegal on a au sommet de l'usine un réservoir régulateur avec trou de vidange, de même qu'au Janicule on a découvert le canal de dérivation de *l'aqua Traina*, avec 2 réservoirs à écluse à rainures réglant le débit d'eau. On a découvert aussi les traces de moulins hydrauliques dans les soutenements des Thermes de Caracalla,[18] ce qui prouve que les eaux conduites à Rome servaient, en partie du moins, au fonctionnement de machines hydrauliques. D'ailleurs la force d'eau était utilisée partout où cela paraissait possible. Ainsi les moulins sur pontons dans les rivières fonctionnaient couramment en Italie et ailleurs.

[12] Bélidor: *op. cit.*, vol. I, p. 321.
[13] Bélidor: *op. cit.*, vol. I, p. 301.
[14] Benoit, F. *op. cit.*
[15] Sagui, C. L. *Croniche d'arte*, fasc. 4, pp. 1–8, anno 1927: *Isis*, No. 91. March 1942, pp. 602–609.
[16] Sagui, C. L., *Econ. Geol.*, vol. 25, pp. 65–86

(1930).
[17] Van Buren, A. W., Stevens, G. P., *Memoirs of the American Academy in Rome, 1* (1915–1916), 1917, p. I, pl. 15; 1927, p. 138, pl. 52; 1933, p. 72, pl. 3.
[18] Ashby, Th. *The aqued. of anc. Rome*, p. 46, Oxford, 1935.

Il ne faut donc méconnaître toutes les applications hydrauliques des anciens, même si les traces de ce lointain passé industriel sont rares et vagues. En *De Rebus bellicis* d'un chroniqueur du Bas-Empire [19] on trouve des choses très intéressantes ayant trait aux mécanismes que les anciens avaient inventés. Il est même question d'un bateau de guerre se déplacant par l'action de roues à aubes mises en mouvement par des manèges de boeufs opèrant sur le pont. L'empereur Commode du reste avait fait installer sur ses voitures des compteurs de distance à engrenage, sur le type du compteur de Héron d'Alexandrie, du 2e siècle. Il est donc possible que les appareils de ce genre fussent connus à Rome bien avant Héron, d'autant plus qu'Archimède avait établi la théorie des engrenages presque trois siecles avant notre ère. Dès cette époque, du reste, les moulins hydrauliques à engrenage devaient fonctionner aussi bien en Asie Mineure et en Afrique du Nord qu'en Europe. Strabon nous en signale un à Cabire sur le Lycos, royaume de Pont, du 2e siècle avant Jésus Christ. Les norias d'arrosage existaient elles aussi bien avant notre ère.[20] Aussi les moulins à huile, à foulon et pour bien d'autres usages, spécialement dans les mines, fonctionnaient hydrauliquement depuis la plus haute antiquité.

La roue motrice de la fig. 3 devait elle aussi nous venir des anciens, puisqu'Archimède a bien dû se rendre compte que si sa vis en tournant pouvait remonter l'eau, cette dernière, animée d'une vitesse suffisante, devait à son tour actionner un tambour portant des éléments de spirale à sa surface. Le moulin hydraulique devait aussi exister du temps d'Archimède puisque ce philosophe a établi la théorie des engrenages. Pour l'établir il fallait bien que des roues dentées fussent appliquées quelque part; leur application aux moulins hydrauliques me paraît du reste celle dont les hommes avaient le plus besoin, et par conséquent leur esprit inventif a dû tout d'abord s'y intéresser. Il est même probable que les scieries hydrauliques de la pierre, surtout du marbre, avaient eu l'honneur d'être les premières usines actionnées par des roues hydrauliques. Pline [21] nous dit déjà qu'on sciait la pierre dans les carrières moyennant des lames en acier, ou en cuivre, et du sable siliceux, et cela depuis la plus haute antiquité.[22]

En Allemagne nous trouvons une scierie hydraulique au XIVe siècle, sur un petit cours d'eau du nom de Roer ou Ruer.[23] Un document du 14 Mars 1328 [24] parle d'une concession du dauphin Guigues à Champagnon de Moras, de gauchoirs et battoirs *tournant* et *battant* à Beaurepaire, c'est-à-dire actionnés hydrauliquement. Le long de la Sorgue, de Vaucluse à Avignon, il y avait au 13e siècle des moulins à blé, à huile, à drap [25] et on signale de ces mêmes moulins dès le XIe siècle à Sorgues.[26] En Dauphiné l'utilisation de la force hydraulique est aussi fort ancienne. On y trouve en effet, en 1269, des moulins à fouler les draps,[27] et en 1266 on établissait une écluse sur la Vésonne pour en utiliser les eaux, comme force motrice.[28] En Piémont, en Lombardie, et surtout dans la Vénétie, les moulins hydrauliques ont de même une très vieille histoire. C'est d'Italie, du reste, que du temps des Romains toutes ces applications hydrauliques ont émigré dans l'Europe tout entière. Les machines pour percer les troncs d'arbres fonctionnaient dans la province de Belluno dès le Moyen âge, et en France, Embrun s'alimentait à la même époque en eau potable venant des sources situées parfois à des distances de 3 km. Des tuyaux en bois servaient de conduite.[28 bis]

Le cabestan et les moufles pour élever de lourds fardeaux étaient aussi d'usage courant dans les temps anciens. Aristote nous rappelle d'un treuil à axe vertical du

[19] Reinach, S. *Rev. Arch.*, 1922; *Amalthée*, p. 256, .930.
[20] Mayence, F. La 3e camp. à Apamée, *Bull. des musées Roy. d'Art et d'Hist.*, No. 1, p. 5, Bruxelles, 1933.
[21] Pline, *35*, 6, 22.
[22] Sagui, C. L., *Econ. Geol.*, Vol. 25, pp. 65–86, 1930.
[23] Poppe, J. H. M., *Gesch. d. Technologie*, Vol. 2, p. 34.

[24] Chan, U. Chevalier, *Regeste Dauphinois*, no. 24415, 1913.
[25] Cartulaire de l'Abb. de Sénanque, *Arch dep. de Vaucluse* H, no. 1.
[26] Chobaut, H. Chef des arch. du Dép. de Vaucluse. Communication personnelle.
[27] *Archives de l'Isère*.
[28] *Archives de l'évêché de Grenoble*.
[28bis] Sclafert, Th., *Le Haut Dauphiné au Moyen âge*. Paris, 1926.

nom de zygón, que Vitruve [29] appelle *ergata*, ce qui en Italien est devenu *argano*. Dans le *polypastos* de Vitruve [30] plusieurs moufles y travaillaient à la fois. Il est même probable que pour la préparation de grandes quantités de mortier on utilisait les *tribomylos*, machine rappelée par Bocklerius [31] avec laquelle on broyait le mortier au lieu d'employer des manoeuvres.

Ainsi, au Bas-Empire l'utilisation des forces hydrauliques, animale et humaine avait été poussée très loin, ce qui aggrava d'ailleurs la crise économique qui déferlait à cette époque sur Rome, crise d'abondance de main-d'oeuvre d'abord, ayant comme résultat un chômage toujours croissant, au fur et à mesure que le pouvoir global d'achat tombait, car les ouvriers qui ne travaillaient pas en entrainaient d'autres, et toujours plus nombreux, dans l'oisiveté forcée. Le chômage développait le chômage avec la rapidité des mauvaises herbes envahissant un champ. Rien n'allait plus, du reste, dans ce vieil Empire mourant. Constantin, en croyant parer à la crise par des méthodes nouvelles et originales, considéra l'activité des moulins et autres industries semblables comme du travail forcé, c'est à dire pareil à celui des mines ou seulement des esclaves y travaillaient. Il obligea même les ouvriers agricoles à ne plus quitter leur emploi, ni le lieu du travail.

C'est dans un étatisme de ce genre qu'on chercha le salut, sans cependant le trouver, car l'origine du mal se cachait dans le développement même du capitalisme devenu gênant lorsque le cycle des conquêtes romaines était terminé, en même temps que la propriété foncière grossissait outre mesure, en transformant les petites fermes laborieuses en *latifundia*, où les propriétaires réduisaient peu à peu l'exploitation intensive, ce qui a transformé tous les immenses domaines le long de la mer Tyrrhénienne, en marécages. De nos jours aussi la puissance mécanique et celle du capital ont abouti à un autre genre de *latifundia* d'où la crise actuelle tire son origine.

Ainsi si Pline avait raison de dire, *latifundia perdidere Italiam*, nous avons peut-être raison aussi de nous demander si les *latifundia modernes* ne menacent de ruiner à la base notre civilisation.

[29] Vitruve, X, 4.
[30] Vitruve, X. 5.

[31] Bocklerius, *Theatrum machinarum*, Nuremberg, 1662.

Carlo Dati on the Invention of Eyeglasses

BY EDWARD ROSEN *

THE first writer to discuss the invention of eyeglasses was formerly thought to be the distinguished naturalist, poet and scholar, Francesco Redi (1626–97). But his priority was asserted [1] before it was known that he addressed to his friend Carlo Dati a letter which begins as follows:

Last night Lorenzo Panciatichi [2] told me that at our Accademia della Crusca you read one of your learned *Veglie*, in which you virtually demonstrated that the invention of eyeglasses is not ancient but modern, and a little before 1300.

I congratulate you, and regret not having had the good fortune to be present. I hope however that I can make up this loss by going to your house some morning to beg you to let me hear it. [3]

This letter, being earlier in date than everything else written about eyeglasses by Redi, proves conclusively that in his investigation of the invention he was preceded by Dati, who must therefore be recognized as the first to treat the subject.

Carlo Roberto Dati (1619–76), having become at the age of twenty-one a member of the Accademia della Crusca, was in the habit of reading his writings at meetings of that scholarly Florentine society. [4] At what meeting did he read his *Veglia* entitled *The Invention of Eyeglasses, Is it Ancient or not; and When, Where and by Whom Were They Invented?* This meeting must have taken place shortly before Redi sent him the letter quoted above. Hence the *Veglia*, which carries no date, can be put not much earlier than the Redi-Dati letter. When this was printed, it was dated 31 May 1663. [5] But there is something seriously wrong with this date, as we shall soon see.

Redi's *Letter concerning the Invention of Eyeglasses* (Florence, 1678) opens as follows: "That evening when Carlo Dati, of celebrated memory, read his learned and erudite *Tuscan Veglia about Eyeglasses* at the home of Orazio Rucellai to Don Francesco di Andrea, the great Neapolitan scholar, and to many other Florentine gentlemen . . . ." The Accademia della Crusca, having no fixed meeting-place, used to assemble at the home of one or other of its members; on the evening when Dati

---

* The City College of New York.
[1] By Domenico Maria Manni, *Degli occhiali da naso* (Florence, 1738; 2nd ed., 1741), p. 53.
[2] He was admitted to membership in the Accademia della Crusca on 12 August 1654; *Lettere di Francesco Redi*, ed. Domenico Moreni (Florence, 1825), p. 179.
[3] Francesco Fontani, *Elogio di Carlo Roberto Dati* (Florence, 1794), p. 187.

[4] Guido Andreini, "Carlo Dati e l'Accademia della Crusca," *Miscellanea di studi critici pubblicati in onore di Guido Mazzoni*, edd. A. della Torre and P. L. Rambaldi (Florence, 1907), II, 101–02. I keenly regret not having been able to consult Andreini's *La Vita e l'opera di C. R. Dati* (Florence, 1913).
[5] Fontani, *Elogio*, p. 188.

read the *Veglia*, it met in the house of Orazio Ricasoli Rucellai.[6] To its sessions would be invited any eminent political or literary figure who happened to be visiting Florence, in this instance Francesco d'Andrea.[7] It is his presence at the reading of the *Veglia* that shows the printed date of our Redi-Dati letter to be in error.

As "Ciccio d'Andrea" ("Ciccio" being the affectionate form of "Francesco" in the Neapolitan dialect) he appears in the dithyramb *Bacchus in Tuscany* (Florence, 1685), on which Redi's reputation as a poet chiefly rests.[8] In his own *Notes . . . on the Dithyramb* Redi explained: "This is Don Francesco di Andrea, the very famous Neopolitan lawyer." [9] Hence there can be no doubt that he is the "Don Ciccio" about whom Redi wrote from Florence to a professor at the University of Pisa: "I send you the news that Don Ciccio has been heard here with pleasure by the Grand Duke [of Tuscany], who has given him special marks of esteem." [10] Redi dated this letter "7 January 1672" in the Florentine style.[10a] The oration which he says the Grand Duke heard with pleasure must have been delivered, therefore, by D'Andrea at Florence early in 1673.

How does it happen that Francesco d'Andrea (1625–98), "the very famous Neapolitan lawyer," was declaiming in Florence early in 1673? He left his home in Naples for a leisurely trip northward through the peninsula. "He traveled through Italy and stayed four years," remarked a contemporary biographer,[11] who unfortunately neglected to specify the four years. D'Andrea's progress can be followed to a limited extent, however, because some letters survive which he wrote while on tour. Thus he was in Viterbo on 13 July 1671.[12] By the autumn of that year he was in Perugia which he, as the chief transmitter of the philosophical outlook of Galileo and Descartes to southern Italy, found to be out of touch with contemporary scientific advances: "Here in Perugia they live profoundly unconcerned with these matters. Last night a physician even wanted me to prove to him, by arguments and not by experiments, that the circulation of the blood was true." [13] Remaining in Perugia through the summer of 1672, he proceeded to Florence, where his presence in January of the following year was reported in Redi's letter, quoted above, to the Pisan professor. More than two decades later, recalling the time "many years ago, when I was in Florence," he asked for information about a certain Frenchman whose name he could not remember, "but I saw him in Redi's house." [14] The latter wrote to D'Andrea: "I have read your book . . . with the same admiration with which I enjoyed your learned discourses." [15] During D'Andrea's stay in Florence, then, we have found him a guest in the homes of Redi and Ricasoli Rucellai. But since he took his extended jaunt through Italy in the early seventies, and spoke before the Grand Duke at Florence early in 1673, he must have heard Dati read the *Veglia* at Ricasoli Rucellai's home in May of that year (not 1663). The printed date of our Redi-Dati letter, I submit, should be emended from 31 May 1663 to 31 May 1673.

At this point a question may occur to those who notice that according to a Florentine historian of the early eighteenth century Orazio Ricasoli Rucellai died in February, 1673.[16] Had his death preceded Dati's reading by several months, surely Redi would not have used the language, quoted above, with which he started his *Letter*

[6] He joined the Accademia della Crusca on 11 August 1626 (*Lettere di Redi*, ed. Moreni, p. 185).
[7] He subsequently became a member of the Accademia della Crusca in 1682; *Lettere di Redi*, ed. Moreni, p. 134 (9 January), p. 155 (3 January).
[8] Ed. 1685, p. 6; *Opere di Francesco Redi* (Milan, 1809–11; Classici italiani, vol. 169–77), I, 4.
[9] Ed. 1685, p. 18; *Opere*, I, 59.
[10] *Opere*, V, 79.
[10a] The Florentine calendar started the year not on 1 January, but on the following 25 March.
[11] Biagio Maioli d'Avitabile, *Vita di Francesco d'Andrea*, in *Vite degli Arcadi illustri*, ed. Giovan Mario Crescimbeni (Rome, 1708–14), I, 51.
[12] *Archivio storico per le province napoletane*, 1919, *44*: 242.
[13] *Op. cit.*, p. 240.
[14] *Op. cit.*, pp. 242–44; letter to Magliabechi from Naples, 23 August 1695.
[15] *Opere*, VIII, 175.
[16] Salvino Salvini, *Fasti consolari dell' Accademia fiorentina* (Florence, 1717), p. 575.

concerning the Invention of Eyeglasses: "That evening when Carlo Dati, of celebrated memory, read his learned and erudite *Tuscan Veglia about Eyeglasses* at the home of Orazio Rucellai . . . ." Actually Ricasoli Rucellai died in February, 1674, since the historian dated his demise in the Florentine style. How much caution is needed nowadays (when a uniform system of chronology prevails) in the handling of details emanating from the period when diversity was the rule may be exemplified by what the genealogist of the Ricasoli family did: in the index he put "† 1673" alongside our Orazio, whereas the same author's text reads: "He died on 16 February 1674, common style." [17]

The Redi-Dati letter, which I have suggested was written in 1673 (not 1663), was reprinted [18] by Giuseppe Albertotti (1851–1936), professor of ophthalmology at the University of Padua. Seeing nothing wrong with the 1663 date, he kept it. What is more, he let it exert a sort of magnetic attraction on other documents, making them an entire decade too early. Thus he assigned Redi's *Letter concerning the Invention of Eyeglasses* (1678) to 1668,[19] and a Redi-Dati letter of 8 November 1673 to 1663.[20] A German admirer declared: "Albertotti even succeeded in fixing with precision the date of Dati's reading as the year 1663 or shortly before." [21] But this admirer, Richard Greeff (1862–1938), professor of ophthalmology at the University of Berlin, was no more reliable in chronological questions than his paragon. Remarking that Albertotti's dating of the *Veglia* rested on the Redi-Dati letter (of 31 May 1673) quoted at the beginning of this article, Greeff gave the letter's date as "8 May 1663." [22] To comprehend how he arrived at this weird concoction in a paper dealing specifically with the *Veglia*, I am compelled to conjecture that somehow he took the day of the month from the Redi-Dati letter of 8 November 1673, mistakenly attributed to 1663 by Albertotti.[23]

Greeff's confusions were not confined to chronology, for he classified the *Veglia* as a letter (Brief), addressed (gerichtet) to Redi.[24] True, he called it also an essay (Abhandlung) and a lecture (Vortrag). He recognized its dialogue form, and saw that it was preceded by a dedication (Widmung). Now an essay may be read to an audience, thereby becoming a lecture. The *Veglia* was indeed both essay and lecture. But it was not a letter. It was not addressed or dispatched to Redi, it was dedicated to him.

Dati's dedication of the *Veglia* to Redi commences as follows:

[17] Luigi Passerini, *Genealogia e storia della famiglia Ricasoli* (Florence, 1861), pp. 90, 272; Salvini (*Fasti*, p. 575) dated the death on 6 February, a discrepancy which need not detain us here. When the *Enciclopedia italiana* (XXVIII, 972) put Redi's death on 1 March 1698, should it not have warned its readers that it was using the former calendar of Pisa, where Redi died? By the common or Roman reckoning, he died on 1 March 1697. The designations of these two styles were interchanged by Ugo Viviani, "L'Autopsia e la data della morte di Francesco Redi," *Archeion*, 1934, *16*: 183–85. It was the Roman calendar that started the year with 25 December, the nativity. At Pisa, on the other hand, the year began on the preceding 25 March or incarnation. Hence, 1 March 1698, incarnation style, Pisan variant = 1 March 1697, nativity style; see Adriano Cappelli, *Cronologia, cronografia e calendario perpetuo* (2nd ed., Milan, 1930), pp. 9–11.
[18] "Note critiche e bibliografiche riguardanti la storia degli occhiali," *Annali di ottalmologia*, 1914, *43*: 330–31.
[19] *Op. cit.*, p. 330; but at pp. 334, 342, he

wrote "1678" without noticing that he was contradicting himself.
[20] *Op. cit.*, pp. 330, 335, 354 (no. 4); cf. *Opere di Redi*, V, 82–84.
[21] R. Greeff, "Die Veglia des Carlo Dati über die Erfindung der Brillen," *Zeitschrift für ophthalmologische Optik* (cited hereafter as **ZfoO**), 1917, *5*: 66. Greeff, *Die Erfindung der Augengläser* (Berlin, 1921), pp. 66, 84.
[22] ZfoO, *5*: 66.
[23] Cf. n. 20, above. Greeff translated this letter into German ("Die Briefe des Francesco Redi über die Erfindung der Brillen," ZfoO, 1918, *6*: 2–3). He gave its date correctly as 8 November 1673, so long as he had Redi's text before him (ZfoO, *6*: 1, 3; *Erfindung*, p. 66); but under Albertotti's influence he shifted to 8 November 1663 (ZfoO, *6*: 9; *Erfindung*, p. 82). He likewise translated Redi's *Letter concerning the Invention of Eyeglasses* (ZfoO, *6*: 3–8) and also Dati's *Veglia*, omitting some passages and making some amazing blunders (ZfoO, *5*: 67–77).
[24] ZfoO, *5*: 65; *Erfindung*, pp. 64, 65.

The honors received from you at various times oblige me to show my gratitude, although without hope of not being ungrateful. For that reason I devoted to your celebrated name this *Veglia* of mine, though blushing somewhat, since I perceive that it is too slight a demonstration in comparison with the *Observations of the Insects* dedicated to me by your most learned self.[25]

Only one of Redi's books was dedicated to Dati, the *Experiments concerning the Generation of Insects, Performed by Francesco Redi, Member of the Accademia della Crusca, and Described by him in a Letter to the most illustrious Gentleman, Carlo Dati* (Florence, 1668).[26] Dati can hardly be blamed for shortening so long a title. But among its twenty-five words (in the original Italian) "Observations" (Osservazioni) does not appear. Redi's first publication, however, was entitled *Observations concerning the Vipers* (Florence, 1664). The fact that the work on the insects cited the *Observations* may have caused the contamination of the two titles in Dati's dedication of the *Veglia*. In any case he must have written the dedication after Redi addressed the insect book to him in the form of a letter in 1668.

How long thereafter did Dati write the dedication of the *Veglia*? The length of the interval is indicated in the remainder of the dedication:

But since later you were pleased to make the *Veglia* valuable, bejeweling it, as it were, by communicating to me that recondite notice which closes, seals and confirms it, I venture to offer it to you, or rather to return it to you, for it seems to me to this extent a thing commensurate with your merit and my obligations. If I do not accomplish my purpose, at least the world will know that I have always been, am, and will be your most devoted and most obedient servant.[27]

The "recondite notice" at the close of the *Veglia* probably consists of material transmitted to Dati by Redi in a letter of 26 February 1674.[28] Hence we reach the conclusion, despite Albertotti and Greeff, that Dati read the *Veglia* to the Accademia della Crusca in May, 1673, and wrote the dedication after February, 1674.

If judged by his working habits, Dati would today be called a perfectionist. Never pleased with what he wrote, he was constantly revising, cancelling, adding. His meticulous method of composition is disclosed in a letter where he was talking about his first group of ten *Veglie*: "I have completed the dedications for all ten, which are settled and finished; yet none is begun, because I haven't begun to make the final draft, and that is just as well on account of the many corrections I am always making." [29] In the same letter he spoke about his writing speed: "so fast a pace doesn't succeed with me, and some think me easy-going and lazy, and they say it's better to work fast and badly." This counsel of imperfection Dati rejected as ill suited to his temperament for, as he modestly remarked in this letter: "[If I wrote] in a hurry I wouldn't be satisfied, though I work badly even [when I'm] slow." When he died in January, 1676,[30] he left the *Veglia* unpublished, and even unfinished. Many of his other *Veglie* remained in like condition. Those preserved by his heirs were listed by title some forty years after his death.[31] But this list does not contain

---

[25] Giovanni Targioni Tozzetti, *Atti e memorie inedite dell' Accademia del Cimento* (Florence, 1780), II, 49.

[26] Not 1688, as Greeff would have it (ZfoO, *6*: 1). He erred again in saying that "Redi was professor of medicine at Pisa" (ZfoO, *6*: 1; *Erfindung*, p. 66). Although Redi took his medical degree there, he did not teach the subject; see Angelo Fabroni, *Historia academiae pisanae* (Pisa, 1791–95). Redi's *Insects* was recently re-issued (Rome: Bardi, 1945).

[27] Targioni Tozzetti, II, 49–50.

[28] As I shall undertake to show in a separate article, where I propose to re-examine our sources for the invention of eyeglasses.

[29] *Lettere di Carlo Roberto Dati,* ed. Domenico Moreni (Florence, 1825), pp. 170–71; undated letter to Magliabechi.

[30] Not 1675, as Greeff would have it (ZfoO, *5*: 66; *Erfindung*, p. 65). According to a portrait of Dati reproduced in *L'Accademia del Cimento,* edd. Giorgio Abetti and Pietro Pagnini (Florence: Barbèra, 1942; Le Opere dei discepoli di Galileo Galilei, national edition, vol. I), pp. 24–25, Dati died in January, 1675. But the local artist was of course using the Florentine style (cf. Redi's letter cited in n. 10, above, and the case of Orazio Ricasoli Rucellai, discussed above).

[31] Salvini, *Fasti,* pp. 557–58.

our *Veglia*, because it probably passed into the possession of Dati's former protégé Antonio Magliabechi (1633–1714), librarian of the Grand Duke of Tuscany. In accordance with the terms of Magliabechi's will, his copious private collection of books and manuscripts was converted into Florence's first public library.[32] One of its directors, finding about a century after Dati's death that "The learned and erudite *Tuscan Veglia about Eyeglasses* . . . survives in manuscript with various other unpublished posthumous works of Carlo Dati in . . . the Magliabechiana Public Library," published the *Veglia*.[33] With the achievement of national unification in Italy the Magliabechiana was merged with another important collection in Florence to form the National Central Library. There the autograph of the *Veglia* was examined some forty years ago by Albertotti, who described it as follows:

Not all the sheets have writing on them; not all the written sheets are written on both sides; and not all the written sides are covered completely. . . .
The *Veglia* is not written continuously but in sections separated by blank spaces. . . . Here and there are seen additions, variants and not a few corrections and cancellations, especially in the last two sheets, which have the character almost of a rough draft.[34]

The unfinished state in which Dati left the *Veglia* is evident not only in the physical appearance of the autograph but in its contents also. Thus, in the letter to Dati of 31 May 1673, at the point where our quotation at the beginning of this article stops, Redi continued: "Meanwhile I venture to ask you to think about the inscription, appended hereto, which was found not long ago at Sulmona." [35] Dati thought about it, and had one of his characters in the *Veglia* say: "Nor do I wish here to omit mention of another inscription, found recently (as I am told) at Sulmona." [36] But after the character has repeated Redi's description of the interesting figures carved on the Sulmona stone, Dati himself interjects: "The inscription in Redi's letter will be put here or at the end." It is clear, then, that after Dati read the *Veglia* to the Accademia della Crusca, he continued to putter with it. He utilized some information furnished in Redi's letter to him of 31 May 1673, though undecided where to include the rest. He likewise constructed the climax of the *Veglia*, as we have already learned from the dedication, out of Redi's letter to him of 26 February 1674.

If the composition of the *Veglia* has been correctly ascribed by us, not to 1663 or shortly before, but to 1673 and the closing phase of Dati's life, its dramatic date must be set some thirty-five years earlier. For it portrays Galileo as already totally blind, his condition after December, 1637.[37] And it treats as still alive his beloved disciple Niccolò Arrighetti, who died on 29 May 1639.[38] The characters in the *Veglia* must have come together for their conversation, therefore, at some time in the interval of eighteen months between the end of 1637 and the middle of 1639.

---

[32] Domenico Fava, *La Biblioteca Nazionale Centrale di Firenze* (Milan, 1939), p. 19.

[33] Targioni Tozzetti, I, 70; II, 49–62. The *Enciclopedia italiana* (XII, 398), said nothing about this, the only, publication of the *Veglia*, but instead mentioned a supposed printing at Florence in 1814. The writings of Dati and Redi on eyeglasses "only gained entry into the literature to the extent that Manni quotes and expounds them," said Greeff, remarking later with characteristic inconsistency that Manni "does not know Dati's *Veglia*" ("D. M. Manni," ZfoO, 1919, 7: 1, 5; cf. *Erfindung*, p. 67).

[34] *Annali di ottalmologia*, 43: 331.

[35] *Ibid.*; Fontani, *Elogio*, pp. 187–88.

[36] Targioni Tozzetti, II, 56.

[37] *Le Opere di Galileo Galilei*, national edition (Florence, 1890–1909; reprinted, 1929–39), XVII, 247.4–6.

[38] *Op. cit.*, XX, 374. Four years later, on 13 May 1643 (Salvini, *Fasti*, p. 450), before the Accademia della Crusca Dati delivered an oration in praise of Arrighetti, which was subsequently published in *Prose fiorentine* (Florence, 1661–1745), part I, vol. III, pp. 307–33; ed. Venice, 1735, tome I, part I, vol. III, pp. 134–45. A newly admitted member of the Accademia della Crusca customarily adopted an appropriate surname. Arrighetti's choice was "Il Difeso" (He who has been defended) and he is so denoted in the *Veglia*. Apparently unfamiliar with this quaint academic custom, Greeff mistranslated "Il Difeso" as "the lawyer" (Advokat), and "Il Ricoverato" as "He who has been rescued, The Refugee) as "the discoverer" (Entdecker; ZfoO, 5: 68; *Erfindung*, p. 70). He also called Galileo's masterly little book, the *Sidereus nuncius*, a periodical (Zeitschrift; ZfoO, 5: 69).

The sense in which Dati used the term "Veglia" may be seen in the following passage:

While I was absorbed all by myself in this study, some friends arrived in my tiny library to pass the evening (veglia) there with me. They asked me what I was doing, and having heard, begged me to tell them something interesting. Therefore, to please them, I began to speak as follows. . . .[39]

For the first volume of his projected collection of essays Dati drafted a "Declaration to the Readers" containing the following explanation:

It pleased me to entitle this work *Florentine Veglie*, because it refers to and imagines nocturnal discussions in bygone years at Florence by gentlemen and scholars, mainly Florentine, most of them members of the Accademia della Crusca; and also because it recalls persons, deeds and stories of this city; it considers authors, writings and idioms of our language; and it describes and illustrates things, sites and customs of the place where I was born.[40]

Dati's intention to use the title *Florentine Veglie* is perfectly plain in the "Declaration," as well as in "The Dedication of the *Florentine Veglie* to the reigning Grand Duke," which was found with the "Declaration" among his unpublished papers. As early as 1660 he told a friend that he "had the first book of the *Florentine Veglie* in order."[41] Less than a year before his death he mentioned to another friend "one of my *Florentine Veglie* prepared by me for the press."[42] The evidence, therefore, is overwhelming that Dati's choice of title was *Florentine Veglie*.

This was no mild preference, but rather the expression of a passionate devotion to his birthplace. He taught at the University of Florence. He sought to revitalize the Accademia della Crusca. Every book that he published in his lifetime was printed in Florence, including his *Discourse on the Duty to Speak your native Language Well*. Pride in the excellence of the local literature spurred him to initiate the publication of *Florentine Prose*[43] as a collection of models worthy of being followed in the various genres. He honored the memory of Galileo despite the condemnation of that great scientist by the Roman Catholic church. In his *True Story of the Cycloid and of the Famous Experiment on Quicksilver* he maintained, with regard to these two discoveries which were claimed for non-Florentine rivals, that priority belonged to Galileo's greatest disciple, Evangelista Torricelli. No wonder he wanted the title *Florentine Veglie*.

Nevertheless, as the attentive reader will perhaps already have twice noticed, in his *Letter concerning the Invention of Eyeglasses* (1678) Redi referred to Dati's *Tuscan Veglia about Eyeglasses*. Nor did Redi use such a designation only after Dati's death (1676). In his epoch-making *Generation of Insects* (1668) Redi said, alluding to the design of the spider's web: "And you yourself have written learnedly about it in one of your erudite *Tuscan Veglie* entitled *Nature, the Geometrician*."[44] In a letter dated 14 May 1675 Redi (who was chief physician to the Tuscan Grand Duke) gave Dati (who was already suffering from the illness that was to send him to his grave eight months later) some medical advice and these words of encouragement: "work hard to finish your eagerly awaited *Tuscan Veglia*."[45] In his *Notes to Bacchus in Tuscany* (1685) Redi remarked: "Worth reading in this connection is one of the *Tuscan Veglie* which the learned Carlo Dati left piled up."[46] During Dati's life, then, as well as afterwards Redi regularly referred to Dati's *Veglie* as *Tuscan*, not *Florentine*.[47]

Besides being the founder of experimental entomology, a poet of genuine talent,

[39] Fontani, *Elogio*, pp. 189–90.
[40] Salvini, *Fasti*, p. 556.
[41] Fontani, *Elogio*, p. 232.
[42] *Lettere di C. R. Dati*, p. 80.
[43] Cf. n. 38, above.
[44] Ed. 1668, p. 92; *Opere*, III, 92; ed. 1945, p. 61.
[45] *Opere*, VII, 258.

[46] Ed. 1685, p. 57; *Opere*, I, 114.
[47] "Then why didn't Dati protest?" (asks my colleague Professor Nathan Berall). I can only surmise that Dati forbearingly chose to avoid rebuking Redi in the confident expectation that a printed edition of the *Veglie* would soon proclaim the true title to the entire world.

and a scholar of enormous erudition, Redi seems also to have taken a perverse pleasure in perpetrating literary and lexicographical frauds. He was capable of creating an imaginary thirteenth-century author, pretending to ownership of a manuscript by this figment, citing examples of his supposed usage and publishing them in the *Vocabolario degli Accademici della Crusca.*[48] Did such a man persist in calling Dati's *Veglie* "Tuscan" because, as a native of Arezzo, he did not share Dati's intense passion for Florence? Redi was content, for example, to conclude that "the art of making eyeglasses is a modern invention and was started in Tuscany."[49] Was it his wider loyalty to Tuscany, in contrast to Dati's Florentine particularism, that motivated his deliberately inaccurate citations of Dati's *Veglie?* The false title he bestowed on them has acquired considerable currency by reason of the immense popularity enjoyed by those of Redi's works in which the misnomer appears.[50] The consequent confusion concerning the title of Dati's *Veglia* is due, then, to the good friend to whom he dedicated it.[51]

---

[48] *Rivista delle biblioteche e degli archivi,* 1909, *20:* 65–72; *Atti della r. Accademia della Crusca,* 1915–16, pp. 33–136.
[49] *Letter concerning the Invention of Eyeglasses,* ed. 1678, p. 10; *Opere,* II, 262. Greeff suffered from the delusion that "Redi writes, and turns and twists the original text, with partiality for Pisa" (ZfoO, *7:* 2); and that "Redi makes the greatest efforts to secure the glory of the invention [of eyeglasses] for Florence's rival, Pisa, his native city" (Vaterstadt; *Erfindung,* p. 84). Although Greeff himself correctly named Arezzo as Redi's birthplace (ZfoO, *6:* 1; *Erfindung,* p. 66), he persisted in calling Redi a Pisan (ZfoO, *6:* 2, *7:* 2; *Erfindung,* pp. 78, 84). Greeff also asserted that "Dati, the Florentine, sought him [the unknown

inventor of eyeglasses] particularly in Florence" (*Erfindung,* p. 84). But in the *Veglia* Dati said: "Hence I conclude that the first inventor of so noble a device probably was a Pisan" (Targioni, II, 60), and Dati's conclusion was translated into German by Greeff himself (ZfoO, *5:* 76).
[50] The editions must be reckoned by the dozens; see Dino Prandi, *Bibliografia delle opere di Francesco Redi* (Reggio-Emilia: Nironi & Prandi, 1941).
[51] Redi may have influenced Targioni, I, 70, 443; and Moreni, ed. *Lettere di C. R. Dati,* p. 170. But was he responsible for the use of "Veglie Toscane" by Jean Chapelain, a French member of the Accademia della Crusca, on 15 September 1667 (Salvini, *Fasti,* p. 558)?

Hero's *Pneumatica*
A Study of its Transmission and Influence

BY MARIE BOAS *

T HE interest in pneumatics that arose suddenly in the late sixteenth century and led in the next century to the work of Torricelli and Boyle has never been properly explained.[1] One important incentive was undoubtedly technological, the increasing use of suction pumps during the later Renaissance, particularly in mining and water-works;[2] but equally important and generally overlooked was the sixteenth-century translation, into Latin and the vernacular, of Hero of Alexandria's *Pneumatica*.[3]

Hero's dates are of extreme uncertainty.[3a] Since he mentions Archimedes and is mentioned by Pappus, he must have flourished somewhere between the second century B.C. and the third century A.D. A recent study by Neugebauer of Hero's *Dioptra* [3b] has shown that he may have referred to a real eclipse of the moon in the problem of determining the distance between Rome and Alexandria. According to the terms of the problem, the eclipse referred to could only be that of 13 March 63 A.D.; this would place Hero conclusively in the first century A.D.

Like much other Hellenistic science, Hero's work awaited translation until the later Renaissance.[4] These later translations appeared in response to specific demand, at a time when interest had turned from the re-appraisal of the science known to the Middle Ages to the study of the newly re-discovered work of the Alexandrians. A consequence of this shift in interest was the translation of these Hellenistic works into Latin.

The earlier engineers and "practical men" of necessity read some Latin,[5] but as their

* Seminar in the History of Science, Cornell University.

[1] This problem was suggested by Professor Henry Guerlac, who has given me much helpful criticism and guidance. Valuable suggestions were made by Professors M. L. W. Laistner and Friedrich Solmsen.

[2] This thesis was developed by R. K. Merton, "Science, Technology and Society in Seventeenth Century England," *Osiris*, **4**, 1938, chap. VII, especially p. 506f. See also L. Hogben, *Science for the Citizen*, New York, 1938, p. 351f.; James B. Conant, *On Understanding Science*, New Haven, 1947, p. 31f.

[3] The standard edition of Hero's works is that published by Teubner and edited by W. Schmidt (Leipzig, 1899) in German and Greek; there is an English translation in *The Pneumatics of Hero of Alexandria*, edited by Bennet Woodcroft, London, 1851; and a French translation by A. de Rochas in *La Science des philosophes et l'art des thaumaturges dans l'antiquité*, Paris, 1882. The *Supplementum* to volume I of the Teubner edition is entirely devoted to the MSS and printed editions of the *Pneumatica*.

[3a] For the older literature on this subject, and for details of Hero's work see George Sarton, *Introduction to the History of Science*, vol. I, 1927, pp. 208–211, and K. Tittel's article on Hero in Pauly-Wissowa *Real-Encyclopädie*, vol. 15, col. 992–1080, 1912.

[3b] O. Neugebauer, "Uber eine Methode zur Distanzbestimmung Alexandria-Rom bei Heron," pp. 21–24, *Det Kgl. Danske Videnskabernes Selskab, Hist.-fil. Meddelelser, 26*, pt. 2, 1938. For a critique, see A. Rome's review of this article in *L'antiquité classique, 7*, 1938, 460–62; Rome agrees that the first century A.D. is the likeliest date for Hero, although he is not sure that Hero refers to an eclipse that actually took place.

[4] For example, the first Latin edition of Apollonius of Perga appeared in 1537; of Archimedes in 1543; and of Diophantus in 1574; the Greek editions were later.

[5] It should be borne in mind that many scientifically inclined men, even those without a humanist education, could decipher scientific treatises in Latin, even though they wrote in the vernacular, and might profess to have no real knowledge of Latin. For example, Leonardo da Vinci repeatedly refers to the works of Greek scientists, including Hero, which were available only in Latin and Greek. See E. Solmi, "Li fonti di Leonardo da Vinci," *Giornale Storico*, supplemento 10 e 11, 1908, for a list of all writers of antiquity and later periods to whom Leonardo refers.

numbers grew there was a demand for vernacular editions of ancient scientific works. In increasing numbers during the late sixteenth and early seventeenth centuries there appeared vernacular translations of various scientific classics, especially those concerned with practical applications like the works of Hero and Vitruvius. The translator, himself usually a humanist,[6] thus formed a link between humanism proper, often decried as antiscientific, and the practical engineer and craftsman, in whom certain writers on the Renaissance have seen the germ of the experimental method which marks the beginning of modern science.[7] A Latin translation might have been made for the use of the scholar or humanist (though this was not always the case) but it is impossible to believe that translations of Greek and Latin science into Italian, French, German or English were made with any other purpose except to provide working textbooks for men not conversant with the language of learning. Thus humanism is seen to have had important consequences for science, though this has perhaps been unduly ignored by those whose attention is exclusively focussed on the socio-economic forces in the early development of modern science.

Hero's *Pneumatica* is essentially a treatise on natural magic, as later centuries called the study of the unexplained properties of nature, in which are described various mechanical contrivances worked by air, water and steam. Most famous is the eolipile, a simple reaction turbine in which an escaping jet of steam causes a pivoted ball to revolve; this is a typical example of the kind of device which Hero discussed: simple, amusing, and usually of no great practical importance. The *Pneumatica* is of interest in the history of scientific theory no less than in the history of technology, since its preface contains a discussion of air and the vacuum which is of great interest.

For Hero, air is a material substance, consisting of minute particles[8] between which there is only vacuum. There is no *continuous* vacuum in nature, though such a vacuum can be produced artificially in various simple ways, but Hero insists on the presence of a discontinuous vacuum separating the particles of all matter.[9] Further, air is compressible suffering expansion and contraction. Hero's theory of matter is summed up at the end of the preface:

It may therefore be affirmed in this matter that every body is composed of minute particles, between which are empty spaces (so that we erroneously say that there is no vacuum except by the application of force, and that every place is full either of air, or water, or some other substance), and, in proportion as any one of these particles recedes, some other follows it and fills the vacant space: that there is no continuous vacuum except by the application of some force: and again, that the absolute vacuum is never found, but is produced artificially.[10]

Hero thus had a very satisfactory theory of elastic fluids, based on a particulate theory of matter.

Although Hero's work was known to the Arabs[11] such knowledge of it as Western

---

[6] The word humanist is used here in the restricted sense of a scholar interested mainly in the recovery, study or translation of the Greek and Latin classics.

[7] The leading exponent of this view is undoubtedly L. Olschki. See his *Geschichte der neusprachlichen wissenschaftlichen Literatur*, 3 vols., Leipzig, 1919–27. The same view was held by the late Edgar Zilsel; see especially "The Sociological Roots of Science," *The American Journal of Sociology*, 47, 4, January 1942.

[8] The Greek word is *sōmata* (bodies). Schmidt translates it as "Molekulen" which has perhaps overly modern connotations.

[9] Hero's theory of matter seems to have been derived from that of Strato of Lampsacus, the last head of the Athenian Lyceum. Strato's atomism was ultimately of Democritean origin, but modified by the Aristotelian doctrines to

which, as a member of the Peripatetic school, he was naturally heir. See H. Diels, "Über das physikalische System des Stratons," *Sitzungsberichte der K. P. Akademie der Wissenschaften zu Berlin*, 1893, 1, 101–127; P. Brunet and A. Mieli, *L'Histoire des sciences; antiquité*, Paris, 1935, p. 321f.

[10] *Pneumatica*, Woodcroft edition, p. 10. Hero was less happy in his attempts to explain the action of a siphon: a continuous void cannot exist; therefore a force is exerted to prevent its formation; this is nearly identified with the pressure of the atmosphere, but never explicitly.

[11] A. Mieli, *La Science Arabe*, Leiden, 1938, p. 22. See the *Legacy of Islam*, ed. by Sir Thomas Arnold, articles by Max Meyerhof and by Carra de Vaux, pp. 321 and 387, for the mechanical contrivances made in imitation of Hero.

Europe had during the Middle Ages came directly from the Greek original.[12] At least a partial translation of the *Pneumatica* was made in Sicily in the twelfth century; this is referred to by Henricus Aristippus as "Eronis philosophi mechanica"[13] and is listed in Richard of Fournival's *Bibliomania* (dated about 1250) as "excerpta de libro Heronis de spiritualibus ingeniis."[14] This translation has been lost[15] and may, in fact, be not the genuine *Pneumatica*, but the work of the much later Hero the Younger, called the Philosopher.[16] There was another translation, as yet unidentified, by William of Moerbeke; this is probably the one referred to in the letter of the Paris Faculty of Arts on the death of Thomas Aquinas,[17] and mentioned in the thirteenth-century *Summa Philosophiae* of the Pseudo-Grosseteste, which, in discussing the problem of the vacuum, refers to the opinions of "Hero egregius philosophus."[18] There is no mention of Hero after this until in the fifteenth century Giovanni da Fontana refers to the *Pneumatica*:[19] in his *Protheus*[20] there is mention of the "work of Hero *de vacuo et inani*," which would appear to be the last trace of the now lost mediaeval translations.

In the late fifteenth and early sixteenth centuries there were signs of growing interest in Hero's work. All the earliest complete Greek manuscripts date from this period.[21] There were even early plans for printed editions; the tradelist of scientific books issued hopefully by Regiomontanus in 1474 contains "Heronis inuenta spiritalia," which would presumably have been in Latin, but which never appeared.[22] The first printed edition of any part of Hero's work is generally conceded to be the Latin paraphrase of the early pages of the *Pneumatica* contained in the *De expetendis et fugiendis rebus* of the humanist Giorgio Valla. This encyclopedia, published at Venice in 1501, contains extracts from much of the more advanced Hellenistic science, including some of the works of Archimedes.[23] The chapter *De spiritalibus*[24] is a quick résumé, in some eight folio pages, of parts of Hero's preface and the theory of siphons, and is close enough to the original to have led some of the more critical minds of the sixteenth century to accuse Valla of plagiarism.[25] It may have been through Valla's

---

[12] For Hero's influence in the Middle Ages see, above all, C. H. Haskins, *Studies in the History of Mediaeval Science*, Cambridge (Mass.) 1924; this includes references to those who read Hero and to translations made in the 12th and 13th centuries. Lynn Thorndike, *A History of Magic and Experimental Science*, 6 vols., New York, 1923–41, has numerous references to Hero, both for the Middle Ages and for the 16th century; it gives useful leads, but is sometimes inaccurate. As a supplement to Haskins, A. Birkenmajer, "Vermischte Untersuchungen zur Geschichte der mittelalterlichen Philosophie," *Beiträge zur Geschichte der Philosophie des Mittelalters*, 20, 5, 1917–23, pp. 1–33, is very valuable. Reference should also be made to V. Rose, "Die Lücke im Diogenes Laertius und der alter Übersetzer," *Hermes*, I, 1866, 388f.

[13] In the introduction to his translation of Plato's *Phaedo*; see Haskins, *Mediaeval Science*, p. 182.

[14] A. Birkenmajer, "Vermischte Untersuchungen," p. 30.

[15] Except for possible fragments identified by Birkenmajer and Haskins. See Haskins, *Mediaeval Science*, p. 182–3, where part of the text is reprinted. These may have been part of the version known to Adelard of Bath; see Thorndike, vol. II, pp. 37–40.

[16] W. Schmidt, *Heronis Alexandrinus Opera I Supplementum*, p. 52.

[17] Birkenmajer, "Vermischte Untersuchungen," p. 19f.

[18] Thorndike, vol. I, p. 189. For the text, see

Ludwig Bauer, "Die philosophischen Werke des Robert Grosseteste," *Beiträge zur Geschichte der Philosophie des Mittelalters*, 9, 1912, pp. 275–643.

[19] A. Birkenmajer, "Zur Lebengeschichte und wissenschaftlichen Tätigkeit von Giovanni Fontana (1395?–1455?)," *Isis*, 17, 1932, 34–53.

[20] This is probably the work of Fontana. See Thorndike, vol. IV, p. 179.

[21] Schmidt, *Heronis Opera I Supplementum*, pp. 3–6, lists only one MS which is earlier than the 16th century, and this may be as late as the 15th. There is, however, a 14th century MS containing excerpts from *Philonis de ingeniis spiritualibus*, which indicates a certain interest in the problem of the vacuum. Quoted by V. Rose, *Anecdota Graeca et Graecolatina*, Berlin 1864, pp. 283–330.

[22] Nor did Regiomontanus, apparently, ever make the projected translation. The tradelist (of which only one item was published) is reproduced by Sarton in "The Scientific Literature Transmitted through the Incunabula," *Osiris*, 4, 1938, 163.

[23] Valla was the owner of the Codex Vallae, from which the important Archimedes MSS are all derived.

[24] Chapter I of Book XV, *De geometria*.

[25] Especially by Conrad Gesner, *Bibliotheca Universalis*, Tiguri, 1545. Under Giorgius Valla: "Nos sane obseruauimus Giorgium Vallam a Graecis permulta dissimulantur esse mutuatum, & non pauca perperam in Latinum sermonem transtulisse." f. 273, *recto*.

summary that Hero became known to Leonardo da Vinci, who cites Hero several times and was apparently influenced by his mechanical devices, though not by his theory.[26] It is possible that Maurolycus intended to follow Valla in excerpting Hero; his *Cosmographia* (Venice, 1543) lists, in the table of contents for the fourth section, "Heronis inuenta spiritalia: ac nonnullae machinae hydraulicae a recentioribus inuentae." Unfortunately and inexplicably, the book ends some time before this topic was to be reached, and the only references to Hero are such as Maurolycus could have got from Pappus and Proclus.[27] An indication of the rising interest in Hero is the amount of space devoted to a discussion of his views by the mathematician and physician Jerome Cardan in his very popular *De subtilitate*, first published in 1550, which shows a considerable acquaintance with at least some of Hero's *Pneumatica*.[28] Petrus Ramus owned a Greek manuscript of Hero's works, and Conrad Gesner referred to Greek manuscripts of the *Pneumatica sive spiritualia* in Italian libraries.[29]

At the end of the sixteenth century this growing interest in Hero's work resulted in a burst of translation into Latin and the vernacular. The first of the Latin editions, which remained the standard edition of the *Pneumatica* until the late nineteenth century, was that published in 1575 as *Heronis Alexandrini spiritalium liber, A Federico Commandino Urbinate, ex Graeco, nuper in Latinum conversus*. Commandino had received a humanist and medical education, and was associated with the court of the dukes of Urbino as a translator of Greek science and as a mathematical tutor.[30] The Commandino edition was reprinted in 1583 (at Paris) and in 1680 (at Amsterdam).

Commandino's was the only published Latin translation, but there were numerous vernacular editions. In 1582 Bernardo Davanzati[31] completed his translation of the preface to the *Pneumatica*, which under the title *Della natura del voto* he dedicated to the architect and painter Buontalenti. The latter had, apparently, a special interest in the work, since Davanzati speaks of an Italian translation of the entire *Pneumatica* made for Buontalenti by Biringuccio; unfortunately this translation is otherwise unknown. More important than Davanzati's work was the Italian translation of the *Pneumatica* which appeared in 1589 as *Gli artificiosi, e curiose moti spiritali de Erone Alessandrino, tradotti da Gio. Batista Aleotti d'Argenta*.[32] Aleotti was an architect and engineer interested in hydraulics, who added some hydraulic "theorems" of his own to the work of Hero. This translation was made not from the Greek, but

[26] Solmi, "Li Fonti di Leonardo da Vinci," LXIX, "Erone," and CLXXXVI, "Valla." For a detailed discussion of the extent of Hero's influence see W. Schmidt, "Leonardo da Vinci und Heron von Alexandria," *Bibliotheca Mathematica*, 3, 3, 1902, 180–187; Schmidt feels that Leonardo was influenced by Hero's devices but not by his theory of matter; there is no discussion of how Leonardo knew of Hero. For Leonardo's references to Hero in the Codex Atlanticus, see *Indici per materie ed alfabetico del Codice Atlantico di Leonardo da Vinci*, compilata da G. Semenza, Milano, 1939.

[27] For example, "Heronis & Procli praeceptū ad uneniēdā visualō solis diametrā" and "Heron & Proclus clepsydrā pendentē aqua plenā constituunt," margin and text, f. 84 *recto*. Gesner, under "Heron Alexandrinus," says "There are also Latin MSS [of the *Pnuematica*]," and refers to f.253 *verso* where he gives the table of contents of the *Cosmographia*. (*Bibliotheca Universalis*, f.309 *verso*).

[28] In volume III of Cardan's *Opera Omnia*, Lugduni, 1663. The French translation of Richard Le Blanc, *Les livres de Hierosme Cardanus . . . intitulez de la subtilité*, Rouen, 1642, was also used.

[29] Petrus Ramus, *Scholarum mathematicarum libri XXI*, first published in 1569. "Studiose vel curiose potius Heronis opera exquisita sunt." Quoted by Schmidt (*Heronis Opera I Supplementum*, p. 41) from the Frankfurt edition of 1627. For Gesner, see *Bibliotheca Universalis*, f. 309 *verso*, "Heron Alexandrinus."

[30] Commandino also translated Archimedes, Apollonius, Aristarchus, Euclid, Pappus. For the humanist court of the later della Rovere dukes of Urbino, see James Dennistoun, *Memoirs of the Dukes of Urbino*, London, 1909, Book IX, "Of Literature and Art under the Dukes Della Rovere at Urbino."

[31] 1529–1606. As a retired merchant, he devoted himself to various studies and seems to have been interested in developing the use of the vernacular. Besides Hero, he translated the *Annals* of Tacitus.

[32] Thorndike, vol. V, p. 364, quoting Doppelmayr's *Historische Nachricht von den Nürnbergischen Mathematicis und Künstlern*, Nürnberg, 1730, p. 17, erroneously ascribes the first edition of Aleotti's translation to 1543. Aleotti was not born until 1546.

from Commandino's Latin edition; it was very popular, being reprinted in 1647 at Bologna and in 1693 at Paris. There was still another Italian translation, the *Spiritali di Herone Alessandrino, ridotte in lingua volgare da Alessandro Giorgi*, published at Urbino in 1592 and reprinted at Venice in 1595. Giorgi was apparently at the court of Urbino, since his work is dedicated to the Duke, and he mentions Commandino as an acquaintance.[33] Giorgi says in his preface that he had planned a translation earlier, but had delayed because of a projected version by Barbaro, the editor and translator of Vitruvius.[34] Giorgi's is a more learned translation than any of the others, not excepting Commandino's, being equipped with critical apparatus and some discussion of the mechanism of various of the devices, with reference to the work of Georgi's contemporaries. In 1687 there appeared the first of three editions of a German translation of the *Pneumatica*. The Greek text was finally published in 1693 in the *Veterum mathematicorum opera* of Thévenot.

That there appeared three Latin editions of Hero's *Pneumatica* between 1575 and 1700 should be sufficient indication of its popularity. The additional vernacular editions (five in Italian alone) supply even more striking evidence. These vernacular editions could only have been for the use of the increasing number of Italian engineers and architects, men without a reading knowledge of Latin, who were eager to study the works of antiquity. The vernacular translation made by men of humanist education are a significant indication of the existence of a bond between humanist and craftsman, and of the contribution that humanism made to the new and growing field of science.

By the beginning of the seventeenth century Hero's work was well known; so well known indeed that casual reference to it was readily understood. Thus Bacon could use Hero illustratively: "the mechanics here understood is that treated by Aristotle promiscuously, by Hero in his Pneumatics, . . ."[35] Or Robert Burton could inquire, "What so intricate, and pleasing withal, as to peruse and practice Hero Alexandrinus' works, on the air engine, the war engine, the engine that moveth itself. . . ?"[36] Or Gilbert, discussing the action of the "effluvium of electrics" could find it natural to compare their action with "the air from vaporized water rushing forth from a pipe (as in the instrument described by Hero of Alexandria in his book *Spiritualia*)."[37] Pascal could refer to "Heron . . . one of the oldest and best of the authors who have written on the raising of water;"[38] and even Robert Boyle, discussing the types of ancient science, added "not to mention what *Hero* teaches in his Pneumaticks."[39] The authority that Hero had acquired in matters hydraulic and pneumatic is well illustrated by the boast with which the Czech Dobrzensky prefaced his book on hydraulics "Redivivi Heronis nova et amenior de fontibus philosophia."[40]

The only aspect of the revival of Hero's work to which much attention has been

---

[33] Giorgi seems to be known only as the translator of Hero, and is not otherwise mentioned by the standard bibliographic works. Dennistoun, *Dukes of Urbino*, vol. III, p. 259, associates Giorgi with the Court.

[34] Daniele Barbaro, whom Giorgi oddly calls Hermalao, the name of several other members of his family, was born about 1514. The Italian translation of Vitruvius appeared first in 1556, and was reprinted in 1567. See *M. Vitruvii Pollionis Architectura . . . ed . . . J. Poleni et Simon Stratico*, Utini, 1825.

[35] *De Augmentis Scientarum* Book III, chap. V. (Creighton edition). Bacon owned the Commandino edition of Hero: see E. Wolff, *Francis Bacon und seine Quellen*, Berlin, 1910, Vol. II, p 188ff.

[36] R. Burton, *The Anatomy of Melancholy*, edited by Floyd Dell and Paul Jordan Smith,

New York, 1938, part. 2, sect. 2, memb. 4, p. 461.

[37] W. Gilbert, *On the Loadstone*, translated by P. Fleury Mottelay, reprinted in the Classics of the St. John's Program, Book II, Ch. II, p. 95.

[38] *The Physical Treatises of Pascal*, trans. by I. H. B. and A. G. H. Spiers, with introduction and notes by F. Barry, New Lork, 1937, p. 71.

[39] R. Boyle, *The Excellency of Theology*, in *Works*, ed. by Birch, London 1772, vol. IV, p. 58.

[40] *Nova, et amoenior de admirando fontium genio (ex abditis naturae claustris, in orbis lucem emanante) philosophiae . . . auctore Iacobo Dobrzenski de Nigro Ponte*, Ferrara, 1659. Though a Czech, Dobrzenski lived mostly in Italy where he practiced medicine; he wrote several works on medical subjects.

given is the influence of his mechanical contrivances on the work of the sixteenth and seventeenth-century writers on machines. Libri went so far as to say that there was practically no interest in machines in sixteenth-century Italy *except* for the attention which the *Pneumatica* attracted from engineers and scholars, and Ewbank regarded the *Pneumatica* as the great reviving influence on hydrodynamics in the sixteenth century.[41] These authorities clearly exaggerate, but it is certain that a flood of useful and amusing machines and devices makes its appearance coincident with the rediscovery of Hero's work, and that many of these show distinct Heronic parentage.[42] In many cases, of course, writers merely copied from one another, and it is often difficult to tell whether or not a particular device is derived directly from Hero. All these mechanical writings were extremely popular, beginning with Cardan's *De subtilitate* and continuing with the work of Besson, Porta, Drebbel, Fludd, Leurechon, Ens, Harsdoerffer, and Kircher until the mid-seventeenth century. Perhaps the works of these authors can best be described as dealing with natural magic, the study of the unexplained forces of nature, of magnetism, change of state, and optical illusion. Hero's treatise was very much in this tradition, which may in part account for the eagerness with which it was studied and copied.

One of the earliest and most successful of these books was Giambattista della Porta's *Magia Naturalis*, originally published in 1558, in four books with no mention of pneumatics. It went through numerous editions, and in 1589 (when Hero's work was available in both Latin and Italian) it was enlarged to twenty books, including one devoted to pneumatics. Many of the devices were adapted from Hero, in spite of Porta's claim "There are extant the famous monuments of the most learned Hero of Alexandria, concerning wind instruments. I will adde some that are new, to give occasion to search out greater matters." [43] And in 1601 Porta published his *Pneumaticorum libri tres*, a strongly derivative work with frequent mention of Hero, though he rejects Hero's theory of the vacuum.

A typical and extremely popular work of the type under discussion was Robert Fludd's *Historia utriusque cosmi*, which appeared in 1617.[44] This was all-embracing,

---

[41] These two authors far underestimate the extent to which engineering had advanced in Italy by the end of the 16th century. The Renaissance engineer, civil and military, must be regarded as being as characteristic of the age as the humanist. But see Libri, *Histoire des sciences mathématiques en Italie*, Paris, 1840, t. 4, p. 68; Thomas Ewbank, *A Descriptive and Historical Account of Hydraulic and Other Machines for Raising Water Ancient and Modern*, 3rd edition, New York, 1849, p. 385. "This little book . . . stimulated, if it did not create that spirit of investigation and experimental research which then commenced and has continued unimpaired to the present times . . . Philosophers, chemists, and physicians, as well as engineers, illustrated their writings by its problems and figures. Porta, De Caus, Fludd, and others, avowedly transferred its pages to their works, while many writers with less candor and less ingenuity made use of it without acknowlegedment."

[42] For the scientists who read and commented upon Hero, the most important reference is W. Schmidt, "Heron von Alexandria im 17. Jahrhundert," *Abhandlung zur Geschichte der Mathematik*, 8, 1898, 197–214. This article is detailed, in that it discusses most (but not all) the scientists and writers on mechanics who mentioned Hero or derived mechanical devices from his work. It is however not exhaustive, and is quite uncritical, making little distinction be-

tween men who leaned heavily on Hero and those who merely mention one or two of his contrivances; and there is little discussion of the influence of Hero upon theory. Similar is A. de Rochas, *La Science des philosophes et l'art des thaumaturges dans l'antiquité*, Paris, 1882. This has a French translation of the *Pneumatica* and notes on authors who were influenced by Hero's machines, pp. 77–175. Though limited, this has more actual details than Schmidt; however it mentions only Oronce Finé, Schwenter, Ens, Schott, Besson, Kircher and Drebbel. Emil Wolff, *Francis Bacon und seine Quellen*, Berlin, 1910, has a chapter on Hero (vol. II, p. 188–197) in which he quotes at length not only Bacon's references to Hero, but those of Gilbert, Kepler, Fludd, and Ramus.

[43] J. B. Porta, *Natural Magick*, London, 1658, p. 385, preface to Book 19.

[44] *Utriusque cosmi maioris scilicet et minoris metaphysica, physica, atque technica, historia*, Frankfurt, 1617. The references to Hero are tract. I, lib. I, p. 32; tract. II, pars VII, lib. III and IV. For a comparison of the relative importance accorded to Fludd in England and on the Continent, compare the articles in the D. N. B. and the *Nouvelle Biographie Générale*. P. A. Cap, *La Science et les savants au XVI siècle*, 1867, pp. 233–5, 252–3, goes so far as to credit Fludd with the discovery that air was a material substance, possessed of elasticity!

and included topics ranging from the creation, described with intimate detail, to the most advanced technology of the day, with a considerable amount of pneumatics: first in connection with the element air, and later in discussions of the vacuum and of pneumatic and hydraulic machines. Fludd was a curious person; an English physician who dabbled rather more in the occult than was quite usual even for his profession; and an ardent defender of the Rosicrucians. His mystical doctrines were ignored in England — perhaps they were not taken seriously — but he was fiercely attacked on the Continent by Kepler, Gassendi and Mersenne.

Less ambitiously encyclopedic were the works of Athanasius Kircher, Jesuit professor of mathematics and oriental languages at Rome. His *Ars Magnetica* (1641) strayed often from its subject, and included a considerable section on pneumatics and hydraulics,[45] with a description of the thermoscope, probably adapted from Drebbel's "perpetual motion" machine.[46] Kircher frequently cited Drebbel as an authority. In spite of his wide and miscellaneous learning, Kircher's physics was thoroughly conservative, and he never accepted the new discoveries of Torricelli and Guericke. Another Jesuit professor of oriental languages, Daniel Schwenter of Altdorff, was co-author with Georg Philip Harsdoerffer, senator of Nürnberg, of a characteristic seventeenth-century potpourri — the *Deliciae physico-mathematicae* (1653) written in German.[47] The authors discussed mechanical and mathematical devices, problems, and tricks, but had a rather baffling tendency to mingle the physical and mystical in inextricable fashion, so that the section on pneumatics ranges from the nature of the soul to the Torricellian vacuum.

More modern in tone are the purely mechanical treatises, such as Jean Leurechon's *Récréations Mathématiques* (1624) and the *Thaumaturgus Mathematicus* (1628) of Gasper Ens. Leurechon was another scientifically-minded Jesuit, whose popular French treatise described simple mathematical and physical problems, theoretical, practical, and amusing, with a section on pneumatic and hydraulic devices. In connection with pneumatic fountains, "Ie laisse les inventions d'Hero, de Cresibius [sic], & autres semblables dont plusiers ont traicté, me contenant d'en produire une plus nouvelle et assez plausible."[48] Ens was an interesting though obscure figure who had studied law but supported himself by writing; the *Thaumaturgus Mathematicus* is very closely based on Leurechon's work.[49]

Perusal of such works as those just mentioned leads to an acquaintance with a seemingly endless variety of pneumatic fountains, automata, trick drinking-vessels, self-trimming lamps, and perpetual motion machines. These contrivances were based on the same simple principles as Hero's: the expansive power of air, the action of a siphon, the fact that a liquid cannot flow from a closed vessel unless air can get in.

---

[45] A. Kircher, *Magnes sive de arte magnetica*, 2nd ed. Coloniae Agrippinae, 1643. Lib. III, Pars II.

[46] Cornelis Drebbel was a very versatile late Renaissance figure: engraver, inventor, court scientist in England and Prague. He was held in high esteem by contemporaries and is frequently cited by Robert Boyle. His most widely read work was *A Short Treatise on the Nature of the Elements and how they bring about wind, rain, lightening, thunder, and why they are useful*, published in Dutch in 1604 and translated into many languages. In a section on the element air, he discussed its powers of expansion and contraction (used in his famous perpetual motion machine, a form of thermoscope), and the change of state from water to "air"; see Gerrit Tierie, *Cornelis Drebbel*, (*1572–1633*), Amsterdam, 1932, (in English), the only useful study. There is a bibliography of the older work on Drebbel in Ferguson's

Bibliotheca Chemica, Glasgow, 1906; there is no really good source in any of the major European languages. For possible influence of Hero on Drebbel, see A. de Rochas, *La science des philosophes*, p. 137.

[47] *Delitiae* [sic] *physico-mathematice oder mathematischen und philosophischen Erquickstunden*. Dritter Theil . . . durch Georg Philip Harsdörffern. Nürnberg, 1653.

[48] *Examen du livre des Récréations Mathématiques et de ses problémes . . . par Claude Mydorge*, Rouen, 1639. Prob. LXXVIII, VII, "D'une autre belle fontaine." The English edition, *Mathematical Recreations* by Henry van Etten, London, 1674, omits this sentence, and other descriptive material.

[49] See the Cologne edition of 1651, Prob. XCIII, VII, "De alio fonte pulcherrimo." "Omissis Heronis, & Cresibi, aliorumve quodam & plausibiliori fontis genere hic cententus ero."

Only the mechanism was changed. For example, Hero described a method by which the door of a temple could be made to open when a fire was lighted upon the altar: the fire caused the air in the hollow altar to expand; this drove water into a bucket, connected through a series of chains and pulleys to the door, so that the weight of the water caused the door to open. Robert Fludd had a contrivance using the same principle, but "the doors may be made to open of themselves by various other methods than that of Hero, of which the following is one invented by us," using neat and elaborate Renaissance gearing.[50] All these devices were popular; John Evelyn, traveling in Holland, saw a "lamp" from which issued streams of water under the force of compressed air; while in Italy he saw in formal gardens artificial birds that sang, and "a coper ball that continually daunces about 3 foote above the pavement by virtue of a wind conveyed secretely to a hole beneath it."[51] Mechanical inventiveness was also stimulated by Hero's eolipile,[52] which was the basis of the earliest attempts at steam-engine design. Poggendorff believes that an eolipile supplied the power for the paddle-wheel boat which Blasco de Garay is supposed to have tested in 1543;[53] and Salomon de Caus was influenced by Hero's work to a considerable extent.[54]

For a thorough knowledge of the properties of air Hero's *Pneumatica* was invaluable, being the standard textbook on the subject[55] until, from the work of Torricelli, Pascal, Guericke, Boyle, and Mariotte, there emerged the modern theories of the vacuum and of elastic fluids. Until its final overthrow, Hero's theory was considered extremely advanced. Cardan, writing in the mid-sixteenth century, was unable to comprehend Hero's ideas on the vacuum; Hero's argument that air is a material substance Cardan readily accepted, and he recognized the compressibility of air, but he ignored Hero's theory of vacua between air particles.[56] The elasticity of air could hardly fail of recognition, since it was on this property that the operation of so many mechanical contrivances rested; its cause was more uncertain. Hero's mechanism, involving a particulate theory of matter, was sometimes rejected, as by Porta, Gilbert, and even Aleotti,[57] but it was always discussed. The recognition of the air's ability to expand and contract was an important step towards the understanding of its true physical nature.

---

[50] *Historia utriusque cosmi*, tract. II, pars VII, lib. III, exp. XIV.

[51] John Evelyn, *Diary*, entries for 19 August 1637 and 5 May 1645, respectively.

[52] Besides Hero's eolipile (a reaction turbine) there was also current in the sixteenth and seventeenth centuries the eolipile described by Vitruvius, a metal retort with a narrow opening, filled with water to provide an air or steam blast when heated. This was a common laboratory instrument of the period. See Vitruvius, *De Architectura*, Book I, chapter VI, section 2, for a discussion of the "figures of Aeolus." For pictures, and a comparison of the two types of eolipile, see F. M. Feldhaus, *Die Technik der Vorzeit, der geschichtlichen Zeit und der Naturvölker*, Leipzig, 1914, articles "Aeolipila" and "Aeolsball."

[53] *Geschichte der Physik*, Leipzig, 1879, p. 529.

[54] W. Schmidt, "Heron im 17. Jahrhundert," pp. 199, 203. See also *The Newe and Rare Inventions of Waterworks* of Isaac de Caus, London, 1701 (first edition 1659) which was closely based on the work of Salomon de Caus. This mentions Hero a number of times, as in Proposition X: "This Pipe [the siphon] is in use in divers Places, and hath been treated of by *Hero of Alexandria*." Interestingly enough, the introductory section of this work, "the theorie of the conduct of water," was issued in 1704 as the introduction to an edition of Thomas Savery's *The Miner's Friend*.

[55] Gaspar Schott in the preface to the *Mechanica hydraulico-pneumatica, Frankfurt*, 1657, gave a list of important pneumatic and hydraulic writers, in which Hero and those influenced by him are prominent: Kircher, Ens, Harsdoerffer, G. Valla, Cardan, Besson, Schwenter, Porta, Aleotti, Leurechon, Mersenne, Fludd, Galileo. And Schwenter and Harsdoerffer gave an interesting bibliography which for pneumatics included Cardan, Drebbel, Ens, Porta, Kircher, Hero.

[56] Cardan discussed air and the vacuum, with a description of pneumatic machines, including one ascribed to Hero, in the first book of the *De subtilitate*, "de principiis, materia, forma, vacuo, corporum, repugnantia, motu naturalia, loco," in connection with the element air.

[57] J. B. Porta, *Pnuematicorum libri tres*, Naples, 1601 (Italian edition 1606). After summarizing in full "Heronis opinio de vacuo" (Cap. V) Porta criticized these views in Cap. VI "Contra Heronem de vacuo, et vinum aqua compressionem 'non patiantur." Here he attacked Hero's arguments: first, wine mixes with water not because of vacua in the water but

Study of Hero inevitably stimulated an interest in the vacuum, and even promoted its acceptance in a restricted fashion. Lucretius, following Epicurus, had made the void all-embracing: matter existed *in* the void and moved *in* the void.[58] Hero had denied the existence of a continuous vacuum in nature — i.e., without the application of force — but he had introduced a sort of minor and manageable vacuum between the particles of all material substances. Whereas Lucretian atomism postulated matter existing and moving in a vacuum, the Heronic theory postulated vacua within matter. This discontinuous vacuum (*commistum* or *disseminatum* the seventeenth-century Latinists called it) was quite generally accepted by later writers. For example, Mersenne in his *Cogitata physico-mechanica* (1644) has a detailed and interesting discussion of the vacuum; this is noted in the preface as one of the more difficult problems to be dealt with, and one "which Hero believed he had demonstrated, in his preface," and which has to be discussed, since it is closely connected with the mechanics of hydraulic devices.[59] That air is a material substance, made up of particles interspersed with "vacuola," is demonstrated by its compressibility. Its elastic action was comparable to that of a sponge or even a bent bow. Mersenne asserts that the assumption of vacua is necessary to explain the passage of light through water and air and the diffusion of wine through water. This is straight out of Hero. In the section of the book entitled "Phaenomena Pneumatica" Mersenne pays particular attention to the properties of compressibility and rarefaction which air possesses, and even makes some experiments to test their extent.

Another important and widely read pneumatic work was the *Mechanica hydraulico-pneumatica* (1657) of the Jesuit Gaspar Schott, professor of mathematics at Wurzburg and a friend of Kircher. It is divided into three parts, a "theoretical" section on pneumatic principles, a "practical" section on the manufacture of pneumatic and hydraulic machines, and finally a description of Otto von Guericke's air pump — with a refutation, by Kircher and others, of the proof of the vacuum given by the Magdeburg experiment. The first two sections lean heavily on Hero's work; but Schott was discriminating, and did not hesitate to criticize errors in Hero or in his

because wine and water are liquids and hence homogeneous; besides the volume is increased when these two liquids mix, as would not be the case if the wine merely filled the vacua in the water. Porta also regarded as invalid Hero's argument that vacua are indicated by the passage of light through a liquid, since for Porta light was incorporeal. However, he had trouble explaining the rarefaction and compression of air on a non-particulate theory.

W. Gilbert, *De mundo nostro sublunari philosophia nova*, (1651), lib. I, cap. 22, quoted by E. Wolff, *Francis Bacon*, II, p. 193. Gilbert referred to "Hero Alexandrinus, who wishes to have a vacuum distributed in little parts throughout nature, so that bodies when compressed fill this vacuum." Gilbert disagreed; it was true that this would account for the compressibility of air, "but we know that denser bodies are transformed into rarer ones, as water by heat is rarefied into air. Truly air is rarefied by heat; by other means it is condensed back into its original nature; and thus it has the power of contraction, even though it may not contain scattered vacua." There is an understandable confusion between the elasticity of atmospheric air, and the change of water to steam, with its subsequent condensation back to liquid form. Change of state remained a problem long after Gilbert's time.

In Aleotti's translation of the *Pneumatica*, there is a section entitled "Aggiunta dell'Aleotti. Intorno al non poter essere alcun vacuo,

ne poter l'Elemento dell'Aria star compresso" in which he denies the possibility of the existence of a vacuum, in fairly theological terms. It is significant that the "theorems" which he added were all purely hydraulic devices; he obviously had no understanding of the action of the air in Hero's pneumatic machines.

[58] Lucretius, *On the Nature of Things*, Oxford 1910, translated by Cyril Bailey. See especially Book I, lines 389–451, p. 40–41. "For there are bodies and the void, in which they are placed and where they move hither and thither." See also *Epicurus to Herodotus*, in *The Stoic and Epicurean Philosophers*, Modern Library edition, New York, 1940, pp. 3–15.

[59] *Hydraulica pneumatica; arsque navigandi; harmonia theoria, practica, et mechanica*, Paris, 1644. A separate title page, but part of the *Cogitata physico-mechanica*. See especially "Phaenomena pneumatica" pp. 137–175, and proposition XXI "An aer tantumdem rarefiere quantum condensari possit, qua ratione condensatur vel rarefiat inquirere." Mersenne was not quite satisfied with Hero's explanation, and felt that there might be other forces at work; just as he rather favored some mechanical form of attraction between air and water to account for the action of siphons. It must be remembered, however, that this was written before Mersenne had heard of Torricelli's experiments, which he himself did so much to publicize.

translators and commentators.[60] From the space devoted to Hero's opinions, and the prominent place given to his name in the table of contents, there is no question but that Schott regarded Hero as his principle authority in the field of pneumatics.

Even more important than the influence of Hero on theories of the vacuum in the seventeenth century, and on the recognition of the compressibility of air, was his influence on theories of matter. In contrast to the Aristotelian plenum, Hero's matter was particulate; in contrast to the Epicurean doctrines reintroduced by Gassendi and others, his theory was non-atomic and non-philosophic. It was a simple physical explanation, requiring no random motion and no unmanageable continuous vacuum. The only vacuum was that small amount necessary to separate the particles of matter, which were themselves simple physical entities with no definitely assigned characteristics except extension and impenetrability. Lucretian and Epicurean atoms were endowed with size and shape as well as with random motion. Heronic corpuscles, on the contrary, were all alike. Hero seems to have explained the different properties of various substances by variation in the size of the vacua: thus diamond, being very dense, had very small pores, whereas presumably the pores between air particles were relatively large. Even Cartesian corpuscles were endowed with more explicit properties, having size, shape, and motion in the aether. Hero's corpuscles were as easy to conceive as the grains of sand to which he compared them; and they accounted, neatly and elegantly, for the observed physical properties of air and water. It was difficult to explain the extraordinary powers of rarefaction and compression which air exhibited if one assumed a plenum, but a particulate theory of air made explanation easy. So this was at least a working hypothesis in the minds of many seventeenth-century pneumaticians. Others besides Robert Boyle found that a corpuscularian hypothesis was by far the best suited to explain the experimentally observed properties of air; and others besides Boyle rejected the philosophic and atheistic overtones of Epicureanism, and the vortex motion and plenum of Cartesianism.

The word used to describe Hero's particles varied, but they were never called atoms, a word too closely associated with Epicureanism. Perhaps the most common expression was *particula*, used by Commandino, who also called them *corpuscula*. Giorgi used *corpi* and *corpicelli*. Davanzati recognized the implicit connection between the particles of Hero and true atoms; in the dedication he referred to Hero's theory of the vacuum as one derived from the doctrines of Democritus and Epicurus, and later he described air as made up of "certain minute and light *corpicelli*, which some call atoms." [61] Gaspar Schott, though conservative, spoke without criticism of "vacuola Heronis inter aeris particulas disseminata;" and in discussing the two kinds of vacuum, continuous and discontinuous, he referred to Gassendi's belief that Hero's opinions on this subject were derived from Epicurus.[62] Mersenne also accepted the particles of Hero, at least for air, in spite of his recognition of their atomic implications; in his explanation of the compressibility of air (caused by the "vacuola" between particles) Hero is merely, according to Mersenne, emulating Democritus.[63]

Francis Bacon favored atomism in general, and was inclined to value Democritus

---

[60] E.g. Pars I, Protheoria I, 1. "Hero Alexandrinus vacuum in aere aqua disseminatum agnoscit; 2. Experimenta quibus Hero vacuum in corporibus disseminatum probat." For his criticism of Hero's errors, cf. Pro. I, 7. "Heronis Alexandrini error in elevanda aqua vi attractiva; 8. Alius Heronis error," etc. Unfortunately, Schott was less discriminating when it came to the work of his contemporaries; he never accepted the implications of the discoveries of Torricelli and Guericke, though he described their experiments, and it was through his book that Boyle first heard of Guericke's air pump.

[61] *Della natura del voto di Erone Alessendrino, volgarizzamento inedito di Bernardo Davanzati,* Firenze, 1862, p. 13. Davanzati himself never called the particles atoms.
[62] Schott, *Mechanica hydraulico-pneumatica,* pp. 19–20.
[63] *Phaenomena pneumatica,* prop. XXI, p. 148. "Qua difficultate motus spiritalium autor Hyeron [sic] plurima vacuola per omnia corpora disseminari credidit (hac in parte Democritum aemulatus) in quae per compressionem coguntur partes, quae ubi violentia desient, ad pristinum locum redeant."

above Aristotle, so it is not surprising to find him speaking approvingly of Hero's particles and discontinuous vacuum.[64] The *Cogitationes de natura rerum* begins with a section devoted to the atomic theory and the vacuum.[65] Hero comes in for high praise — "vir ingeniosus et mechanicus" as Bacon described him elsewhere [66] — because of his belief in the vacuum and in particulate matter. That Bacon recognized the peculiar nature of Hero's particles is indicated by his comparison of Hero and Democritus. Hero, "utpote hominis mechanici" was inferior to Democritus, because he denied the existence of a continuous vacuum, which he did not find in "nostro orbe," the terrestrial sphere.

By far the most important follower of Hero's atomism was Galileo, who was also the most clearly derivative. That Galileo was an atomist is well known, and the passages in the *Two New Sciences* in which he outlines his atomic theory are familiar; what is less generally recognized is Galileo's debt to Hero, a debt strikingly apparent when once Galileo's discussion has been read with Hero's theory in mind.[67] To account for the resistance to fracture exhibited by solid bodies, Galileo had need of a force holding the body together; this force he postulated to be the "resistance of the vacuum" between the particles of matter. The idea of minute vacua between particles is directly inherited from Hero — it is definitely not Lucretian — though Hero would not have recognized this force of resistance displayed by the vacuum. The cause of the melting of metals Galileo assigned to the penetration of the pores between the metallic particles by particles of fire, which, as Hero had said, were finer than air particles. That Galileo read Hero we know; he owned a copy of the Italian translation of Alessandro Giogri and seems also to have been familiar with Commandino's Latin edition.[68] There is no reason to doubt that Galileo's atomic theory is closely related to that of Hero.

For a hundred years after its first appearance in 1575, Hero's work was much read and widely discussed. Essential to an understanding of the basic principles of pneumatics, it became a starting point for that intensive study of air and the vacuum which led the seventeenth century to develop our modern theory of elastic fluids. That the Heronic vacua between particles were extensively discussed and frequently accepted could not fail to lead to a consideration of the continuous vacuum, and the forces which prevented its existence under ordinary conditions. Hero's atomism, a simple, non-Lucretian and non-philosophic particulate theory of matter, was highly useful in physical discussion; and it reached an immensely wide audience, whether directly through any one of the numerous editions of the *Pneumatica*, or indirectly through the seventeenth-century pneumatical writers who leaned so strongly on Hero's work, and whose books were available in many editions and in many languages. This is a hitherto unsuspected source of that non-Epicurean corpuscularianism of the seventeenth century, by no means exclusively derived from Descartes, which reached its culmination in the "corpuscular hypothesis" of Robert Boyle.

[64] See Kurd Lasswitz, *Geschichte der Atomistik*, Hamburg, 1890, pp. 425 ff., for a discussion of Bacon's use of Hero's ideas on the vacuum. However here, as elsewhere, Lasswitz discusses only Hero's possible contributions to the acceptance of the vacuum, and ignores Hero's atomism.

[65] Ellis and Spedding edition, vol. V, *Cogitata I* "De sectione corporum continuo et vacuo." This begins "Doctrina Democriti de atomis aut vera est, aut ad demonstrationem utiliter adhibetur," a nice example of the state of atomic theory at the beginning of the seventeenth century.

[66] *Descriptio globi intellegi*, Ellis and Spedding, vol. VII, caput VI is concerned with the vacuum and the views of Hero, Leucippus and Democritus are all cited.

[67] *Dialogues Concerning Two New Sciences*, translated by Henry Crew and A. De Salvio, Evanston, 1946. The relevant passages are on pp. 18–19; also 24, 39, 58. For the influence of Hero on Galileo, Ernst Goldbeck, "Galileis Atomistik und ihre Quellen," *Bibliotheca Mathematica*, III, 3, 1902, 84–112, *passim*, is very good; clear and detailed.

[68] According to Schmidt, who ("Heron im 17. Jahrhundert," p. 206–7) quotes a letter from Galileo to Alvise Mocenigo of 1594, in which Galileo discusses the construction of a lamp which is wrongly interpreted in the *Pneumatica*. Schmidt has compared the letter with the phrasing of Commandino, and believes that it is this edition which Galileo is discussing.

FIG. 1. — Floating dock. Woodcut included in the *Descrittione* of Venice 1560.

FLOATING DOCKS IN THE SIXTEENTH CENTURY

By GEORGE SARTON

MR. PHILIP HOFER has recently acquired and deposited in the collection of Printing and Graphic Arts in the Houghton Library, Harvard University, a curious little booklet printed in Venice in 1560. The *Descrittione dell' artifitiosa machina* is a pamphlet of six leaves (24.5 x 17 cm.), including title-page, two full-page woodcuts and nine pages of text with four small woodcuts. Thanks to Mr. HOFER's courtesy we reproduce the second of the larger woodcuts (Fig. 1) and the title-page (Fig. 2).

The woodcut explains itself. It shows a floating dock to be used for the salvaging of a grounded ship. A vessel had been lying for a whole year in the Venetian laguna and efforts to raise her had failed. The unknown author of this booklet asked for the privilege of using a new method which he described and illustrated. This would justify an investigation

of early dry docks and floating docks which I have no time to undertake at present. Were not similar efforts made by English and Dutch engineers?

According to FELDHAUS [1] the earliest dry dock in England (and presumably in the world) was built in Portsmouth in 1495/96 by order of HENRY VII. In the *Theatrum instrumentorum* of JACQUES BESSON, privileged in 1569, we find drawings (Figs. 53 to 60, chiefly 58) of devices to pull or lift ships, but nothing comparable to the Venetian drawings of 1560.

JACQUES BESSON of Grenoble was a contemporary of the Venetian anonym, and perhaps an older one, for his earliest book, *Le cosmolabe*, had appeared in Paris as early as 1537. His *Theatrum instrumen-*

[1] F. M. FELDHAUS: Die Technik (933, Leipzig 1914).

DESCRITTIONE
DELL'ARTIFITIOSA MACHINA
FATTA PER CAVAR'IL GALEONE,
COL RITRATTO DI QVELLA, ET DI
ALTRI SVOI ORDEGNI MARAVI-
GLIOSAMENTE FABRICATI.

AL CLARISSIMO ET VALOROSO SIGNOR
Chriftoforo da Canal Dignifsimo Proueditor
dell'armata della Serenifsima Signoria
di Venetia.

C.O.N. P R LV I.L E G I O.

I N   V E N E T I A.

INSTRVMENTORVM
ET MACHINARVM, QVAS
IACOBVS BESSONVS DELPHINAS
MATHEMATICVS ET A 'MACHINIS PRATER ALIA
excogitauit, multifque vigiliis & laboribus excoluit, ad
rerum multarum intellectu difficillimarum expli-
cationem, & totius Reipublicæ vtilitatem,

Liber primus.

Cum Priuilegio Regis.

FIG. 2. — Anonymous, Venice 1560 (Hofer Collection).

FIG. 3. — JACQUES BESSON. First edition of his *Theatrum instrumentorum* printed between 1569 and 1574 (Hofer Collection). Folio 38.5 cm. high.

torum, a collection of sixty inventions each of which is represented by a large copper plate with a brief description, received a royal privilege for ten years in Orléans, June 27, 1569. The first edition (Fig. 3) was published within the author's lifetime without date or place. It was dedicated to CHARLES IX who died in 1574, and hence the date is restricted to one of the years 1569 to 1574. The edition of Lyon 1578 (Fig. 4), generally quoted as the first edition, is, according to its own preface, a posthumous one. The date of BESSON's death is not mentioned in it, which suggests that it was not much anterior to 1578. The plates of both editions are the same, but in the second (1578) they have been spoiled by ugly letterpress; the first edition is far more pleasant to the eye. The title-pages of both editions are here reproduced thanks to Mr. HOFER's courtesy.

BESSON's *Theatrum* was very popular, for in addition to various Latin-French editions, it was published in Italian and German before the end of the

century, and in Spanish in 1602. The Venetian booklet, on the contrary, seems to be a very rare item. One would like to know whether the floating dock which it described was actually built and the ship rescued from its precarious position in the harbor. Venetian chronicles might provide information on the subject. If that dock was built and used, how is it that the example was not imitated? Or was it? At any rate, I do not recall any new invention in that field until that of the "camel" invented by the Dutch engineer MEEUWES MEINDERTSZOON BAKKER a century later (in 1688 or 1690) to lift ships from one water level to a higher one.[2]

[2] The "camel" ("kameel" in Dutch) was a floating water tank. Two of them or more were placed on both sides of the ship, filled with water and securely attached to her; then they were emptied and their buoyancy lifted the ship (WINKLER PRINS' *Geïllustreerde Encyclopaedie*, vol. 10, 163, Amsterdam 1909).

Oct. 17, 1944

THEATRVM
INSTRVMEN-
TORVM ET MACHINA-
rum Iacobi Beſſoni Del-
phinatis,Mathematici in-
geniofiſsimi.

THEATRE
DES INSTRV

LVGDVNI,
Apud Barth.Vincentium.
Cum priuilegio Regis.
1 5 7 8.

FIG. 4. — JACQUES BESSON. Second edition of same work,
Lyon 1578 (Hofer Collection). Folio 40.5 cm. high.

The Science of Gunnery in Elizabethan England

By Henry J. Webb *‡

I

GUNNERY PRACTICE

THE practice of gunnery by Englishmen during the early years of Queen Elizabeth's reign was in its rudimentary stages. Artillerymen, both on land and at sea, knew how to make powder after the continental method, being aware of the theory that, not only should the ingredients be pure, but that different proportions of saltpeter, charcoal, and sulphur should be used for different sizes of artillery; and they adhered to the customary — and often dangerous — mode of charging their pieces with powder that weighed two-thirds of the weight of the ball.[1] When lading their pieces, they also followed the custom of using wads (generally wisps of straw or pieces of wool cloth) to keep powder and shot solidly in place.[2] Besides ordinary solid projectiles, they experimented with fragmentary shot [3] and incendiary shells.[4]

But in aiming their weapons, they simply sighted along the barrels of their pieces, from the breech to the muzzle, until the target was covered;[5] consequently — assuming their pieces were truly bored — they could be expected to do fairly well only at point-blank range, a range, with most artillery, too close to the enemy to be comfortable.[6] Targets beyond point-blank range could be hit only by chance; for without the aid of fixed front sights and adjustable rear sights and with no mechanism for determining the proper muzzle elevation necessary to deliver a shot a certain distance, Elizabethan cannoneers had to guess themselves onto a target. They observed their shots carefully, however, and, by altering the elevation of their pieces with "coynes" or wedges beneath

* University of Utah.

‡ Material for this paper was gathered with funds granted by the University Research Committee, University of Utah.

[1] Peter Whitehorne, *Certain Waies for the Orderyng of Souldiers in Battelray* (London, 1562), fol. 28.

[2] *Ibid.*, fol. 33.

[3] William Bourne, *Inventions or Devises. Very Necessary for all Generals* (London, 1578), pp. 40–41.

[4] Whitehorne, *Certain Waies*, sig. Lii–Liii.

[5] *Ibid.*, fol. 34.

[6] The effective range of Elizabethan artillery varied widely with the size of the cannon, the excellence of its construction, and the type of powder employed. Bourne mentions point-blank ranges of 26, 40, and 80 yards, and a maximum range of "almost a mile," *The Arte of Shooting* in *Great Ordnaunce* (London, 1587), pp. 36–37. Thomas Smith notes a range of 700 yards, but he mentions the maximum range for wall-pounding to be 240 paces, *The Arte of Gunnerie* (London, 1600), pp. 51, 67–68. Cyprian Lucar indicates that the ideal distance for wall-pounding was 80 paces, adding that cannon be "in no wise (without constraint) more farther from that wal than 150 paces," *A Treatise Named Lucar Appendix* (London, 1588), p. 59. John Sheriffe (fl. 1590) indicates that the greatest point-blank range of the farthest shooting cannon was 400 paces. At the same time, he notes that such cannon "be most serviceable for battery being within 80 paces of their mark." See "The Brevity and the secret of the Art of great ordnance" as reproduced in A. R. Hall, *Ballistics in the Seventeenth Century* (Cambridge, 1952), p. 166.

the tails, approached their targets by "creeping" or "bracketing" fire. Since their guns recoiled six to eight feet,[7] and so had to be completely remounted after each firing — without the use of gauges or sights — it is not surprising that the effects were sometimes discouraging.

By the late 1570's, however, decided improvements were made in Elizabethan gunnery methods. Front sights came into general use, although, since cannon were not equipped with them in the gun foundries, gunners had to manufacture their own. The process of preparing such sights was quite simple. Elizabethan ordnance was generally tapered down from breech to muzzle, so that the bore of the piece was not level when the top of the barrel was level. Therefore, a front sight had to be devised in such a way as to take this tapering into consideration. Gunners figured the diameter of the breech (for instance, by using calipers when they were available or by placing a string around the breech and taking 7/22 of the result) and the diameter of the muzzle, subtracted one from the other, and divided the result by two. This figure represented the correct height of the front sight. It was an easy matter to cut a length of straw the right number of inches and affix it to the muzzle with wax.[8] This procedure was termed "disparting" the piece, and the front sight was therefore called "the dispart." [9]

Of course, such a method would not work unless the gun were "truly bored," so a means was devised for determining whether or not the bore was centered in the barrel. The means, as described by William Bourne, was as follows:

> Take two straight staves, and make them fast at the one ende, that they be not wider asunder at one ende than . . . at the other, and then put one of the staves into the mouth of the peece neere unto the tutchhole, and then trie the peece round about on every side with an ynche rule. . . .[10] [See Fig. 1.]

Were the bore not true, the "dispart" could be lengthened or shortened, put to the left or right, to allow for its inaccuracy, although such a gun, Bourne declared, would never shoot accurately.[11]

The rear sight at this time was merely another piece of straw affixed to the breech. As most of us are aware, an immobile rear sight is useful only when the target is within point-blank range. Beyond that range, the sight must be elevated, little by little, according to the distance of the piece from the target. Instead of manipulating their rear sights, however, Elizabethan gunners did what amounts to the same thing: they placed a quadrant in the muzzle of their cannon [see Fig. 2] and adjusted the muzzle elevation to the degree required to project a ball the desired distance.

Two things were requisite before this practice could produce good results. In the first place, the cannoneers had to know how far their weapons would fire with every degree of muzzle elevation; and secondly, they had to be able to judge ranges. In general, the first time gunners had a chance to fire their

[7] Humphrey Barwick, A Breefe Discourse, Concerning the Force of All Manuall Weapons of Fire (London, 1594?), fol. 12.

[8] Bourne, The Arte of Shooting, p. 15.

[9] Ibid.

[10] Bourne, Inventions or Devises, p. 33. Bourne borrowed from Tartaglia.

[11] Bourne, The Arte of Shooting, pp. 45–46.

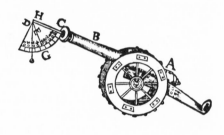

Fig. 1. Instruments for checking cannon bores. From William Bourne's *The Arte of Shooting in Great Ordnaunce* (London, 1587).

Fig. 2. Elevating cannon with a gunner's quadrant. From William Bourne's *The Arte of Shooting in Great Ordnaunce*.

cannon was in battle.[12] If they kept their heads, however, they might work out a rough table of ranges with two shots — assuming, of course, that they had level fields of fire. For they could determine the point-blank range of their pieces with one shot, the range of one degree elevation with a second shot, and by noting the distance between these two marks, have an approximation of how much farther their pieces would throw a cannon ball "at the mount of every degree" up to twenty degrees.[13] Since the ranges involved never exceeded the range of a modern rifle, most gunners probably estimated distances by eye, a method, however, that experience can make very accurate. They may also have paced off distances to fortified walls if they could do it without jeopardizing their lives.[14]

Even guns with good sights manned by gunners who could estimate ranges correctly would not fire properly without good powder; and in spite of the fact that in Elizabethan times "the making of the pouder and also the making of the

[12] Not until the late seventeenth century was regular artillery practice instituted in England. See Hall, *op. cit.*, p. 31.

[13] Smith, *The Arte of Gunnerie*, p. 49. Bourne declares that many gunners did not use quadrants in making these elevations but made "a gesse what advantage will reach the ' marke . . . ." *The Arte of Shooting*, p. 19.

[14] Bourne declares that few gunners knew any other method. See *The Arte of Shooting*, sig. Aiv recto.

saltpeter" had "become . . . a common thing," [15] gunners could never be sure that the powder they received in barrels was good or that its explosive force would be consistent from keg to keg. As a result, if they wanted to know where their shots would fall, they had to be prepared to test the powder. This they did in two ways. First, upon opening a keg, they noticed whether or not the powder was dry, as it should be; they tasted it, to see that it was "sharp" enough; examined its color ("blewish" was considered to be the best); felt it to note if it were as "fine as sand, and as soft as floure"; and finally lit a portion of it to determine whether or not it would fire in "the twinckling of an eye" and burn with a white smoke.[16] Second, by making for themselves a small can with a hinged lid, a notched metal arc above the lid to catch it, and a touch hole, they were able to fire a portion of the powder and note how high it forced up the lid. Such a procedure taught them what quantities to use out of different barrels.[17]

When cannon were first employed on the battlefield, any size and weight would serve for any purpose. But toward the end of the Elizabethan period, careful distinctions in the use of pieces began to be made. The double cannon and demi-cannon, varying in weight from 8,000 pounds to 5,000 pounds, were used as siege guns to batter down walls; quarter cannons and most culverins, weighing from approximately 5,000 pounds to 4,000 pounds, were mounted on fortified walls to repel the besieging enemy; and some culverins and all sakers, falcons, and falconets were employed as field pieces.[18] Mortars, of course, were used against targets hidden by walls or hills. At sea, the most frequently used cannon were culverins and demi-culverins, although some ships carried demi-cannon. Naval gunners also had smaller pieces of ordnance, not normally used on land, such as bases, slings, fowlers, robinets, hail-shot pieces, and port pieces, which were used against enemy personnel at close range.[19]

Distinctions were also made in the use of various types of projectiles. Thus, whole iron shot was employed against distant targets, small base shot against intermediate targets, and chain shot, clive shot, and dice shot were used against targets close at hand.[20] Gunners constantly devised new explosive shells and "sundry sorts of fire-works for the annoyance of their enemies," [21] using wild fire against buildings or tents within a fortified area, and "certaine little vesselles full of Nailes and Bullets chained togeather" or "little sacks full of Musket Bullets" against congregating troops and civilians.[22] Solid balls were used against personnel as well as against walls.

These projectiles were normally loaded into pieces with ladles and rammers, a slow and cumbersome method which, in the heat of battle, would result in unequal charges and spilled powder. Consequently, Elizabethans were intro-

[15] *Ibid.*, p. 5.
[16] *Ibid.*, p. 6.
[17] Although Bourne describes this device in the late seventies, Hall states that it "had been used since at least the mid-sixteenth century," p. 61.
[18] An examination of the various extant lists of gun weights would indicate that gun foundries varied widely in their casting of cannon. The reader might want to compare these figures

with several gun tables gathered by Hall, *op. cit.*, pp. 166–71.
[19] L. G. Carr Laughton, "The Navy: Ships and Sailors," *Shakespeare's England* (Oxford, 1917), *I*, 159.
[20] Bourne, *The Arte of Shooting*, p. 61.
[21] Bourne, *Inventions or Devises*, p. 41.
[22] Edward Grimestone, *A True Historie of the Memorable Siege of Ostend* (London, 1604), pp. 30–31.

duced to a mode of charging cannon which, though hardly new, had not been practiced very often, even on the continent. Instead of lading powder directly from a keg into the bore, the gunners prepared cartridges of paper or canvas before the battle, making sure that all the cartridges contained the same amount of powder. In an engagement, gunners provided with such cartridges were able to fire with greater rapidity and accuracy than when "charging . . . with a Ladell." [23]

As might be expected from a people whose ancestors had perfected the use of the long bow, Elizabethan gunners were well aware of the method of hitting targets that were in rapid motion across their front. Instead of firing directly at a galloping troop of horsemen or a sailing ship, they took what the modern soldier calls "leads." That is, they noted a spot which the horsemen or ship would cross, aimed their cannon at it, and just before the spot was reached, fired.[24] Greater difficulty in getting good results was naturally experienced by sailors, since cloud formations rather than land marks were used for aiming points.[25]

In general, the practice of artillerymen on land, as I have already suggested, was the practice of naval gunners, except that the latter had to worry about more matters. Thus, besides all the problems of correct boring, good powder, and accurate sights, naval gunners had to deal with heaving seas, wet powder and barrels, constantly moving targets, and unsteady emplacements. But in spite of Elizabethan success at sea, we cannot say that naval gunners were any more scientific than their brothers on land. They were counted good gunners, William Bourne points out, because they were "hardy or without fear about their ordnance," not because of their "knowledge";[26] and when it comes down to sheer effectiveness against fortifications, it would seem that army gunners were sometimes worthy of the applause usually reserved for Elizabethan seamen.[27]

II

SOURCES OF THE ELIZABETHAN SCIENCE OF GUNNERY

The sources of Elizabethan gunnery practice were three-fold. First of all, during the reign of Henry VIII, artillerymen learned the barest elements of gunnery from experience in the field with the Dutch and the Flemish.[28] Secondly, from 1560 onward, Englishmen were confronted with an increasing number of books — some of them foreign works, some of them translations of foreign works, and some of them the product of native Englishmen — on the art of war, gunnery, and ballistics;[29] and from these works they slowly developed improved methods of employing cannon. Finally, from 1572 until well into the seventeenth century, Englishmen volunteered or were pressed into the

[23] Bourne, *The Arte of Shooting*, pp. 30–31.
[24] *Ibid.*, pp. 61–62; Lucar, *op. cit.*, pp. 54–55.
[25] Bourne, *The Arte of Shooting*, pp. 51–52.
[26] Bourne, *The Arte of Shooting*, sig. Aiii^r.
[27] For instance, during Elizabeth's campaigns in Ireland, "practically no castle could be maintained by the Irish, provided the English could reach the scene with cannon of adequate weight." Cyril Falls, *Elizabeth's Irish Wars* (London, 1950), p. 344.
[28] Bourne, *The Arte of Shooting*, sig. Aiii^r.
[29] See M. J. D. Cockle, *A Bibliography of English Military Books up to 1642* (London, 1900).

army for service in France, the Low Countries, and Ireland, there learning from the French, the Dutch, and the Spanish still further methods of improving their science of gunnery.

Improvement was not rapid, however, in spite of books and experience. For more than twenty-five years after Elizabeth ascended the throne, soldiers and sailors were still employing the elements of gunnery learned during the reign of Henry VIII.[30] One of the reasons for the slow development of English artillery was that Elizabethan military science had its roots in the classics. The tactics of war, which had emerged in unorganized form from ancient histories, were patched together in such a way as to produce a recognizable system — if not exactly a science — of warfare, and this system was presented to Englishmen as the most logical manner in which to win battles. In deriving stratagems of war from ancient histories, the English were doing nothing particularly new. Frontinus, Onosander, and Vegetius — names to be reckoned with in Elizabethan times — had done it long before them; and, more recently, Machiavelli in Italy and Fourquevaux[31] in France had published military treatises in an effort to convince their countrymen of the wisdom of returning, in part at least, to ancient methods of warfare.

In 1560, two years after Elizabeth ascended the throne, Peter Whitehorne presented to Londoners the first English translation of Machiavelli's *L'arte della Guerra* as *The Arte of Warre*. Nothing of note on military matters, except for Christine de Pisan's *Fayttes of Armes and of Chyvalrye* (1489) and Frontinus' *The Strategemes, Sleyghtes and Policies of Warre* (1539), had appeared in English before this time; and, except for Onosander's *Of the Generall Captaine and of His Office* (1563) and Vegetius's *The Foure Bookes of Martiall Policye* (1572), little of importance appeared after that date until, in 1574, the second edition of Machiavelli was printed. For the first two decades of Elizabeth's reign, therefore, English military writings emphasized Roman tactics based upon the legion, an infantry unit supported in a very minor way by cavalry and artillery.

Now while a return to Roman military science was a definite improvement over medieval methods of warfare, with its emphasis on heavy cavalry and its minimization of infantry, a close adherence to Roman methods and, particularly, to the theories of its most articulate admirer, Machiavelli, inhibited the development of gunnery. In field engagements, the Romans eschewed artillery (or, more correctly, engines of war) because they found such engines relatively ineffective except when used against fortified walls. There are instances in ancient history, of course, in which the employment of weapons like the ballista and the catapulta materially affected the tide of battle; but on the whole their value was essentially one of harassment. Machiavelli likewise dismissed artillery as "unprofitable," except against fortifications, because his observations taught him that on the battle-field it generally had a chance to fire but once before it was masked by advancing friendly troops or neutralized by

[30] Bourne, *The Arte of Shooting*, sig. Aiii^r.
[31] Niccolò Machiavelli, *L'Arte della Guerra*   (c. 1520); Raimond de Beccarie de Pavie, Sieur de Fourquevaux, *Instructions sur le Faict de la Guerre* (1548).

enemy cavalry.[32] Thus discouraged, Englishmen but slowly produced anything like a science of gunnery.

Another reason for the slow development of English artillery was undoubtedly due to the fact that the first half of Elizabeth's reign was relatively peaceful, and there was no pressing need for the development either of artillery or of an art of war.[33] However, once Elizabeth was forced to desert diplomacy for warfare, mathematicians and physicists, in cooperation with experienced gunners, devised scientific methods of increasing the effectiveness of artillery, publishing their findings in short, readable, and often well-illustrated textbooks.

The cooperation of the scientists and the gunners was probably not very "scientific" in the modern sense of the word. Thomas Digges, one of the more learned mathematicians of the age and author of several military books, says that he was aided in his studies by the "Conferences" of his father with "the rarest Souldyoures of his time";[34] and Humphrey Barwick, author of *A Breefe Discourse, Concerning the Force of All Manuall Weapons of Fire*, also speaks of "conferences with persons of sundrye callings."[35] However, most thinkers seem to have drawn upon the extant works of scientists,[36] foremost of whom was Niccolò Tartaglia (1506–57), an Italian mathematician who published two important works on ballistics: *La Nova Scientia* (Venice, 1537) and *Quesiti et Inventioni Diverse* (Venice, 1546).[37] The latter text was presented to Henry VIII of England in manuscript form[38] and either from copies made therefrom or from copies of the Italian printing, Tartaglia's theories circulated among Englishmen. As A. R. Hall has pointed out in *Ballistics in the Seventeenth Century*, they translated him (Cyprian Lucar brought out his *Quesiti* as *Three Bookes of Colloquies* in 1588), imitated him, and plagiarized his statements.[39] Indeed, "there were few further contributions to the theory of gunnery before the middle of the seventeenth century," although, as Hall adds, a few useful footnotes were contributed by Thomas Digges and William Bourne of England, Diego de Alaba y Viamont and Luys Collado of Spain, Vanoccio Biringuccio and Girolamo Cardano of Italy, and Daniel Santbech of Austria.[40]

[32] Three interesting evaluations of Machiavelli as a military theorist are in Sir Charles Oman, *A History of the Art of War in the Sixteenth Century* (New York, 1937); Joseph Kraft, "Truth and Poetry in Machiavelli," *Journal of Modern History*, 23 (June 1951), 109–21; and Felix Gilbert, "Machiavelli: The Renaissance of the Art of War," *Makers of Modern Strategy*, ed. by Edward Mead Earle (Princeton, 1944), pp. 3–25. Oman points out that all Machiavelli's "recommendations of a practical sort bear no relation whatever to the actual development of tactics," and that his evaluation of artillery was "hopelessly erroneous," pp. 93–4. Kraft agrees, in much the same words. Gilbert, on the other hand, states that "Machiavelli raised military discussion to a new level and established the principles according to which intellectual comprehension and theoretical analysis of war and military affairs progressed," p. 20. It might be added that Machiavelli's low estimate of the value of artillery certainly seems justified

by events in the Italian wars of the twenty-five years before he wrote his *L'Arte della Guerra*.
[33] For a general treatment of artillery development in the sixteenth century, see Oman, *op. cit.*, esp. ch. 3 and pp. 351–52.
[34] *Stratioticos* (London, 1579), sig. Aij[r].
[35] Barwick, *A Breefe Discourse*, sig. A2[v].
[36] Lucar lists twenty-five scientists from whose works he borrowed, including such well-known authorities as Tartaglia, Biringuccio, Santbech, Leonard and Thomas Digges, Collado, Cardano, and the soldier-scholar Whitehorne.
[37] Complete discussions of the impact of Tartaglia on ballistics of the 16th and subsequent centuries may be found in Charbonnier's *Essais sur l'Histoire de la Balistique* (Paris, 1928) and Hall, *op. cit., passim.*
[38] Tartaglia's dedication to King Henry was later used to preface the first English edition.
[39] Hall, *op. cit.*, p. 42.
[40] *Ibid.* Portions of their theories and experiments were presented to English readers from

There is no proof, of course, that the works of these men were immediately accessible to interested Englishmen during the period of our study. Indeed, it is well-nigh impossible to state to what extent the science of gunnery percolated down to the rank and file of Elizabethan gunners. Hall feels that these works really influenced the science of gunnery in the field very little, contending that the "emphasis of the experts and of the artillery schools was on a sound education in straight forward field gunnery in which scientific ballistics played a very small part." [41] Bourne, writing in the late seventies, supports Hall's contention by remarking that among gunners of his acquaintance there were "divers that will have instruments, and yet be utterlie voide of the use of them." He assumed, moreover, that many gunners, who "wold not have their ignorance knowen," might be displeased with his attempt to explain the details of gunnery. [42]

III

POSSIBLE IMPROVEMENTS

Had Elizabethan gunners studied available military literature, they could have improved their accuracy and speed of fire, but they would have had to have the cooperation of the government to do it. One of their greatest faults — inability to place shots on given targets at various ranges — was owing in part to the fact that they were unfamiliar with their weapons. Although Bourne stated that "Ordnance hath beene had into the field [for range practice] both in maister Bromefields time when that he was Liefetenant of the Ordnance, & at divers times since," [43] he found that the methods of testing weapons were inadequate. And Thomas Smith, writing in 1600, complained that he had "never heard nor reade of any that hath as yet fully put the same [i.e., range firing] in practice." [44]

The suggested methods for zeroing in cannon were as follows. After leveling their piece with the quadrant and shooting across horizontal ground until they found the point-blank range of their weapon, gunners could elevate their piece from minute to minute and from degree to degree, firing after each change in elevation. Then, by marking down the distance the shot was conveyed at every elevation, they could construct a table of ranges or "randoms." [45] In time of battle, gunners would merely have to estimate a target's distance from their piece, consult the table, elevate the piece to the proper degree, and, with a plumb line or a piece of straw as a rear sight, lay on the target and fire.

Another method was to construct a rear sight out of a rule and a sliding eye-piece and, by practicing on a target range, translate degrees of muzzle elevation into inches of breech depression. [46] [See Fig. 3.] Gunners could then either mark yardages off on the rear sight or consult a table of randoms.

---

time to time by Smith, Barwick, and Lucar. Eventually they were compiled and made available in one volume by Robert Norton in *The Gunner* (London, 1628).
[41] *Ibid.*, p. 52.
[42] Bourne, *The Arte of Shooting*, sigs. Aiii^v–Aiv^r.

[43] *Ibid.*, sig. Aiii^r.
[44] Smith, *The Arte of Gunnerie*, p. 48.
[45] Bourne, *The Arte of Shooting*, pp. 35–36; Smith, pp. 51–57.
[46] Lucar, *Treatise*, pp. 53–54; Bourne, *The Arte of Shooting*, pp. 35–37.

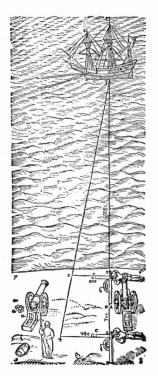

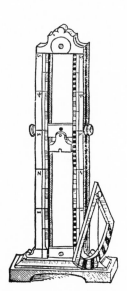

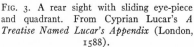

Fig. 3. A rear sight with sliding eye-piece   Fig. 4. Estimating range. From Lucar's *A*
and quadrant. From Cyprian Lucar's *A*   *Treatise Named Lucar's Appendix.*
Treatise Named Lucar's Appendix (London,
1588).

Having once prepared a table of randoms or a graduated rear sight, gunners also could have hit targets on hills without wasting innumerable shots to discover the proper number of degrees to elevate their weapons. Assuming that they knew the distance to the target and the point-blank range of their piece, gunners could, in four movements, lay on their target — and the method described to them was precisely the method used by gunners today. They could (1) raise their piece the number of degrees it would take to reach the target on level ground, (2) determine with their quadrant the number of degrees the target on the hill stood above the piece, (3) raise their piece this additional number of degrees, and (4) align target, dispart, and rear sight.[47] In other words they could do what modern gunners do when they add the angle of elevation to the angle of site. Were their powder good, their measurement of it accurate, their ball of the proper size, their dispart of the correct length, and

[47] Lucar, pp. 55–56; Bourne, *The Arte of Shooting*, pp. 47–51.

their weapon truly bored, they could have hit their mark, or close to it, when they fired.

A special, if obvious, skill needed before gunners could possibly hit targets was that of estimating the range. As has already been pointed out, most gunners probably judged distances by eye or, when the terrain was favorable, paced off distances between gun emplacements and walls. But Elizabethans were presented with another way of resolving distances which, though slow and therefore most useful against stationary objects, was nevertheless safe and accurate. As described by Cyprian Lucar, it was not greatly different from the method used by modern gunners. One of the gunners first placed his quadrant on a level spot, #1, [see Fig. 4] and sighted the target, #5. Second, without moving his quadrant, he sighted back along it several hundred paces to another point, #3, which he marked. Third, he turned his quadrant 90°, and sighted a point, #2, several hundred paces from point #1, which he also marked. Fourth, he took his quadrant to point #3 and, after aligning it with points #1 and #5, turned it 90° and marked a point, #4, which was in alignment with points #2 and #5. By measuring distances between points #1 and #2, and #1 and #3, and #3 and #4, he had enough information to calculate the range to his target. The formula was as follows:

$$\frac{(\text{distance from 1 to 3}) \times (\text{distance from 3 to 4})}{(\text{distance from 3 to 4}) - (\text{distance from 1 to 2})}.$$

For instance, suppose (as Cyprian Lucar does in the accompanying diagram) that the gunner found the distance from #1 to #3 to be 300 paces, the distance from #3 to #4 to be 240 paces, and the distance from #1 to #2 to be 200 paces. He would then find that the distance to his target was 1,800 paces, as follows:

$$\frac{300 \times 240}{240 - 200} = \frac{72,000}{40} = 1,800 \text{ paces.}$$

By planting his piece at point #1, raising the muzzle the necessary number of degrees to convey a ball 1,800 paces, and aligning his sights on the target, the gunner (theoretically, at least) would hit his mark.

Elizabethan theory for wall-pounding was likewise quite scientific. Faced with a curtain or cullion point that was successful in repelling besiegers, the master of ordnance could plant his cannon in three positions, each approximately the same distance from the target, and have his gunners aim in such a manner that "the 2 side mountes would coine or cut out that which the Ordinance from the midle mount doth batter or pierce."[48] Or, he could set up two batteries of three guns each and have the No. 1 guns in both batteries shoot at the bottom of the mark, the No. 2's one foot higher, and the No. 3's one foot still higher — all at once.[49] These methods were obviously better than blasting away indiscriminately at a stubborn fortification.

During this period, gunners were also presented with a new theory concern-

[48] Smith, *op. cit.*, pp. 67–69.   [49] Bourne, *The Arte of Shooting*, p. 65.

ing the amount of powder which should be used to convey cannon balls the maximum distance with the minimum harm to their weapons. Instead of charging their pieces with powder weighing two-thirds of the weight of the ball, as was customary at the time, they were directed to divide the weight of their shot into the weight of their cannon and apply the following rule:

Pieces which had		Would use powder weighing
100–150 lb of metal	⎧ *for* ⎫	⅔ the weight of the shot
150 lbs of metal	⎪ *every* ⎪	⅞ the weight of the shot
150–200 lb of metal	⎨ *one* ⎬	⅞ the weight of the shot
200 lbs of metal	⎪ *pound* ⎪	the same weight as the shot
300 lbs of metal	⎩ *of* *shot* ⎭	1⅑ the weight of the shot

For instance, according to this rule, a double cannon weighing 8,000 pounds and being serviced with a ball of seventy pounds, would need forty-six pounds of powder to cast its projectile; while a little saker weighing 1,800 pounds and being serviced with a ball of nine pounds, would need nine pounds of powder to cast its projectile.[50]

These powder and shot weights were figured out so as to obtain the greatest force at the maximum range without bursting the cannon. To make sure that cannon did not become over-heated and were not subjected unduly to the strain of constant firing, gunners also were instructed to limit the firing of their weapons to a predetermined number of shots a day. Thus, one table of firings indicates that the ordinary double cannon could be fired thirty times within twenty-four hours, while the falcon could be fired one hundred twenty times.[51]

It is quite possible that all or some of these methods for increasing the accuracy of cannon were used by Elizabethan cannoneers at one time or another. One suspects, however, that the use was not widespread; for, in spite of the fact that gunners were notably successful at sea and against Irish fortifications, there is plenty of evidence in contemporary histories and military newsbooks to the effect that on the continent, either because of poor gunners, poor gun founders, or superior fortifications, cannon were not always especially effective. The contempt in which artillery men were sometimes held is amusingly illustrated by the defenders of Steenwijk in the early nineties, who came to their ramparts after a cannonading "with broomes to sweep the walles in mockage."[52] And it seems particularly significant that the Dutch and English troops, assembled in great numbers to undertake the momentous Flanders campaign of 1600, brought only six pieces of artillery with them.[53] Hall explains this situation by pointing out that there is always a "lag of artillery training behind the science of each age."[54] This lag toward the end of the Elizabethan

[50] *Ibid.*, pp. 10–11.
[51] Lucar, p. 48.
[52] *A True Declaration of the Streight Siedge Laide to the Cytty of Steenwich* (London, 1592), p. 4. Apparently the gunners pulled themselves together after this insult, because Steenwijk eventually fell to artillery pounding.
[53] *The Battaile Fought betweene Count*

Maurice of Nassaw, and Albertus Arch-duke of Austria (London, 1600) is one of several interesting texts containing an account of this expedition. A complete list of contemporary published accounts in English of this and related actions may be found in Henry J. Webb, "Military Newsbooks during the Age of Elizabeth," *English Studies*, 33 (December, 1952), 1–11.
[54] Hall, *op. cit.*, pp. 52–53.

period, however, was not as perceptible as at the beginning. Englishmen, after all, trained in the Low Countries under Maurice of Nassau who, as Oman relates, was a master of siege craft. With artillery he caused the surrender of Zutphen, Deventer, Hulst, Nijmegen (in 1591) and Steenwijk, Cveorden, and Gertruidenberg (in 1592), and he did it with amazing tactical perspicacity, concentrating on the employment of weapons more than on the clash of men.[55] It was only a question of time before tacticians and scientists got together and these gunnery theories, proved by practice on the range and in the field, became the common property of cannoneers.[‡]

[55] Oman, *op. cit.*, pp. 568 ff.

[‡] Figures 1 and 2 are reproduced by permission of The Library of Congress; Figures 3 and 4 are reproduced by permission of The Folger Shakespeare Library.

دری

The First Epicycloidal Gear Teeth

By Robert S. Woodbury *

THE gear has become so much a part of our technology today that we take it for granted. But its ability to carry extremely heavy loads and to operate quietly at high speeds stems from the marriage of a little known branch of mathematics with one of the most ingenious of machine tools — the gear-cutting machine. To perform as they should, the teeth of gears can have a number of forms, of which only the epicycloid and, much later, the involute have been commonly used in practice.

The few writers on the history of gears [1] have all repeated the claim of Ole Rømer, the Danish scientist who first measured the speed of light, to have been the first to apply the epicycloid to the teeth of gears. More careful examination of all the sources indicates a more complex problem, and that these writers' common assumption that the scientific design of gears grew out of the desire of clock and instrument makers for greater precision is also open to serious doubt.

The mathematicians' interest in the epicycloid had been aroused very early. The cycloidal curve had first been studied by Nicholas of Cusa (1401–64) in 1451,[2] and the epicycloid had been investigated by Albrecht Dürer (1471–1525) in 1525.[3] During the seventeenth century, Galileo, Torricelli, Descartes, Roberval, and Mersenne discovered the important properties of this family of curves. In early 1658 Pascal created quite a controversy with his Dettonville Problems, in which Christopher Wren, Wallis and Lalouère had been interested.[4] By the middle of the seventeenth century the mathematics of the cycloids had been very well worked out from purely mathematical interests.

The results of the mathematicians' work had not, however, penetrated into the practice of the engineers. To be sure, there were in the seventeenth century close relationships between the scientists and the instrument and clockmakers, but their mutual interests seem not to have extended to the scientific study of gears. The "mechanicians," as they were called, were content with empirical solutions.

In Leonardo da Vinci we find some drawings of gear tooth form — one very like a buttress tooth and the other looking much like modern teeth, but he does not say enough in the text for us to be sure.[5] That Leonardo was interested in reducing the friction of gear teeth is indicated in his drawing of gears using roller teeth.[6] But of course Leonardo's manuscripts were largely unknown in the seventeenth century.

The first mathematics of gear teeth is to be found in Cardano's work of 1557, where he gives empirical rules.[7] These rules, based on circular arcs,

* Massachusetts Institute of Technology.

[1] Feldhaus, Franz, *Die Geschichtliche Entwicklung des Zahnrades in Theorie und Praxis*, Berlin, 1911. Kammerer, O., "Die Entwicklung der Zahnrader," in *Beiträge zur Geschichte der Technik und Industrie*, 1912. Kutzbach, Karl, *Bemerkungen zur Entwicklung der Verzahnung*, Berlin, 1940. Matschoss, Conrad, *Geschichte des Zahnrades*, Berlin, 1940.
[2] Nicolaus Cusanus, *Opera*, Paris, 1514, vol. II, pp. 33–59.
[3] Dürer, Albrecht, *Underweysung der Messung mit dem Zirckel vnd richtscheyt in Linien*, (no title page, but of 1525).
[4] For Pascal's side of the story see his *Oeuvres*, La Haye, 1779, t.V, pp. 135–275.
[5] Beck, Theodor, *Beiträge zur Geschichte des Maschinenbaues*, Berlin, 1899, p. 100 and fig. 100.
[6] *Codex Atlanticus*, folio 391.
[7] Cardano, Girolamo, *De rerum varietate*, Basel, 1557, pp. 363–372.

were also known in Germany at this same time.[8] These practical rules gradually evolved by 1724 into the "rule of seven" as given in Leupold.[9] Well down into the nineteenth century the commonly accepted method of designing gear teeth, both for mills and for clockwork, was based on these rules.[10]

The claim of Ole Rømer (1644–1710) to have been the first to suggest in 1674 the use of epicycloidal teeth for gears is found in both Leibniz and Huygens. Leibniz does not give any date for Rømer's discovery; he only says that it was made while Rømer was at the Royal Observatory in Paris.[11] This claim is also to be found in a letter which Leibniz wrote to Wolf on 20 August 1705.[12] Wolf repeats much the same information, evidently depending upon Leibniz.[13] On the other hand, Leibniz cannot have been ignorant of the prior claims of others, for Bernoulli had written him a letter as early as February 1698 crediting Desargues with the discovery.[14]

The credit is also given to Rømer in du Hamel[15] and in Huygens.[16] In fact, Huygens repeatedly credits Rømer in work of his own on this same subject written in late 1674. But only three years earlier he had attributed the discovery to Desargues, in a letter which he wrote to Lodewijk Huygens on 29 October 1671.[17] The editors of Huygens' works seem to feel that de La Hire should also be given credit for an independent discovery, but they ignore Desargues' claim entirely. Leibniz and Huygens both seem to imply that Rømer announced his discovery in a paper before the Académie des Sciences, but Huygens' editors state (t. XVIII, p. 602) that this paper has not been preserved. The application of the epicycloid to gear teeth is not to be found in Rømer's published work, but since his papers were unfortunately lost in a fire in Copenhagen in 1728, we have no choice but to accept the statements of Leibniz and Huygens as evidence of an independent discovery.

It seems likely that the French mathematician Phillipe de La Hire (1640–1718) had also arrived at the concept of epicycloidal gear teeth independently and at about the same time as Rømer. Certainly he was the first to attempt a systematic application of the epicycloid to gear teeth,[18] and he is said to have applied this discovery in practice in his design of a large waterworks.

In the preface to a separately published edition of his paper before the Académie des Sciences [19] he tells us that he had been working on the problem twenty years earlier. This would be at about the same time as Rømer's discovery.

However, in de La Hire's original paper and again in the preface to his *Traité de Mechanique* [20] he describes the work of Gérard Desargues (1593–

[8] Holzschuher, Berthold, "Drey Kamphreder," Germanisches National-Museum MS Sig. 2°, no. 28893, folio 19.
[9] Leupold, Jacob, *Theatrum machinarum generale*, Leipsic, 1724, p. 49 and fig. XIV.
[10] Langsdorf, C. C., von, *Ausführliche System der Maschinenkunde*, Heidelberg, 1826 (Langsdorff was a Professor at Heidelberg); Hawkins, John I., *Teeth of Wheels*, London, 1806; Reid, Thomas, *Treatise on Clock and Watchmaking*, Edinburgh, 1826.
[11] Leibniz, Gottfried W., "Tentamen de natura et remediis resistentia . . .", in Societati Regiae Scientiarum, *Miscellanea Berolinensia*, Berlin, 1710, vol. I, p. 315.
[12] Gerhardt, C. I. (ed.) *Briefwechsel zwischen Leibniz und Christian Wolf*, Halle, 1860.
[13] Wolf, Christian, *Elementa Matheseus Universiae*, Halle, 1758, t. II, par. 960.

[14] *Virorum celeberr. G. G. Leibnitii et Johan. Bernouillii Commercium Philos. et Math.*, Lausanne & Geneva, 1745, vol. I, pp. 347, 349, 352.
[15] du Hamel, Jeanne, Baptista, *Regiae Scientiarum Academiae Historia*, Lipsiae, 1700, anno 1675, p. 162, par. 1.
[16] Huygens, Christiaan, *Oeuvres Complètes*, La Haye, 1934, t. XVIII, pp. 607–620.
[17] Huygens, C., *Oeuvres*, La Haye, 1888–1950, vol. III, pp. 112–113.
[18] La Hire, Phillipe de, "Traité des épicycloides et leurs usages dans la méchanique," in *Mém. de Math. & Phys. de l'Ac. R. des Sciences*, Paris, 1694, t. 9, p. 342.
[19] La Hire, Phillipe de, *Mémoires de Math. et de Phys.*, Paris, 1694.
[20] *Ibid. Traité de Méchanique*, Paris, 1695, p. 10.

1661). Besides his mathematics, Desargues was also interested in architecture and in engineering. De La Hire only says that in the course of building some machinery near Paris, Desargues designed and constructed the first gears having epicycloidal teeth. Unfortunately de La Hire does not give us a date, nor can the buildings be dated, although they can be identified. But despite Desargues' various travels, the dates of the two periods when he was working near Paris would lead us to believe that the work was done in 1644–1649, or possibly in 1657–1661. At any rate, it is clearly prior to the work of either Rømer or de La Hire.

Unfortunately this discovery is not mentioned in Desargues' published works, nor is it among his papers.[21] But it is clear that Desargues was the first to suggest and use the epicycloidal form of gear teeth and thereby to begin the scientific study of gears, even though the credit for their first systematic analysis must go to de La Hire.

[21] Taton, René, *L'Oeuvre mathématique de G. Desargues*, Paris, 1951, p. 65.

Latent Heat and the Invention of the Watt Engine

BY DONALD FLEMING *

MUCH has been written, early and late, on the connection between Joseph Black and James Watt; and few if any writers have entered a radical dissent from the proposition that Watt could not have introduced the separate condenser without the aid of Black.[1] The materials for this view of their relationship lay ready at hand in the oldest layer of traditions concerning the two men. Their common friend, John Robison, in dedicating his edition of Black's chemical lectures to "Dr. Black's most illustrious Pupil," spoke of Watt's "improvements on the steam engine, which you profess to owe to the instructions and information you received from Dr. Black."[2] In the text proper Black made the same point:

I have the pleasure of thinking, that the knowledge which we have acquired concerning the nature of elastic vapour, in consequence of my fortunate observation of what happens in its formation and condensation, has contributed, in no inconsiderable degree, to the public good, by suggesting to my friend Mr. Watt of Birmingham, then of Glasgow, his improvements on this powerful engine.[3]

That is, the theory of latent heat was decisive for the invention of Watt's steam engine. Of Robison at least, no reader of the several passages in which he recurs to this point will doubt that he means as far as he can to vindicate the social utility and historical significance of the quiet and selfless academic who shakes the world at one remove. The claims made by Robison and Black have been repeated from generation to generation; and may be found in several works of scrupulous contemporary scholarship.[4]

The present article proposes to substitute for the traditional view an alternative resting on three propositions: first, that Watt discovered certain empirical consequences of the phenomenon of latent heat, independently of Black; second, that the knowledge of these consequences would have been sufficient for Watt's purpose as a mechanic, without the construction which he learned from Black to put upon them; and third, that the fundamental innovation of a separate condenser did not require a knowledge either of the empirical consequences or of the theoretical doctrine of latent heat. Substantially these points were made by Watt in 1822.[5] Though his testimony might be regarded as suspect, it has not been refuted but ignored. The case for his indebtedness to Black in the matter of latent heat is asserted rather than argued. Before examining the thesis propounded by Watt, we ought to bear in mind that he kept his peace for many years, dealt respectfully with Black and Robison when he spoke out, and gave little evidence of exasperated vanity. He began by drawing up a short list

* Brown University.
[1] A. Wolf, *A History of Science, Technology, and Philosophy in the Eighteenth Century* (London, 1939), pp. 618–620, fails to make the conventional claim for Black, but says nothing in refutation of it.
[2] Joseph Black, *Lectures on the Elements of Chemistry*, John Robison, ed. (Edinburgh, 1803), I, iii.
[3] Black, I, 184.
[4] Cf. H. W. Dickinson and Rhys Jenkins, *James Watt and the Steam Engine* (Oxford,

1927), p. 22; H. W. Dickinson, *A Short History of the Steam Engine* (Cambridge, Eng., [1939]), p. 175; Douglas McKie and Niels H. de V. Heathcote, *The Discovery of Specific and Latent Heats* (London, 1935), p. 122; J. R. Partington, *A Short History of Chemistry*, 2d ed. (London, 1948), p. 95.
[5] "Letter to Dr Brewster from Mr Watt," in John Robison, *A System of Mechanical Philosophy*, David Brewster, ed. (Edinburgh, 1822), II, iii–x.

of facts known before his time or discovered by others in his time: first, that "steam was condensed by coming into contact with cold bodies"; second, that "water and other liquids boiled in vacuo at very low heats; water below 100°"; third, that "the capacity . . . of heat . . . was much smaller in mercury and tin than in water"; and fourth, that "evaporation caused the cooling of the evaporating liquid, and bodies in contact with it." [6] To this tabulation he added a list of his own experiments to determine: the capacities for heat of certain substances as compared with water; the bulk of steam compared with that of water; the quantity of water evaporated in a given boiler by a pound of coal; the elasticities of steam at various temperatures above the boiling point of water; the quantity of steam required for each stroke of a Newcomen engine of given proportions; and the quantity of cold water required in every stroke to condense the steam in the cylinder of the Newcomen engine. [7] The last experiment taught him that steam could heat six times its own weight of water to 212° F.

Being struck with this remarkable fact, and not understanding the reason of it, I mentioned it to my friend Dr Black, who then explained to me his doctrine of latent heat, which he had taught for some time before this period, (sum- mer 1764,) but having myself been occupied with the pursuits of business, if I had heard of it, I had not attended to it, when I thus stumbled upon one of the material facts by which that beautiful theory is supported. [8]

To my knowledge this statement has never been challenged; and in spite of the lateness of the date, it has the ring of truth about it, with the enthusiastic acknowl- edgment by Watt that the *theory* of latent heat is entirely the achievement of Black. [9] Watt's recollection would indicate that he discovered for himself an unexpected reservoir of heat in steam; and if the existence of this reservoir had been the decisive clue for the improvement of the Newcomen engine, Watt could have done his work without consulting Black. He got from Black an access of understanding; but better machines can sometimes be built on a foundation of brute empirical fact into which no great theoretical insight has yet been afforded. In all good logic, men need not have passed from the Edison effect to the Fleming valve over the bridge of sub-atomic physics.

Yet all of this, in Watt's view, would have been beside the point. In his words:

. . . this theory [of latent heat], though useful in determining the quantity of injection neces- sary where the quantity of water evaporated by the boiler, and used by the cylinder, was known, and in determining, by the quantity and heat of the hot water emitted by Newcomen's engines, the quantity of steam required to work them, did not lead to the improvements I afterwards made in the engine. These improvements proceeded upon the old-established fact, that steam was condensed by the contact of cold bodies, and the later known one, that water boiled in vacuo at heats below 100°, and consequently that a vacuum could not be obtained unless the cylin- der and its contents were cooled every stroke to below that heat.

These, and the degree of knowledge I pos- sessed of the elasticities of steam at various heats, were the principal things it was *necessary* for me to consider in contriving the new engine. [10]

To put the matter in another way, the inconvenience and much of the economic waste of alternately cooling and heating the same cylinder would not have been obviated by the *non-existence* of latent heat (regarded not as a theory but as a natural phenome- non).

One difficulty remains to be cleared away. If, as a psychological and historical fact, Watt did not pass from the conception of latent heat to that of a separate condenser, how had he come to make the famous experiment which established that steam could

  [6] *Ibid.*, II, vii.
  [7] *Ibid.*, II, vii–viii.
  [8] Watt, note supplied to Brewster; Robison, *Mechanical Philosophy*, II, 116n.
  [9] Ivor Hart, *James Watt and the History of Steam Power* (New York, 1949), p. 162, makes the point that Watt had uncovered certain em- pirical consequences of the latency of heat, inde- pendently of Black. Cf. Dickinson and Jenkins, *Watt*, p. 22.
  [10] Watt, "Letter to Brewster," Robison, *Me- chanical Philosophy*, II, viii.

bring to the boiling point six times its own weight of water? The answer would seem to be that this experiment was merely part of a larger enterprise, namely, an effort at understanding the phenomenon of "back pressure." The down stroke of the piston in a Newcomen engine ought ideally to work against a perfect vacuum induced by condensing the steam required for the up stroke. The cold injection water used to produce condensation may, however, fail of its purpose and be brought by the heat of steam to the boiling point. The result is back pressure, impeding the down stroke of the piston and producing less of a lift from, say, the mine shaft to which the engine is applied. The problem was greatly complicated by the circumstance, well known to Watt and his contemporaries, that the boiling point of water is drastically lowered by the very process of evacuating the vessel in which the water is contained. Cooling the cylinder of the engine, therefore, to a temperature slightly below 212° F. will not suffice to prevent back pressure. In the light of this knowledge, antecedent to the discovery of latent heat, a given quantity of steam would possess the power to bring a given quantity of water to a boil at temperatures of less than half the normal boiling-point. This fact, of itself, would require very sharp alternations of cooling and heating the cylinder; and so contribute to that waste of steam which Watt had seized upon as the central attribute of the Newcomen engine. In this engine, the avoidance of back pressure required that steam, on being introduced to effect the up stroke, be diverted in considerable part to re-heating the walls of a cylinder which had just been cooled, and markedly cooled, to produce the down stroke. Now, it is a particular aspect of this matter that owing to the release of latent heat by steam on condensation, an astonishingly large injection of cold water is needed to prevent back pressure. This fact Watt discovered for himself. But on the basis of the records now remaining, one must suppose that he regarded his discovery as merely a further complication of the problem of back pressure. This problem did not arise out of the latency of heat. One may, indeed, imagine that some one, having discovered the latency of heat, and the consequent necessity for very large injections of water into a Newcomen engine, might have concluded that a separate condenser would be a good thing. Yet this is not history, but speculation.

The relationship between the author of the concept of latent heat and the inventor of the separate condenser ought not to be taken as the validating image of the reliance of practice on theory, the dependence of the mechanic Watt on the theorist Black. Another kind of reliance of Watt on Black may perhaps be discerned.

Although [Watt writes] Dr Black's theory of latent heat did not *suggest* my improvements on the steam-engine, yet the knowledge upon various subjects which he was pleased to communicate to me, and the correct modes of reasoning, and of making experiments of which he set me the example, certainly conduced very much to facilitate the progress of my inventions. . . .[11]

To say of Black that he inspired the process of reasoned experimentation by which Watt successively improved the steam engine would be a remarkable tribute to a great scientist; and this tribute is authorized by Watt himself.

---

[11] *Ibid.*, II, ix.

Sadi Carnot and the Steam Engine Engineers

Introduction

IN the year 1824, in Paris, Nicholas Léonard Sadi Carnot published his *Reflections on the Motive Power of Heat*[1] which was destined to lay the foundations of thermodynamics and to distinguish him as one of the very great scientific geniuses. Although he was an engineer[2] and wrote primarily for engineers, his work was almost completely neglected by them. A quarter of a century later it was exhumed by two physicists, Kelvin and Clausius,[3] and then only slowly diffused into engineering theory and practice.

The reason for this indifference towards Carnot's work, especially on the part of the steam engine engineers, is either avoided by historians of science or is meshed with some sweeping generalization such as "he was before his time."[4] S. Lilley[5] and L. Rosenfeld[6] have suggested that the physicists failed to develop Carnot's ideas immediately because they belonged to a different social world from the engineers, had different perspectives and were thus interested in different kinds of problems. However, there is no comment on why the steam engine engineers, who were vitally concerned with the same problems as Carnot, ignored him. The thesis of this essay is that by the usual

* Clarkson College of Technology, Potsdam, New York. This paper was read before the International Congress of the History of Science at Barcelona, 4 September 1959. I should like to acknowledge the kindness of M. Lehanneur in making available to me the facilities of the library of L'Ecole Nationale des Ponts et Chaussées during a period when the library is normally closed.

I should also like to express my appreciation to the American Philosophical Society for a grant which enabled me to spend some time at the Bibliothèque Nationale and Ecole des Ponts et Chaussées in Paris; also to the Shell Companies Foundation for a travel grant which enabled me to use the Cornell University library.

[1] The two English translations are by R. H. Thurston, New York and London, 1897 and by W. F. Magie in *The Second Law of Thermodynamics* (New York, 1899). A French paperback facsimile of the 1878 edition is now available with the imprimerie of A. Blanchard (Paris, 1953). Both this and the Thurston

edition also contain some posthumous notes.

[2] There is included, in the *Histoire de l'École Polytechnique* by A. Fourcy (Paris, 1828), a list of graduates by classes. The present affiliation of each man is given. Carnot is cited as a "constructeur de machines à vapeur à Paris." We are indebted to Professor Henry Guerlac for drawing our attention to this point.

[3] R. Clausius, "On the Motive Power of Heat," *Poggendorff's Ann.*, 1850, *79*: 376,500. W. Thomson, "On the Dynamical Theory of Heat," *Trans. Roy Soc. Edinburgh* (March 1851).

[4] Henry W. Dickinson, *A Short History of the Steam Engine* (New York and London, 1938), p. 177.

[5] S. Lilley, "Social Aspects of the History of Science," *Archives Internationales d'Histoire des Sciences*, 1949, *2*: 376-443.

[6] L. Rosenfeld, "La genèse des principes de la thermodynamique," *Bull. de la Soc. Roy des Sciences de Liège*, 1941, *10*: 197-212.

criteria—the availability and clarity of the work, the social and technological requirements of the age, the stated objectives of the practicing engineers, the logical development of the science—Carnot's work should have been recognized for its true worth by his fellow engineers shortly after publication. It is certain that a leading steam engine engineer, Clapeyron, studied Carnot's work and thoroughly comprehended it on at least a technical level, and that Poncelet, the dean of the French mechanical engineers, had read it. It is likely that others, such as Pambour, were aware of its existence. The application of Carnot's explicitly stated results could have been of assistance in some of the problems with which the engineers were wrestling such as the merits of fluids other than water as the working medium or a quantitative estimate of the benefits derived from using high pressure engines. Even in the design of certain mechanical features, Carnot's injunction against permitting conduction between the hot and cold parts of the engine could have hastened developments that came about only slowly. That the steam engine actually did evolve in the "right" direction without the guidance of Carnot's theory, only points up the consistency of the theory with nature itself and demonstrates the perspicacity with which the engineers might have been endowed. Certainly, the use of Carnot's theory would have, at the very least, prevented many engineers from spending time on hopeless projects. What obscure veil it was that impeded their perception provides yet another enigmatic thread to the fabric of the sociology of discovery.

Reflections on the Motive Power of Heat

Sadi Carnot was born 1 June 1796 in the palace of Luxembourg in Paris, where his father, Lazare Nicholas Marguerite, then lived as a member of the Directory. The elder Carnot had already established his niche in the history of science when, as a young officer before the outbreak of the revolution, he had published a number of important works in mathematics and engineering. A meteoric rise during the revolution led to his participation in the top administrative echelons of the revolutionary regimes. For a time, he served as Napoleon's minister of war.

Sadi prepared to follow in his father's footsteps by entering the École Polytechnique in 1812. Upon graduation in 1814, he was commissioned in the engineer corps and in 1819 succeeded in procuring an appointment to the general staff corps in Paris. This provided him with some leisure to pursue the studious life and upon his resignation from the army in 1828, he devoted himself completely to his intellectual and technical pursuits until his premature death from cholera on 24 August 1832.[7]

[7] The dearth of biographical material on Sadi Carnot is remarkable not only because of his importance in the history of science, but also because of his connection with one of France's most illustrious families. There is only a very short biographical sketch prepared by his younger brother, Hippolyte, in 1878 which appears in the Thurston edition. Hippolyte makes no mention of Carnot's connection as a "constructeur de machines à vapeur" but presents, rather, a picture of a many-sided dilettante. "He diligently followed the course of the Collège de France and of the Sorbonne, of the École des Mines, of the Museum and of the Bibliothèque. He visited the workshops with eager interest, and made himself familiar with the process of manufacture, mathematical sciences, natural history, industrial art, political economy, — all these he cultivated with equal ardor. I have seen him not only practice

The problem to which Carnot addressed himself in the *Reflections* was an analysis of the factors that determine the production of mechanical work from heat in the steam engine and heat engines in general. The youthful officer pointed out that "already the steam-engine works our mines, impels our ships, excavates our ports and our rivers, forges iron, fashions wood, grinds grains, spins and weaves our clothes, transports the heaviest burdens, etc. It appears that it must some day serve as a universal motor, and be substituted for animal power, waterfalls and air currents . . . yet, its theory is very little understood, and the attempts to improve it are still directed almost by chance." Questions were being raised for which no answers had been forthcoming. How was the work developed by the engine related to the heat supplied? Was there an upper limit to this work and what condition could lead to its release? Was water the best material to use, or might not some other liquid such as alcohol provide a more effective medium? Might not a gas such as air be more advantageous than a condensable vapor?

Carnot pointed out that in a heat engine work is obtained by passing heat from a body at a high temperature—a boiler—to another body in which the temperature is lower—the condenser. In fact, an analogy could be set up between the production of heat through a difference of temperature and the work produced by a water wheel upon the passage of water through a difference of gravitational potential.

The condition for the maximum production of work was that there should not occur any change of temperature in the bodies employed which was not due to a change of volume, the main offender being direct conduction of heat through the parts of the engine. Such direct transference of heat was equivalent to wasting a difference of temperature which might have been utilized to produce motive power. This condition of maximum efficiency was characterized by its *reversibility*. If the reverse of such a process were carried through, all of the effects would be of the same magnitude but reversed in direction.

Carnot was able to demonstrate that the maximum effect was obtained when

---

as an amusement, but search theoretically into, gymnastics, fencing, swimming, dancing, and even skating."

Hippolyte had earlier written a two volume biography of their father, *Mémoires sur Carnot par son fils* (Paris, 1861, 1863), in which Sadi is hardly mentioned and his work only vaguely alluded to. The later sketch was commissioned on the occasion of the formal recognition of Carnot, by the publication of an edition of the *Reflections* by the Academy of Sciences. Undoubtedly the aged Hippolyte depended primarily upon his own reminiscences for it.

There are only passing references to Sadi in a family biography, *Les Trois Carnot — Histoire de Cent Ans, 1789-1888* (Paris, n.d.), by Maurice Dreyfuss. This is devoted primarily to Lazare, Hippolyte and the latter's son Sadi, who was the fourth President of the Third Republic. In *Une Famille républicaine: Les Carnot 1753-1887* (Paris, 1888), par un deputé, there is a short chapter on Sadi which is a rehash of Hippolyte's sketch.

F. Arago, as *sécrétaire perpetuelle* of the Academy of Sciences, read a 97-page *éloge* of Lazare Carnot in 1837, *Comptes Rendus*, 1837, 5; 294. There is no mention of Sadi in this biography which Arago submitted for publication without change in 1850, *Mémoires de l'Académie des Sciences*, 1850 (2), 22; 1. Arago's neglect of Sadi is all the more remarkable because of his interest in the history of the steam engine. First published in 1829 in *L'Annuaire du Bureau de Longitudes*, this "Notice Historique sur les Machines à Vapeur" was reissued in 1830, 1837 and 1860. (The 4th edition forms volume V of Arago's *Œuvres Complètes*.) The purpose of this 117-page work is to negate the assertion by many Englishmen that the steam engine was entirely an English invention. Arago emphasizes, especially, the role of Papin, but the contributions of Carnot are completely ignored, both in this work and in the biography of Lazare.

an engine operated reversibly and that all reversible engines operating between the same two temperatures must have the same efficiency, regardless of the medium utilized as the carrier of the heat. Hence, it was the reversible operation of the engine, not the use of steam, alcohol, or anything else, that determined its efficiency in producing mechanical work. He also concluded that, for a given quantity of heat transferred, the work produced was greater, the greater the difference of temperature between boiler and condenser. Furthermore, for the same difference of temperature, the engine would operate more efficiently, the lower these temperatures.[8] The principles to be considered in the design of heat engines were now clear. We may summarize them as follows.

1. Maintain the greatest possible temperature difference between boiler and condenser.
2. If faced with a choice between equal temperature intervals, select the one lower on the temperature scale.
3. The actual working medium is unimportant from the point of view of thermodynamic efficiency, except as its properties affect the working temperatures.
4. Seek to operate as closely to the reversible conditions as is practical.

Modern students of thermodynamics are well aware that in the heat engine, work appears as the result of the conversion of some of the heat being transferred and that not all of the heat which leaves the boiler finds its way into the condenser. It is at this point that Carnot's analogy with the water wheel breaks down. In the water wheel, the amount of water leaving at the lower level is equal to the amount entering at the upper level. In his treatment, Carnot considered that work appeared as the result of the fall of heat through a difference of temperature. Carnot adhered to the caloric theory of heat. There was no conversion of heat—rather, there was a conservation of heat. His result, then, was erroneous whenever he dealt with the question of the origin of the work. However, Carnot was concerned primarily with determining the conditions under which maximum work could be obtained from the transfer of a given quantity of heat from boiler to condenser. His results in this area stand, and because the reasoning which led to them does not involve the question of the origin of the work, Carnot's reasoning as well as his conclusions remain valid.

Clapeyron and Carnot

Ten years passed with Carnot's work finding hardly an echo[9] until 1834,

[8] Carnot's argument for using lower temperatures requires a proof that the isothermal expansion of a gas through a given volume ratio is greater at higher temperatures. His proof of this is erroneous in that it utilizes the caloric theory plus some poor experimental data. Thus, although this conclusion stands, Carnot's reasoning in this case does not.

[9] We will refer to Poncelet's reference to Carnot in the next section. No mention is made of Carnot in the following works which we have consulted in the libraries of Columbia, Cornell and Harvard Universities, the University of Illinois, Massachusetts Institute of Technology, the Library of Congress and the New York Public Library and which we would presume to be representative. C. F. Partington, *An Historical and Descriptive Account of the Steam Engine* (London, 1826); same author, *A Course of Lectures on the Steam Engine*; Elijah Galloway, *History of the Steam Engine* (London, 1826, 1832); John Farey, *A Treatise on the Steam Engine* (London, 1827); Thomas Tredgold, *The Steam Engine* (London, 1827); James Renwick, *Popular Lectures on the Steam Engine* (New York, 1828); same author, *Treatise on the Steam Engine* (New York, 1830); P. and J.

when Benoit-Pierre-Émile Clapeyron published a paper[10] which is a detailed exposition of the *Reflections*. In it, he transformed Carnot's verbal analysis into the symbolism of the calculus and represented the Carnot cycle graphically by means of the Watt indicator diagram, familiar to engineers. The paper also appeared in translation in England and Germany,[11] so that despite the rarity of the original, Carnot's work was generally available and associated with the name of Clapeyron who was widely recognized as a leading steam engine engineer. However, not only was Clapeyron's original paper ignored by the other engineers, but he himself made only one passing reference to it until the work of Kelvin and Clausius made its true significance generally known.

Clapeyron[12] was born in Paris on 26 February 1799 and died there on 28 January 1864. He graduated from the École Polytechnique in 1818 and then attended the École de Mines. In 1820 he went to Russia with his friend and classmate, Gabriel Lamé, where they taught pure and applied science at the École des Travaux Publics de Saint-Petersburg and did construction work.[13] While in Russia they published a number of papers in the *Journal des voies de communication de Saint Petersburg*, the *Journal du génie civil* and the *Bulle-*

Grouvelle, *Guide du chauffeur et du proprié-taire de machines à vapeur* (Paris, 1830) ; M. A. Alderson, *An Essay on the Nature and Application of Steam* (1834) ; Hugo Reid, *The Steam Engine* (Edinburgh, 1840, also London, 1851) ; P. B. Hodge, *The Steam Engine* (New York, 1840, 1849) ; E. Alban, *The High Pressure Steam Engine* (London, 1847-48), 2 vols., translated by Wm. Pole from the German, *Die Hochdrückdampfmaschine* (1843) ; E. Partwine, *The Steam Engine* (London, 1847) ; J. A. Armengaud, *Traité Théorique et Pratique des Moteurs à Vapeur*, 2 vols. (Paris, 1861). We will discuss Pambour's *Théorie de la Machine à Vapeur* later. W. Whewell in the third edition of the *History of the Inductive Sciences* (1859), discusses the contributions of Joule and Thomson to the conservation law in his section of the Dynamical Theory of Heat. However, there is no mention of Carnot's work despite the fact that Thomson had discussed and championed it more than ten years earlier. William Rankine, along with Thomson and Clausius, was among those first to recognize the importance of Carnot's work and he utilized it without making reference to Carnot by name. His *Manual of the Steam Engine and Other Prime Movers* appeared in numerous editions from 1859 on. After this Carnot's work slowly diffused into the steam engine treatises until by 1870 the treatment is quite modern. For the rediscovery of Carnot by Kelvin see: M. Kerker, "Sadi Carnot," *Scientific Monthly*, 1957, *85:* 143.

[10] B. P. E. Clapeyron, "Mémoire sur la puissance motrice de la Chaleur," *J. de l'école polytech.* (Paris), 1834, *14:* 153.

[11] *Scientific Memoirs, selected from the Transactions of Foreign Academies of Science and Learned Societies and from Foreign Jour-* nals by Richard Taylor, 1937, *1:* 347-376. In the preface, Taylor laments the lack of success of his journal. "Hitherto, as I can hardly yet boast of the sale of 250 copies, I am very far from being repaid the cost of publication, to say nothing of the care and labour which have been required ; nor could I be expected, having now finished a volume, which, from the nature of its materials, may be considered a complete work in itself, then proceed further unaided, until I have ascertained whether I may calculate upon adequate support."

The German translation by Poggendorff appeared in *Annalen der Phys. u. Chem.*, 1843, *59:* 446, with the following preface: "Dieser bisher nur von wenigen beachtete Aufsatz schien seiner Wichtigkeit wegen noch jetzt ein volles Recht zur Aufnahme zu haben."

[12] Much of the biographical material on Clapeyron was obtained from Ch. Combes, *Discours prononcés aux funerailles de M. Clapeyron*, le 30 janvier 1864 (Paris: F. Didot). We are indebted to the archivist of the Academy of Sciences for a copy of this brochure. In addition, biographical sketches of Clapeyron as well as other leading graduates of the École Polytechnique appear in *L'École Polytechnique* (Paris, 1932) by E. Estaunié and *École Polytechnique, Livre du Centenaire, 1794-1894* (Paris, 1895).

[13] Towards the end of 1809, Emperor Alexander created a corps of engineers which was to encompass the areas of highways and bridges as well as military engineering. He requested some engineers from the French government to provide a nucleus for this corps as well as to engage in instruction. This program was reinstituted after the Restoration. *Histoire de l'École Polytechnique*, A. Fourcy (Paris, 1828).

tin Ferussac as well as various works published in France.[14] They left, following the revolution of 1830, when their position became somewhat difficult due to their well-known liberal tendencies.

Upon returning to France, Clapeyron engaged in railroad engineering,[15] specializing in the design and construction of steam locomotives. In 1836, he traveled to England to order some locomotives that would negotiate a particularly long continuous grade along the Saint-Germain line. When the illustrious Robert Stephenson declined to undertake the commission because of its difficulty, the machines were built in the shops of Sharp and Roberts, according to the designs of Clapeyron.[16] He extended his activities to include the design of metallic bridges, making notable contributions in this area.[17]

He was elected to the Academy of Sciences in 1848, replacing Cauchy,[18] and served on numerous committees of the Academy, including that which awarded the prize in mechanics. the investigation of the project for piercing the Isthmus of Suez and the application of steam to the navy.

Clapeyron had a continuing interest in steam engine design and theory throughout his career. His most important research paper[19] dealt with regulation of the valves in a steam engine. The purpose of this work was to deter-

[14] Lamé, G., and Clapeyron, B. P. E., *Mémoire sur la stabilité des voûtes avec un rapport de M. de Prony sur ce mémoire* (Paris: Huzard, 1823). Lamé and Clapeyron, *Mémoire sur les chemins de fer considérés sous le point de vue de la défense des territoires* (Paris, 1832). Lamé, Clapeyron and Flâchet, *Vues politiques et pratiques sur les travaux publics* (Paris: Carelian-Goewy, 1832).

[15] Clapeyron and Lamé came into the railroad business at an early stage. The period 1823-33 saw several concessions to private companies, but except for some short lines radiating from St-Étienne, these were failures. In 1833, under pressure from a group of brilliant young followers of Saint-Simon, 500,000 francs were authorized for an engineering study of the problem, including the sending of engineers to England and the United States for study and observation. The engineering talent for this and the earlier assistance to the "concessionaires" was provided by the Corps des Mines and included Clapeyron and Lamé. Clapeyron conceived the idea of a railroad from Paris to St. Germain, but while waiting for financing went to Saint-Étienne as professor at the École des Mineurs where he taught the course in construction. In 1835, upon authorization of a line from Paris to St. Germain, Clapeyron and Lamé were charged with direction of the work. Lamé left shortly thereafter to accept the chair of physics at the École Polytechnique. For the early history of the French railways, see "The French Railroads, 1823-1842" by George LeFranc, *J. Eco. & Business History*, 1929-30, *2:* 299; *The French Railroads and the State* by Kimon A. Doukas (New York: Columbia U. Press, 1945); "How the First French Railways Were Planned" by

Arthur L. Dunham, *J. Eco. Hist.*, 1941, *1:* 12 and *Les Chemins de fer en France pendant le règne de Louis Philippe* by Ernest Charles (Paris, 1896).

[16] B. P. E. Clapeyron, "Expériences faites sur le chemin de fer de Saint-Germain avec une nouvelle locomotive," *Bulletin de la Société d'Encouragement de l'Industrie Nationale* (1846) *45:* 413. "Note sur une expérience faite le 17 juin, 1846 au chemin de fer de Saint-Germain," *Comptes Rendus,* 1846, *22:* 1058.

[17] B. P. E. Clapeyron. "Calcul d'une poutre élastique reposant librement sur des appuis inégalement espacés," *Comptes Rendus,* 1858, *45:* 1076. "Mémoire sur le travail des forces élastiques dans un corps solid deformé par l'action de forces exterieures," 1847, *Comptes Rendus,* 1858, *46:* 208.

[18] He was not elected upon his first presentation as a candidate, losing to Ch. Combes. *Comptes Rendus,* 1847, *24:* 502. He was later presented and elected receiving 43 votes over Borre de Saint Venant, 12 votes. Foucault 3 votes, Phillips 2 votes. *Comptes Rendus,* 1848, *26:* 545, 564, 667.

[19] "Mémoire sur le règlement des tiroirs dans les machines à vapeur," *Comptes Rendus,* 1842. *14:* 632. In 1843, Clapeyron communicated with the Academy in order to point out that the commission, consisting of Poncelet. Coriolis and Piobert, which had been charged with examining and rendering a report on this memoir, had not discharged its duty. Since a vacancy had been created on the commission by the death of Coriolis, Lamé was designated as a replacement. *Comptes Rendus.* 1843, *17:* 1289. A report was finally rendered, authored by Lamé, *Comptes Rendus,* 1844, *18:* 275, 345.

mine the optimum position for the piston at which the various valves should be opened and closed. For example, as the piston moves outward under pressure from the boiler the maximum effect is obtained if the steam pressure is cut off at some point before the full extent of the piston is reached. A similar problem is faced in considering the exact moment when the valve to the condenser is to be opened and closed. These matters are discussed in terms of the Watt diagram which Clapeyron had so skillfully exploited in his exposition of Carnot's work.

Although Carnot's theory cannot yield a specific solution for this problem, it does give the maximum possible effect for which the mechanician can strive. In such a situation it is important to know how close to the limit one is working since it would be futile to try to improve upon a mechanism that is already operating at nearly the ideal level. Carnot's theory sets the framework within which these matters must be considered. It is remarkable, then, that at no point in this paper does Clapeyron even allude to Carnot's work.

From 1844, Clapeyron was a professor at the École des Ponts et Chaussées where he taught the course in the steam engine. His teaching career covered a span of years (1844-1859) from a time when Carnot's work was hardly known to several years after the establishment of the general laws of thermodynamics by Kelvin and Clausius. Fortunately there are extant in the library of the École des Ponts et Chaussées several manuscript editions of notes of his lectures[20] (taken by students) which enable us to learn just what Clapeyron was teaching about Carnot's work during this time.

In the 1844-45 course there is absolutely no consideration of Carnot's work. However, by 1851, Clapeyron commences the course with a general discussion of the motive force of heat using essentially the same point of view as his 1835 paper. He applies the theory to the efficiency of Cornwall engines explaining the difference between the theoretical efficiency and that obtained practically as due to conduction of heat between parts of the engine at different temperatures. He then points out how thermal contact between the cylinder and boiler is an important factor in this loss of efficiency and how improvements in this regard were being currently effected in certain of the Cornwall machines. In his treatment of the gas cycle, Clapeyron continues to use the caloric theory. This is not surprising in view of the fact that it wasn't until 1851 that Kelvin himself was able to resolve the apparent contradiction between Carnot's and Joule's theorems. There is no direct mention of Carnot's paper in all of this or even of Clapeyron's 1834 paper.

In the 1853-54 edition Clapeyron clearly discusses the principle of the equivalence of heat and work which he attributes to Regnault, omitting any reference to Joule, Kelvin, Mayer, etc. He now cites Carnot and his own earlier work but the discussion is a verbatim repetition of the 1851 lectures,

---

[20] Notes prises par les élèves aux conférences sur les machines à vapeur locomotives, Conférence de M. Clapeyron. Session 1844-45. Notes prises par les élèves aux conférences sur les machines à vapeur fixes, Conférences de M. Clapeyron, 1851. Notes prises par les élèves au cours de machines à vapeur. M. Clapeyron, professeur, 1853-54. There is a second impression of this in 1858.

The *Catalogues des livres, composant la Bibliothèque de l'École des Ponts et Chaussées* (Paris, 1872), list an 1844-45 edition instead of the above 1845-46 edition.

with no attempt to reconcile the new principle of equivalence with his treatment of the Carnot cycle which used the caloric theory.

In a scientific biography of 1847,[21] prepared to support his candidacy for election to the Academy, Clapeyron goes into considerable detail about his mechanical and mathematical work and refers to his paper on Carnot only briefly. Even in an expanded version published in 1858 he only adds a short paragraph referring to a citation of his 1835 paper in a lecture before the Academy given by Reech. Indeed, Clapeyron is quite apologetic about his contributions to theory complaining that "depuis cette époque (1835), le pratique a absorbé presque exclusivement tout mon temps ... je n'ai pu consacrer à l'étude des sciences proprement dites, qu'un temps très limité. ..."[22]

Poncelet

The first reference to Carnot's work which we know of is by Jean Victor Poncelet.[23] Poncelet became a lieutenant in the Engineers upon graduation from the École Polytechnique in 1812 and was sent to Russia shortly thereafter. Taken prisoner, he took advantage of his captivity by pursuing mathematical researches. Upon his return to France in 1814, he was stationed at his native city of Metz where his studies led to his receiving a prize in mechanics from the Academy of Sciences and to his being placed in charge of the course on machines at the Artillery and Engineering School. Here his reputation grew, but despite his being known as the "Newton de la mécanique industrielle," he refused all invitations to leave the provinces for Paris until the death of his mother in 1834 when a special chair in "Mécanique physique" was created for him by the Academy of Sciences. He continued to remain in the army, rising to the rank of general and to the command of the École Polytechnique.

There is a reference to Carnot's treatise in a footnote in one of Poncelet's early works[24] as follows: "Le calorique, pouvant être considéré comme un

[21] Notice sur les travaux de M. Emile Clapeyron (Paris, 1847), 7 pp.; *ibid.* (Paris, 1858), 11 pp. These are located in the Bibliothèque Nationale, Paris.

[22] Although F. Jacqmin, Clapeyron's successor at the École des Ponts et Chaussées, continued to discuss Carnot's and Clapeyron's contribution, the course was altered towards a more practical point of view. In the introduction to his treatise, *Des Machines à Vapeur, Leçons faites en 1869-70 à l'école impériale des ponts et chaussées,* 2 vol. (Paris, 1870), Jacqmin points out that his course will be on a more practical level and describes an interview just several days prior to Clapeyron's death at which the elder engineer gave his approbation for this scheme. "Appelé à l'honneur bien imprévue de remplacer Clapeyron à l'École des Ponts et Chaussées, nous ne pouvions songer à conserver à son cours le caractère scientifique si élevé qu'il lui avait imprimé. Nous avons entrevu un but plus modeste: nous avons considéré la machine comme un outil et nous avons cherché à en enseigner l'usage. Soumis à Clapeyron quelques jours avant sa mort, cet

ordre d'idées pratique reçut sa complète approbation et cet ingénieur éminent, cet homme de bien, toujours préoccupé du désir d'être utile au plus grand nombre, voulut bien nous dire que le moment d'étudier la machine à vapeur au point de vue purement scientifique était passé, qu'il faillait desormais s'attacher à en vulgariser l'emploi et à montrer le rôle qu'elle remplissait comme instrument de transformation et de progrès." The emphasis on practical work may have been due to the fact that the students at the École des Ponts et Chaussées were already graduates of the École Polytechnique where they had been subjected to a fairly extensive theoretical treatment of mechanics and machines.

[23] For biographical material on Poncelet, Cf. 10 and "Éloge de Jean Victor Poncelet" by J. Bertrand, *Mémoires de l'Academie des Sciences,* 1879, *41* (2).

[24] *Introduction à la Mécanique Industrielle,* Deuxième Édition (Metz, Paris, 1839), page 203. The existence of this reference was first pointed out to me by Professor Thomas S. Kuhn of the University of California.

fluide éminemment élastique, sans inertie ou pesanteur, et dont l'état de tension est indiqué par la température thermométrique, il en résulte qu'on peut lui appliquer, jusqu'à un certain point, les mêmes raisonnemens qu'aux gaz matériels, et dire qu'une certaine quantité de chaleur, introduite dans un corps ou soustraite de ce corps, doit développer, contre les résistances directment opposées à son action, des quantités de travail absolues qui sont toujours les mêmes ou indépendantes du mode de cette action et de la nature des corps, mais dont une certaine partie est, dans les solides et les liquides, employée à contre balancer la force d'agrégation des molecules. Ce principe offre quelque analogie avec celui qui a été mis en avant par M. S. Carnot, ancien élève de l'École Polytechnique, dans un petit ouvrage intitulé: *Réflexions sur la puissance motrice du feu* (Paris, Bachelier, 1824). Quant à ce que nous venons de nommer *quantité de chaleur,* elle se mesure, non pas simplement par la température, mais par le nombre des kilogrammes de glace à 0°, qu'elle peut convertir en eau à la même temperature de 0°."

In the preface, Poncelet explains that the second edition was put together piecemeal under pressure and that the part up to page 224, which includes the above footnote, was completed prior to 1830 and hence prior to Clapeyron's paper.[25]

The footnote is particularly interesting because it cites as one of the properties of calorique that the work produced by its expansive action is independent of the manner of application or the nature of the body. This does bear a superficial resemblance to Carnot's conclusions regarding the operation of the reversible heat cycle and it is in this connection that Carnot is cited. However, Poncelet is rather vague and although the footnote is part of a section on the work of expansion of gases and is followed by a section on the work produced in the steam engine, there is no further reference to Carnot. The footnote is designed merely to point up the analogy between the properties of gases and the gas-like material, calorique. The implications for the theory of the steam engine, and the production of work from heat engines in general, are completely ignored.

Pambour

Francois Marie Guyonneau, le Comte de Pambour, was an outstanding steam engine engineer who might have been expected to be familiar with Carnot's work and yet he makes no mention of it. This certainly was not due to a lack of interest in problems of steam engine efficiency for this was one of Pambour's areas of interest.

He attended the École Polytechnique during 1813-1815,[26] a member of the

[25] The first edition is a manuscript in the Bibliothèque Nationale, Paris, in three parts. *Résumé des leçons du Cours de mécanique industrielle* professé par M. Poncelet, redigé par M. Le capitaine du génie Gosselin, 1827-28. *Cours de mécanique industrielle professé de 1828-29* par M. Poncelet, 2° partie. *Cours de mécanique industrielle professé du mois de janvier au mois d'avril 1830* par M. Poncelet, 3°

partie. There is no treatment of heat or pneumatics here, the entire work being exclusively devoted to mechanics, both theoretical and practical. There is an 1841 reprint of the second edition. The third edition, Paris, 1870, is a posthumous reprint of the second edition annotated by X. Kretz, Ingénieur en Chef de Manufactures de l'État.

[26] Fourcy, *op. cit.,* p. 450.

class following that of Carnot.[27] Upon being commissioned, he entered the artillery, and, like Carnot, later transferred to the general staff.[28]

His *Théorie de la machine à vapeur*, which went through several editions and translations,[29] had a fundamental and mathematical approach such as might be expected from an applied physicist rather than a practical engineer. As late as 1876, it was authoritatively referred to as "the most celebrated treatise of de Pambour . . . published in 1844, then far superior to other works and still in many respects one of the best standards on the subject."[30] In his definitive treatise, R. H. Thurston[31] frequently refers to Pambour's work in the highest terms. He points out that much of his original work has been "demonstrated anew by a certain number of modern writers who appear to ignore the works of Pambour."[32] Pambour was certainly not a mere empiricist. His original researches were reported in papers communicated to *Comptes Rendus*.[33] In addition to his treatise on the seam engine, he wrote an equally successful practical work, *Traité des Locomotives* (1835).

Pambour's most important contribution to the theory of the steam engine dealt with the calculation of the work obtained under a given set of operating conditions. An earlier treatment, developed by Poncelet and Arthur Morin,[34] calculated the work of expansion by using the Boyle-Mariotte law, not taking into account the drop in steam temperature upon expansion. Pambour, on the other hand, assumed that the steam remained saturated throughout the engine and since the temperature of saturated steam varies wih pressure, the Boyle-Mariotte law is quite incapable of representing this situation. Instead, Pambour used an empirical formula involving two experimentally determined constants. He assumed various pressure situations between the boiler and the cylinder and, using his formula, calculated the work for these cases. The assumption that the steam is saturated during the expansion is not used today,

[27] Pambour must have known Carnot, at least by reputation, not only because of his father's position, but because in December 1813 Carnot organized a successful appeal to the Emperor requesting that the students of the École be mobilized for active service at the front. His leadership in this dramatic episode must have certainly brought his name to the attention of every student in attendance at the time.

[28] From the title page of *Théorie de la Machine à Vapeur* (Paris: Bachelier, 1839).

[29] We have located the following editions all of which are in the Cornell University Library: Brussels, 1837; Paris, 1839; London (English), 1839; Philadelphia (English), 1840; Liège, 1847; Berlin (German, Introduction by A. L. Crelle), 1849. There is a Paris, 1844 edition in the Columbia University Library. We possess a Liège, 1848 edition.

[30] R. S. McCullock, *Treatise on the Mechanical Theory of Heat and its Application to the Steam Engine*, etc., 1876.

[31] R. H. Thurston, *Traité de le Machine à Vapeur* (Paris, 1893).

[32] However, in Thurston's earlier work, *Die*

Dampfmaschine, Geschichte ihrer Entwickelung, translated by W. H. Uhland (Leipzig, 1880), no mention of Pambour is made. The introduction points out that "Die Grundlage des vorliegenden Werke bildet der allgemein interresante Theil einer Reihe von Vortragen die im Winter 1871-2 im Stevens Institute of Technology, Hoboken vor einem gemischten Publiken."

[33] There are forty-four papers by Pambour on the steam engine in volumes 4 to 21. Later he developed an interest in hydraulic turbines, on which subject he published seventeen papers in volumes 32 to 75.

[34] Arthur Morin attended the École Polytechnique from 1813-16 with time off during the interval for military service. He joined Poncelet at Metz in 1829 and in 1835 replaced him as Professor when Poncelet left for Paris. In 1839, he joined the Conservatoire des Arts et Métiers as professor and rose through the administrative ranks to become director. He remained in the army rising to the rank of three star general. He was elected to the Academy of Sciences in 1846.

Pambour's scheme being replaced by the Rankine Cycle where the expansion is from superheated steam into wet steam. However, the improvement over the assumption of the Boyle-Mariotte law was tremendous and represented a major advance.[35]

Despite his productivity, Pambour failed to be elected a member of the Academy of Sciences. He was presented as a candidate for the Section de Mécanique on three occasions; in 1837 in competition with François for the seat of Moled (Comptes Rendus *4*, 556), in 1840 with Morin for the seat of de Prony (ibid. *10*, 504) and in 1843 with Combes and Séguin (ibid. *17*, 1310).[36]

Pambour was primarily concerned with the dynamics of the steam engine. Given the boiler conditions, the resistance and the load of the machine, he asks what speed the cylinder might attain and what are the relations among the quantities—speed, load and work. The emphasis is different from that of Carnot who is interested in the relationship between heat and work. Pambour, like Clapeyron, is primarily interested in the utilization of the potential motive force already made available in the boiler. Given this, he wants to know how much work can be obtained, how rapidly it may be mechanically utilized and

---

[35] In his *Treatise on the Steam Engine* (New York, 1848), 3rd edition, James Renwick refers to "the successful investigations of Pambour" and gives a detailed exposition of the theory in a rather long exposition. Clapeyron also used Pambour's formula in his 1851 lecture notes (see footnote 18) but recognized its shortcomings due to the assumption that the steam was "dry." In *Die Theorie der Dampfmaschinen* (Braunschweig: F. Vieweg und Sohn, 1857), Fr. Zernikow says "Vom praktischen Standpunkte aus lässt sich gegen die Resultate der Theorie wenig einwenden: da die empirische Formel, welche der Theorie zur Grundlagen dient, ziemlich einfach ist, da die Entwickelung von dort aus tadelos fortschreitet und da die erhaltenen Rechnungsresultate mit den Werthen, welche sich aus den Versuchen ergeben haben, gut übereinstimmen. . . ." Zernikow states that the theory was universally accepted by the German engineers.

[36] It is quite possible that Pambour's failure to be elected to the Academy was a result of scientific differences with Poncelet, probably aggravated by a personal clash. There is a record of a polemic between Pambour and Poncelet's protégé Morin regarding the choice of "frictional coefficients" in calculating the work of piston expansion. This quantity deals with the relationship between the volumes occupied by a unit weight of steam in the boiler and in the cylinder. According to the older theory of Poncelet and Morin, it can be correlated by a constant coefficient. With the new theory of Pambour the coefficient is no longer constant, varying with operating conditions. Pambour's denunciation of earlier work done by Poncelet elicited a response from the latter which was introduced politely as follows: "Malgré le répugnance que j'éprouve à prendre la parole dans la discussion qui vient de s'élever entre M. M. Morin and de Pambour, candidats dont les utiles travaux sont justement appreciés par l'Académie, mon nom ayant néanmoins été plusieurs fois prononcé par ces messieurs d'une manière à la verité très honorable, je crois ne pouvoir garder davantage le silence. . . ." After Poncelet's presentation, Pambour responded once again after which the following entry appears: "Lors de la lecture faite par M. de Pambour devant l'Académie, M. Poncelet, à qui sa qualité de membre ne permet pas de répondre verbalement, s'est borné à protester purement et simplement contre les assertions erronées de l'auteur, dont quelques-unes se trouvent ici rectifiées. Mais si le Réglement s'oppose à ce qu'un membre puisse prendre la parole dans de telles circonstances, il est un autre motif qui doit encore empêcher M. Poncelet de continuer une discussion à laquelle il n'a pris part qu'à regret et par les provocations de M. Pambour; ce motif, que tout le monde appréciera, est relatif à sa position de juge vis-à-vis d'un candidat pour la place resté vacante dans le sein de la section de Mécanique. Le même motif l'engage à refuser de continuer faire partie de la Commission chargée d'examiner les Mémoires des M. M. Morin et de Pambour. (M. Regnault est designée pour remplacer M. Poncelet dans le commission.)" *Comptes Rendus*, 1843, *17*: 971, 1048-1058.

Not only was Pambour rejected by the Academy but his name does not appear in the *École Polytechnique, Livre du Centenaire* (see note 10), which includes biographical sketches of considerably less distinguished graduates.

the relation between rate and efficiency. He carries the efficiency back only to the stage where the motive force becomes available. That the energy reservoir is a boiler is only incidental and Pambour does not concern himself with Carnot's problem—the efficiency of conversion of heat into the motive force.

Time has proved that Carnot's approach has led to the solution of one of the most fundamental problems in nature whereas Pambour merely worked out practical problems. However, it was not apparent at the time which approach was more fundamental. There is little doubt that Carnot himself would be amazed at the ultimate ramifications of his work.

Did Pambour know of Carnot's work? The fact that he does not refer to it does not mean he was unaware of it. Pambour and Clapeyron were both active candidates for membership in the Academy, both were engaged in the same type of professional work, both were graduates of the École Polytechnique and were contemporaries. It would seem that Pambour might very likely have been aware of Clapeyron's paper on Carnot in the *Journal de l'École Polytechnique*[10] and had possibly seen Poncelet's footnote.[24] However, since Clapeyron himself did not refer to Carnot in his later work, Pambour's omission is hardly surprising. That none of these men, whose training and interests were so similar to Carnot's, could see the broader meaning of Carnot's work is understandable for it took a genius of Kelvin's stature to do this. What is remarkable is their failure to apply Carnot's views to the narrower problems of steam engine technology.

Heat Engines Operating with Fluids other than Steam

The possibility of using a fluid other than steam as the working substance of a heat engine intrigued a number of engineers during the first half of the nineteenth century. The idea seemed to be that all vapors at the same pressure would be equally effective in producing work. Therefore, a liquid with a lower boiling point and lower latent heat would produce the same amount of work with a lesser heat input.

Carnot addressed himself to this problem in *Reflections on the Motive Power of Heat* and showed that the efficiency of a heat engine was independent of the medium except as it defined the temperature range over which the engine operated:

> The maximum of motive power resulting from the employment of steam is also the maximum of motive power realizeable by any means whatever ... [since] the motive power of heat depends also on the quantity of caloric used, and on what may be termed, on what in fact we will call, the *height of its fall,* that is to say, the difference of temperature of the bodies between which the exchanger of caloric is made.

The main effort at replacing the steam engine was on the development of a heat engine which utilized air or permanent gases as the working substance and on the steam turbine. However, there were also serious attempts to develop the analogue of the steam engine using volatile liquids other than water.[37]

---

[37] Henry Adcock, *Rules and Data for the Steam Engine, Railways, Canals and Turnpike Roads* (London, 1839). Although he disagreed with these efforts, Adcock pointed out that "in some of the treatises on chemical science, many persons have inferred that the vapors of alcohol and ether might be beneficially introduced, as the motive power of the steam engine."

These culminated in the use of the condenser of the steam engine as a heat source for an auxiliary engine utilizing a low boiling liquid. In 1840, Trembley[38] built several commercial engines of this sort using ether. One of these was employed in a factory at Lyons and another 70-horsepower motor was in use on a steamboat plying between Marseilles and Algiers. However, the project was soon abandoned because of the escape of the noxious and inflammable fumes.

Lafond,[39] a naval lieutenant, proposed to substitute chloroform for ether, since it was less flammable. This was done, and such an engine was operated on the steamboat Galilée. Although the problem of flammability was resolved, the fumes were hardly less toxic than ether and in addition the chloroform proved to be highly corrosive.[40]

If the failure of Carnot's principles to penetrate into engineering practice need further emphasis, one might consider that as late as 1852 John Ericsson went to considerable expense and effort to construct an enormous atmospheric marine engine which he presumed would operate in the absence of a temperature difference.[41] However, this failure to comprehend Carnot's work is generally appreciated. What we wish to emphasize is that Carnot's conclusions could have been of direct and immediate practical value to the engineer. Carnot's maxims for the steam engine designer were not super-sophisticated concepts, couched in a language alien to the engineers, nor did they involve a point of view or of interest different from that of the engineers. It is true that the steam engine was developed without practical assistance from Carnot's theory. But it could have been given such assistance.

Regnault stated the situation most succinctly in the introduction to his mammoth memoir. "Le problème général que je me suis proposé de résoudre par ces longues recherches, commencés en 1840 et dont la première partie a été publiée en 1847, peut s'énoncer ainsi: Une certaine quantité de chaleur étant donnée quel est théoriquement, le travail moteur que l'on peut obtenir en l'appliquant au développement et à la dilation des fluides élastiques, dans les diverse circonstances pratiquement réalisable?" Of course this problem was precisely the one solved by Carnot. Although Regnault was thoroughly aware of the significance of Carnot's work at the time he wrote this statement,[42] it does point up the fact that Carnot was in the mainstream of engineering practice and theory.

A point of entry, a bridgehead, into the engineering literature had already been effected by Clapeyron. Clapeyron was not a mere dilettante who dabbled for a short time and then proceeded to other matters. He was concerned with the problem of the efficiency of the steam engine throughout his long professional career. The leading steam engine engineers were a closely knit group. In addition to Clapeyron, Poncelet and Pambour there were Combes, Lamé,

[38] Cited by F. Jacqmin, op. cit.
[39] Comptes Rendus, 1848, 26, 408.
[40] F. Jacqmin, op. cit.
[41] A detailed description of this is given in the paper, "John Ericsson and the Age of Caloric," read by Eugene Ferguson of the Smithsonian Institution at the annual meeting of the History of Science Society, 30 December 1958, Washington, D.C.

[42] V. H. Regnault, Mémoires de l'Académie des Sciences, 1862 (2), 26: 1-928. The experiments were terminated in 1852 and the memoir read in 1853. Regnault refers to a delay in publication due to a serious accident in 1856. The introduction was probably composed considerably after that.

Séguin, Regnault and others, all graduates of the École Polytechnique, who met and discussed their work at the sessions of Academy of Sciences. They were all vitally interested in the steam engine and certainly technically competent to follow the logic of even the most erudite parts of Carnot's text or Clapeyron's exposition of it. Even if all these men were completely oblivious of Carnot's work, why didn't Clapeyron promote it among them? What obscure veil was it that impeded his complete perception?

Sadi Carnot and
the Cagnard Engine

By Thomas S. Kuhn *

A CONTINUING search of the early nineteenth-century literature on power engineering [1] has recently brought to my attention the document reprinted in part immediately below. I reserve discussion until after the presentation of evidence but must first say why the material seems worth reproducing. Two sets of reasons combine: first, the document is well suited to suggest essential features of the Carnot ideal heat engine; second, it is all but certain that Sadi Carnot was fully acquainted with its contents before he undertook the classic investigation that culminated in his *Réflexions sur la puissance motrice du feu*. It could well, therefore, have provided him with important clues during the genesis of his novel and significant approach to the mechanical action of heat.

What follows is the first two-thirds and conclusion of a report presented by Sadi Carnot's father, Lazare Carnot, to the *Classe des sciences physiques et mathématiques* of the *Institut national* on 8 May 1809: [2]

M. Cagnard Latour a présenté à la Classe l'invention d'une nouvelle machine à feu, que MM. de Prony, Charles, Montgolfier et moi [Lazare Carnot] avons été chargés d'examiner.

On sait que tout corps plongé dans un fluide perd une partie de son poids égale à celle du fluide qu'il déplace. C'est sur ce principe qu'est établie la nouvelle machine proposée par M. Cagnard.

Le moteur dans cette machine n'est point la vapeur de l'eau bouillante, comme dans les machines à feu ordinaires; mais un volume d'air qui, porté froid au fond d'une cuve remplie d'eau chaude, s'y dilate, et qui, par l'effort

qu'il fait alors pour se reporter à sa surface, agit à la manière des poids, mais de bas en haut, conformément au principe énoncé ci-dessus.

Ce moteur une fois trouvé on peut l'employer de bien des manières différentes. Voici celle de M. Cagnard.

Sa machine est, à proprement parler, composée de deux autres qui ont des fonctions tout à fait distinctes. La première a pour objet d'amener au fond de la cuve d'eau chaude, le volume d'air froid dont il a besoin. La seconde a pour objet d'appliquer à l'effet qu'on veut produire l'effort que cet air, une fois dilaté par la chaleur, fait pour se

---

* University of California, Berkeley.

[1] For a highly condensed report on the results of that search see my " Engineering Precedent for the Work of Sadi Carnot," in *Actes du IXᵉ Congrès International d'Histoire des Sciences* (Barcelona, 1959), pp. 530-535.

[2] *Institut de France, Académie des sciences: Procès-verbaux des séances de l'Académie, tome IV, an 1808-1811* (Hendaye, 1913), pp. 200-202.

reporter à la surface supérieure du fluide.

Pour remplir le premier objet qui est d'amener l'air au fond de la cuve, M. Cagnard emploie une vis d'Archimède. Si une pareille vis fait monter un fluide en la faisant tourner dans tel ou tel sens, il est évident qu'elle devra le faire descendre si on la tourne en sens contraire. Si donc elle est plongée dans l'eau de manière que la seule partie supérieure de son filet spiral reste dans l'air, elle devra, lorsqu'on la retournera en sens contraire, comme nous venons de le dire, faire descendre au fond de cette masse d'eau l'air qu'elle saisit par sa partie supérieure à chaque tour de sa rotation. C'est ce qui a lieu en effet dans la machine de M. Cagnard. L'air dont il a besoin est porté d'abord au fond du réservoir d'eau froide où est plongée la vis; de là il est conduit par un tuyau au fond de la cuve d'eau chaude. La chaleur de cette eau le dilate aussitôt et crée ainsi la nouvelle force qui doit servir de moteur. Ainsi se trouve rempli le premier objet du mécanisme proposé.

Le second objet, comme nous l'avons dit, est d'appliquer ce nouveau moteur à l'effet qu'on veut produire. Pour cela l'auteur emploie une roue à augets entièrement plongée dans la cuve d'eau chaude; l'air dilaté et rassemblé au fond de cette cuve trouve une issue qui lui est menagée pour le diriger sous ceux des augets dont l'ouverture est tournée en bas. Alors sa force ascentionnelle chasse l'eau de ses augets et, le côté de la roue où ils se trouvent devenant plus léger que l'autre côté où les augets restent pleins, la roue tourne continuellement comme les roues à pots ordinaires.

Cette roue une fois en mouvement peut transmettre à d'autres mobiles quelconques, soit par engrenage, soit par d'autres moyens, l'action du moteur. Dans la petite machine exécutée pour modèle par M. Cagnard, l'effet produit consiste à lever au moyen d'une corde attachée à l'essieu de la roue un

poids de 15 livres, avec la vitesse uniforme verticale d'un pouce par seconde, tandis que la force mouvante appliquée à la vis est seulement de trois livres avec la même vitesse. L'effet de la chaleur est donc de quintupler l'effet naturel de la force mouvante.

On conçoit que, l'effet de la force mouvante étant quintuplé, on peut prélever sur cet effet même de quoi suppléer à cette force mouvante, et qu'il restera encore une force disponible quadruple de cette même force mouvante. C'est ce qui a lieu en effet dans la machine de M. Cagnard. Il établit par un joint brisé la communication entre l'axe de la roue et celui de la vis; celle-ci tourne alors comme si elle étoit mue par un agent extérieur, et consomme par ce mouvement un cinquième de l'action du moteur. Le reste sert à élever un poids de 12 livres avec la vitesse constante d'un pouce par seconde; c'est-à-dire que la machine se remonte continuellement d'elle-même, et que de plus il reste une force disponible quadruple de celle que devroit employer un agent extérieur qui auroit a entretenir par lui-même le mouvement de cette machine.

Il résulte de cet exposé que dans la machine de M. Cagnard, la chaleur quintuple au moins le volume de l'air qui lui est confié, puisqu'il est évident que l'effet produit doit être proportionnel au volume de cet air dilaté. Je dis au moins à cause des frottemens qu'il faut vaincre; mais ces frottemens sont peu de chose, parce que la vis et la roue étant l'une et l'autre plongées dans l'eau, perdent une partie considérable de leur poids et pressent par consequent peu sur leurs tourillons; d'ailleurs les mouvemens sont toujours lents et non alternatifs, et il ne se fait aucun choc. Ainsi cette machine est exempte des résistances qui absorbent ordinairement une grande partie de la force mouvante dans les machines et en accélèrent la destruction.

Nous ne croyons pas que la machine

inventée par M. Cagnard soit un objet de pure curiosité; elle peut devenir fort utile dans un grand nombre de circonstances. Comme elle produit son effet dans une masse d'eau échauffée seulement à 75° et même moins, elle donne lieu à profiter des eaux chaudes que dans plusieurs manufactures ou établissemens on rejette souvent comme inutiles. Par example dans les salines, l'ébullition des eaux salées pourroit servir, au moyen de la machine de M. Cagnard, à faire mouvoir les pompes destinées au service des chaudières; dans les forges la chaleur seule du haut fourneau pourroit faire mouvoir les soufflets; aux pompes à feu ordinaires qui, comme celle de Chaillot, fournissent une grande quantité d'eau très chaude; on pourrait en tirer une action équivalente à celle de beaucoup d'hommes ou de chevaux; enfin dans les bains, les distilleries, les fours à porcelaine, les fours à chaux, les verreries, les fonderies et tous les établissemens

où il y a production d'eau chaude ou de chaleur, on peut tirer partie de la machine de M. Cagnard. Cette machine qui, comme nous l'avons déjà dit, est peu sujette aux frottemens et aux réparations, a de plus l'avantage d'être facile à conduire, et lorsqu'on suspend son action pour quelque tems sans éteindre le feu, la chaleur n'est point perdue, parce que, l'eau n'étant point bouillante, le calorique s'y accumule et fournit ensuite une action plus considérable. . . .

Le machine de M. Cagnard nous a paru renfermer plusieurs idées nouvelles et ingénieuses. L'application en a été dirigée par une bonne théorie et par la connoissance approfondie des véritables lois de la physique. Elle nous a paru aussi pouvoir être utile dans nombre de circonstances à la practice des arts; nous pensons donc que l'auteur mérite l'encouragement de la Classe et nous vous proposons de donner votre approbation à cette nouvelle machine.[3]

The section of the report omitted above deals with the application of Cagnard's inverse Archimedean screw to an ingenious pump and bellows, but these do not concern us. What does is the description of Cagnard's working model. Let me briefly recapitulate the principal features of its operation: An Archimedean screw is placed in a tank of cold water and turned backwards so that it takes in air at the surface and releases it underwater. On emerging from the screw the air bubbles through a tube which conducts it into a tub of hot water where it expands. In rising through the hot water the expanded air strikes the inverted buckets of a paddle wheel fully immersed in the water, and it then causes the wheel to turn. Tests show that five times as much power is delivered by the wheel as is needed to turn the Archimedean screw, and the wheel is therefore coupled to the screw which it thereafter turns while continuing to do external work.

Though I know of no relevant direct evidence, Sadi Carnot was almost certainly aware of this report and its contents. A long extract from the report, including all its essentials, was reprinted in J. N. P. Hachette, *Traité élémentaire des machines* (Paris, 1811), and this treatise was officially adopted, even before its publication, by the *Conseil de perfectionnement* for

---

[3] The report was signed only by Carnot, Charles, and Prony. Montgolfier appears to have suffered a stroke about which a few words were said at the next meeting.
Note that in the title and text of this paper

I am following the spelling adopted in the report above. Cagnard Latour's name is more often found in one of the forms: Cagniard de Latour, Cagniard-Latour, or Cagnard-Latour.

the use of students at the *Ecole polytechnique*.[4] Sadi Carnot entered that school, at which Hachette then taught, in 1812, the year following the book's first publication.[5] He could scarcely have avoided being exposed to its contents, including the report on Cagnard's work.

Furthermore, if exposed to this report at all, Sadi Carnot is very likely to have studied it with care. In the first place, it had been presented to the *Institut* by his father. More important, it dealt with a working air engine, and these engines were a topic that particularly concerned him, at least during the decade after completing the *Polytechnique* course. The single concrete question posed by Carnot in introducing his *Réflexions* is, " La puissance motrice de la chaleur est-elle immuable en quantité, ou varie-t-elle avec l'agent dont on fait usage pour la réaliser [,] avec la substance inter- médiaire, choisie comme sujet d'action de la chaleur? "[6] That question was, he suggested, particularly natural and important because there were so many proposals to substitute some other working substance—a solid, a liquid, a permanent gas, or another vapor—for the steam commonly employed in heat engines. But, in fact, air seems to have been the principal alternate working substance seriously considered by engineers during the early decades of the nineteenth century. The 1811 edition of Hachette's *Traité* also contains a report on an air engine suggested by Niepce, and the 1819 edition (from which the report on Cagnard's engine was dropped) mentions two other investigations, by Laroche and Montgolfier, with the same aim.[7] There are, however, in these and the other engineering works I have examined, no reports of attempts to construct engines using solids, liquids, or other vapors as working substance. A man concerned, as Sadi Carnot was, to compare the effectiveness of various working substances was particularly concerned to compare air with steam. When Carnot, close to the end of his memoir, undertook a concrete computation of the motive power of heat, air was the first substance he considered.[8]

---

[4] For the official adoption of Hachette's book see p. iv of the work itself. The extract from the preceding report there occupies pp. 149- 154. It includes much of the material omitted above and omits only the first of the para- graphs here reprinted. The only other differ- ences are the occasional omission in Hachette's version of informal phrases like " Je dis," etc. These omissions, however, occasionally result in awkward readings, and I have preferred to reprint the original form. In all essentials the two are identical.

[5] Milton Kerker, " Sadi Carnot," *The Scien- tific Monthly*, LXXXV (1957), 143-149. This excellent brief account of Sadi Carnot's life and work also includes useful bibliography as well as an elementary description of his ideal engine cycle and its applications. I have as- sumed an acquaintance with the latter below, and readers in need of additional background will find Kerker's article particularly helpful.

[6] In the convenient facsimile edition (Paris:

Blanchard, 1953) the quotation occurs on pp. 14 f. Other citations below refer to the same edition.

[7] The report on Niepce's machine is on pp. 144-149 of the 1811 edition and on pp. 225- 229 of the edition of 1819. The reference to the work of Laroche (more often called De- laroche) and Montgolfier is on p. 224.

[8] *Op. cit.*, pp. 78 ff. The air computation is followed by one for water and another for alcohol vapor.

One should notice the extent to which Sadi Carnot's concern with engine economy in gen- eral and with air engines in particular is char- acteristic product of France's economic and industrial situation at the beginning of the nineteenth century. In the first place, France's coal deposits were concentrated in the North, far from its main iron mines and from most of its scattered industry. Transport costs made coal expensive, and economy of use was there- fore particularly important. Furthermore, in

There is another reason to suppose that in preparing his *Réflexions* Carnot was particularly concerned with air engines and would therefore have paid particular attention to a proposal like Cagnard's. His memoir itself indicates that he did most of his constructive thinking in terms of an air (or permanent gas) engine. All his detailed and rigorous arguments are carried through with an ideal gas as working substance. Only in the introductory outline of his argument does Carnot discuss an ideal heat engine run by steam, and that argument — probably introduced because the steam engine was the only type familiar to most of his readers — is wrong. Carnot's attempt to cover the gap in the argument seems to me the only truly clumsy argument in his memoir.[9] Very probably, then, the contemporary concern with air engines was more directly relevant to the genesis of Carnot's ideas than was the concern with steam. All of which makes it that much more likely that Carnot, if aware of Cagnard's engine as he must have been, would have studied it.

We may, I think, therefore safely assume that when Sadi Carnot first took up the problem of a general heat engine theory, the Cagnard engine was among those he contemplated. It may even — both because of its great simplicity and because of its peculiarity — have been felt to present a particular challenge. That makes it worth asking what Carnot could have learned from this engine that he would not have learned with equal ease from other engines described in the literature of his day. Three unique aspects of Cagnard's work may, I believe, have had a significant effect upon the subsequent development of his thought.

First and most important, no engine then known can be so immediately, directly, and completely described as a device which raises a weight by simply taking heat from a high-temperature body (the hot water) and delivering it to a low-temperature body (the surrounding atmosphere).

---

these years an often-noted lack of venture capital and of private entrepreneurial initiative kept French industry small. There were very few of the large-scale factories which the Industrial Revolution had brought to England (see Henri Sée, *Histoire économique de la France* [2 vols., Paris, 1939-42], I, 351-364, II, 153-157). As a result the French were particularly concerned to produce small engines, a drive illustrated especially clearly by the prize announced in 1806 by the *Société d'Encouragement pour l'Industrie Nationale* for the best design of a heat engine to be used in small plants (" Prix proposé pour l'année 1809 pour une petite machine a feu," *Bull. Soc. d'Enc.*, V [1806], 238). I am indebted to my former student, Mr. John Esty, Jr., for calling my attention to this significant connection.

9 Carnot's preliminary sketch (which he says "ne doit être considérée que comme un aperçu ") is on pp. 16-22. His difficulty with it is that, because he imagines steam in the cylinder, he cannot employ his normal four-

stage cycle. Water cannot be vaporized by adiabatic compression. As a result Carnot considers only three stages of the cycle explicitly and implies that water in the cylinder is vaporized by direct contact with the high-temperature reservoir, a step which violates his condition that two bodies at different temperatures must never be put in contact.

Carnot recognizes the difficulty and attempts to remove it on pp. 25-27 by supposing that the difference of temperature between his hot and cold reservoirs is infinitesimal. In his case the loss due to direct conduction of heat will be negligibly small. But so will the work done by such an engine. Furthermore, if a set of such engines is compounded, as Carnot suggests, to give a finite amount of work per cycle, the losses due to heat conduction will be compounded also, apparently in the same way. This is no proof at all. The thermodynamic cycle applicable to steam engines is inherently far more complex than Carnot ever recognized.

Other engines, of course, do that too, but their structure makes the thermo-dynamic essentials harder to see. Partly the unique suggestiveness of the Cagnard engine results from its simplicity: it has no pistons, valves, and mechanical linkages. Partly the unique suggestiveness results from the sim-plicity of the engine's operation: all other engines then known work in cycles composed of apparently incommensurable steps, and, before Carnot, engi-neering theory had therefore concentrated upon the power stroke and ignored the rest of the cycle. But, above all, Cagnard's engine is suggestive because, unlike all other known steam and air engines, *it takes nothing from the high-temperature reservoir except heat.* Caloric transfer is the only *net* environmental change required to raise a weight. That view of the relation between heat and mechanical effect is, however, one of Carnot's most novel and most fundamental contributions to physical science. The first substantive section of his memoir is devoted to its development, and his summary statement of the new abstraction is the occasion for his first use of italic emphasis: " La production de la puissance motrice est donc due, . . . non à une consommation réelle du calorique, *mais à son transport d'un corps chaud à un corps froid.*" [10] Though Carnot elaborates this view by considering normal engines, he could far more easily have learned it from Cagnard's, the only engine then known in which nothing was taken from the heat source but heat.

Two other central conceptual elements in Carnot's *Réflexions* could also have emerged directly from the contemplation of Cagnard's engine. Early in his memoir Carnot develops a parallelism between water wheels, which draw motive power from a " chute d'eau," and heat engines, which draw power from a " chute du calorique." [11] The image of caloric's falling from the high-temperature to the low-temperature reservoir recurs constructively throughout the work, and has there ordinarily been taken as metaphor. Logically it can, of course, be no more than that, but originally it may well have had literal meaning. Remembering that since Lavoisier the volume of gases had been supposed to consist overwhelmingly of pure caloric, Cagnard's engine is quite literally one in which an actual physical transport of caloric does work by impact upon a water wheel.[12]

Finally, it is at least possible that the linkage introduced by Cagnard between his wheel and his Archimedean screw may have prepared the way for Carnot's proof that his ideal gas engine was the most perfect heat engine possible. Cagnard's wheel can be coupled to the screw because it produces more work than the latter requires and can therefore still raise a weight. Carnot's engine is the best possible because any engine that did more work for the same transfer of caloric could be coupled to Carnot's engine and thus, by simultaneously raising a weight and cancelling the caloric transport, produce perpetual motion.[13] Though the parallelism is far from complete,

[10] *Op. cit.*, pp. 10 f.
[11] *Ibid.*, p. 28.
[12] For the literature on the caloric theory of gases see: T. S. Kuhn, " The Caloric

Theory of Adiabatic Compression," *Isis*, IL (1958), 132-140.
[13] *Op. cit.*, pp. 29-38.

the coupling of two engines — a coupling permitted by the excess of work produced by one of them — is central both to Carnot's argument and to Cagnard's machine.

Cagnard's engine is not, of course, identical with Carnot's. Given all the suggestions that the former could conceivably have supplied, the very best in creative imagination would still be required to substitute a gas-filled cylinder for Cagnard's wheel and screw and to recognize that a similar over-all effect would be obtained by transporting this cylinder from hot to cold reservoir in a particular four-stage cycle. Yet, though genius was undoubtedly required, most of the remaining elements with which genius had to work were available in works that Carnot either cited or must have known.[14]

The standard text of the *Ecole polytechnique*, and many other engineering works besides, taught how to compute — in terms of boiler pressure, cylinder diameter, and piston stroke — the maximum work performed by a steam engine per cycle.[15] Poisson, whose work in this area Carnot knew, had shown how to take account of adiabatic cooling in this computation.[16] Watt's patent for expansive working, which Carnot cited, had provided a technique for handling pressure variation during stroke and had simultaneously illustrated in both a graph and a table what were subsequently to become the first two stages of Carnot's cycle.[17] Carnot's father, in his famous *Principes fondementaux de l'équilibre et du mouvement* (Paris, 1803) had shown the necessity of completing the cycle. At the end of that work the elder Carnot had insisted that the computation of work done by an engine involving springs (and confined air was often conceived as a spring in this period) demanded considering the engine in identical positions at the

[14] For a fuller discussion of these precedents see the papers cited in notes 1 and 12. Together with the conjecture offered in this paper, they offer sources for all but one of the essential elements of Carnot's memoir (*but not for the way they are there combined*). The missing element is reversibility, and a hint of that might conceivably have been provided by Cagnard's striking application of an Archimedean screw run backwards.

[15] The 1811 edition of Hachette outlines the calculation briefly on pp. 122-126, and the 1819 edition describes a more complete mode of computation on pp. 212-216. But the source is unimportant. Some form of this computation is found in most books that deal with engines, and there were many of these before Carnot wrote.

[16] "Sur la chaleur des gaz et des vapeurs," *Ann. chim. phys.*, XXIII (1823), 337-352, is Poisson's most fully relevant paper, for it contains an explicit steam-engine theory. Carnot almost certainly knew it, for he cites another paper by Poisson that deals with a closely related topic and that appeared in the same volume of the journal. That citation occurs

on p. 43 n. of the *Réflexions* and refers to "Sur la vitesse du son," *op. cit.*, pp. 5-16. All the information about adiabatic cooling that Carnot needed is actually contained in this slightly earlier paper and in the works by Laplace there cited.

[17] Carnot discusses and partially reproduces Watt's patent in a long note whose relevant section begins on p. 100. I am still not sure from which of several possible sources Carnot took this information (probably from the 3rd edition of the *Britannica*—see note 12 of the reference cited in note 1, above), but most of the discussions of expansive working reproduced Watt's graph of pressure as a function of piston position. This shows a horizontal line during the period while steam is being admitted from the boiler. Then, after the boiler is cut off, the pressure curve declines hyperbolically for the rest of the stroke. Conceptually, the distinction between the pre-cut-off and post-cut-off stages of the stroke corresponds closely to Carnot's distinction between the first isothermal and the first adiabatic stage of his cycle.

beginning and end of its performance.[18] Given these and other elements in the contemporary literature of physics and engineering, the creative man concerned to assimilate Cagnard's model to the more usual engineering concepts and techniques might plausibly have done what Carnot did.

Did the model actually have a role in the development of Carnot's thought? In the absence of a research notebook or similar documentary evidence one can only speculate. Yet three consequences of the preceding argument make the speculation worth recording: Carnot almost certainly knew the Cagnard engine. If he knew it, he would probably have studied it. And if he did that, the engine could have led him to several of the least precedented conclusions that underlie his memoir. Furthermore, it could have done so far more directly than could any other engine or engine theory described in the literature of his day. Because it helps to bridge what has previously seemed a gigantic conceptual leap, the existence of Cagnard's engine makes it far easier to understand the direction taken by Carnot's research.

[18] The very last paragraph of Lazare Carnot's book states a general theorem for engine computations and closes (p. 262) with the condition: "pourvu, toujours, que . . . si l'on emploie des machines à ressorts, on laisse ces ressorts dans le même état de tension où on les a pris." For the assimilation of gas to springs see A. Guenyveau, *Essai sur la science des machines* (Lyon, 1810), p. 232. "On se sert de deux espèces de corps élastiques: les ressorts proprement dits, qui sont des corps solides, et les *gaz* ou fluides élastiques." Guenyveau then discusses both in the same chapter.

LEOPARDI AND THE MACHINE AGE

By HILDA L. NORMAN

GIACOMO LEOPARDI, in his *Discorso di un Italiano intorno alla poesia romantica*,[1] written in answer to LODOVICO DI BREME's defense of modern poetry,[2] mentions a curious mechanical invention. A search through the poet's other works revealed no further allusion to this invention, but showed that LEOPARDI both in his verse and in his prose refers to a number of other inventions. The poet was aware that a mechanical age, unfortunately inescapable, was fast overtaking civilization. Notwithstanding the rebellion of his sensitive nature, his alert mind took note of the changes and commented on them. The quest for the curious invention alluded to above has been successful only in throwing light on a little studied aspect of LEOPARDI's thought and in revealing inventions which, now either forgotten or considered as matters of course, were the cause of much public curiosity during the early decades of the past century. An examination of the casual and unsystematic allusions found in LEOPARDI's work brings nearer to us the nineteenth century and the poet himself.

And now to return to the aforesaid essay and the elusive invention. In the part of this essay with which we are concerned,[3] LEOPARDI flays the Romanticists for their misinterpretation of the theory of imitation. They, according to LEOPARDI, understand imitation to be merely the reproduction of things as they are: this, then, is what they mean by *il vero*. If this is art, protests LEOPARDI, then a doll with a waxen face and glass eyes would surpass a statue by CANOVA. This Romantic theory, he continues, which imitates the beat of horses' hooves with a *trap trap trap* and the sound of bells with a *tin tin tin* might well be compared to the said doll, or, should you prefer, to a "burattino che ha la mobilità da vantaggio." If we must

have such poetry, then why does not the poet abandon writing and invent "vedute e figure" of all sorts, imitating "il suono col suono," so that not only the imagination but also the senses of the (we can no longer say *reader*) *spectator* may be stirred? And even as he writes, adds the poet,

> viene con un nome infernale da un paese romantico uno strumento non dissimile in quanto all'ufficio da questo ch'io m'andava immaginando quasi per giuoco . . . .[4]

and here LEOPARDI smiles to think that he had foreseen what the new school of poetry was coming to, and then he expressed mock regret that no one can suggest even in fun anything so extravagant but that the Romanticists think it, and speak it, and, when they can, put it into execution.

If, as the author says, the invention was contemporaneous with the writing of his essay, we must try to establish the date of the *Discorso*. LEOPARDI writes that he began his essay immediately upon the appearance of DI BREME's *Osservazioni*.[5] He first mentions the *Osservazioni* in his *Zibaldone*[6] (entry undated) in which he says he has just read the article. He then comments on it for several pages, but without mentioning the new Romantic invention. On March 27, 1818,[7] LEOPARDI wrote to the publisher STELLA relative to the first part of a *Discorso* on the *Osservazioni* to be followed by more if STELLA liked the first part. STELLA did not publish the article and the only explanation seems to be that found in the author's *Avvertimento* appended to the *Discorso* which was finally completed but which remained unpublished until it appeared in the Le Monnier

---

[1] *Scritti vari* in *Opere* a cura di G. ROBERTIS, I Classici Rizzoli (Milano-Roma, 1937), II, 484 ff.
[2] *Spettatore italiano*, X, 46 (*Milano*, 1818), pp. 113–143.
[3] *Ed. cit.*, 567–568.

[4] *Ibid.*, 568.
[5] See the *Avvertimento* at the close of the *Discorso*, *ed. cit.*, 574.
[6] In *Tutte le opere*, a cura di FRANCESCO FLORA, *I Classici Mondadori* (Milano, 1937), I, 21.
[7] *Epistolario*, a cura di FRANCESCO MORONCINI (Firenze, Le Monnier, 1934), I, 166.

edition of the *Scritti vari* in 1906.[8] LEOPARDI assigns as his reasons for not having published the article: that others had already replied to DI BREME; that he preferred to keep out of the mêlée; and that he could not complete the essay in "un batter d'occhio" because material kept increasing; and that DI BREME's article had not stirred Italy sufficiently to warrant further refutation. Did LEOPARDI finish the essay between March and August of 1818, as indicated by GIUSEPPE DE ROBERTIS in a note on the essay,[9] or did he retouch his work at a later date, as is implied in his *Avvertimento?* In an entry of the *Zibaldone* for April 22, 1821,[10] LEOPARDI discusses imitation and quotes the *trap trap trap*, etc., referring to a review of LONDONIO's *Cenni critici sulla poesia romantica* of 1817, in the *Biblioteca italiana*, VIII, of that year, in which the author ridicules the use of imitative words in BÜRGER's *Lenore*. Apparently LEOPARDI had only just read this review which had appeared before he had begun his *Discorso*. It would seem probable that he then inserted the allusion to *Lenore*. This might mean that the Romantic machine, invented even as LEOPARDI was writing, belongs to the spring of the year 1821. It is obvious, however, that the dating can be only approximate and therefore the machine difficult, if not impossible, to verify. Perhaps, however, the by-products of this paper may justify the seeming futility of the quest.

What is this *strumento* with an *infernal name* invented in a *Romantic* country, even as the author was writing his essay? It was evidently an invention which would display scenes and figures and produce sound. The Romantic country of its invention might be Germany, England, or France, though most likely Germany. The word *strumento* would suggest a musical instrument, though not necessarily so. There was, in fact, as we shall see later, no dearth of "infernal" names applied to fantastical musical instruments. The author, however, implies that the invention was made especially to serve the purpose of the Romanticists whom he accuses elsewhere of giving birth to monsters.[11] And so this limitation would have to be taken into consideration. Perhaps, then, LEOPARDI is referring to a musical instrument, but it would be a pity to solve our problem too hastily, as it is little more than a pretext to write of many other things. Let us be content, for the present, to know that we are dealing with a mechanical invention which will serve to introduce the inventions made during the early years of our mechanical age.

What was LEOPARDI's attitude to this mechanical era and what are the inventions he singles out as of especial importance or of casual interest? LEOPARDI, the poet of the golden age of simplicity, could hardly be expected to praise anything that would render life more complicated and remove us even farther from nature. Unhappiness is the penalty man pays for the loss of contact with nature, and the poet, in his *Discorso*,[12] reproaches the Romanticists with drawing their metaphors from civilization to the neglect of nature, replacing mountains and forests with "cannocchiali e strumenti manufatture officine d'ogni sorta, e cose simili." In his *Proposta di preme fatta dall'Accademia dei Sillografi*[13] of 1824, he characterizes his age as "l'età delle macchine" in which "non gli uomini, ma le macchine, si può dire, trattano le cose umane e fanno le opere della vita." Hence the Accademia expects machines to accomplish in the future not merely material, but spiritual things as well and looks to automatons for the moral perfection unattainable by men. LEOPARDI's sarcasm does not seem ill placed when we read of an American invention of 1818 for the teaching of Latin.[14] An entry in the *Zibaldone*,[15] 1826, shows us LEOPARDI shrugging his shoulders at the ultimate utility of machines, although he recognizes their probable perfectibility and probable influence on civilization. Men of a later age, says he, will wonder how we managed to endure life in a period when inventions were so imperfect, but we ourselves are content enough; from this we may deduce that it is foolish to wonder how men possibly lived without this or that invention, and we may feel sure that the savage, before the discovery of fire, was as contented as we are. In the array of inventions mentioned in this passage, lightning rods are condemned as of little use; balloons as of no use at all; steamboats, the telegraph, etc. as highly imperfect. Years later, in 1835, LEOPARDI again vents his hostility toward the modern *aureo secolo* in his satirical *Palinodia*. Here,[16] with irreverent pen, he jumbles together modern ideas and modern inventions: universal love is lumped with railroads, steam, and the press, and with new sorts of furniture, new pots and pans. Machines, which have been steadily growing more gigantic, will, says the poet, continue to increase and the human race will ride to perfection with the rush of trains and conveniences like that of the tunnel under the Thames and gas lighted streets. These are the principal passages in which LEOPARDI ridicules the mechanical aspect of his time.

---

[8] The date 1910 is given by MORONCINI in his already cited edition of the *Epistolario*, I, 166, note 3. This, however, is the date of the "seconda impressione."

[9] *Ed. cit.*, p. 1004.

[10] *Ed. cit.*, I, 654 and note referring to p. 655.

[11] *Zibaldone, ed. cit.*, I, 13.

[12] *Ed. cit.*, 506.

[13] *Le Operette morali* (Firenze, Sansoni, 1931), 30 ff.

[14] *Il Raccoglitore* (Milano, 1819), II, 7–16.

[15] *Ed. cit.*, II, 1026.

[16] *I Canti di G. Leopardi* (Firenze, Sansoni, 1934), 30 ff.

LEOPARDI's interest in modern inventions is not entirely satirical, however, and perhaps BENJAMIN FRANKLIN is to some degree responsible for this more serious attitude, for we find that LEOPARDI proposed about 1826[17] to write a treatise on common sense in the matters of morality, politics, etc. "alla maniera di FRANKLIN." He had in mind works on *Arte o industria, Elettricità, Moto, Magnetismo, Calor centrale, Sole* . . .[18] and these topics would seem to suggest Franklinian influence as does LEOPARDI's interest in the lightning rod. But if LEOPARDI planned a serious work on electricity, it was never written, and of the two allusions to lightning rods, one is satirical, the other legendary. In the *Proposta* already mentioned, LEOPARDI, after calling attention to the numerous and varied inventions of the day, among which are those protecting us from lightning and hail, suggests the advantage of similar inventions to improve our spiritual condition:

qualche parainvidia, qualche paracalunnie o paraperfidia o parafrodi, qualche filo di salute o altro ingegno che ci scampi dall'egoismo, dal predominio della mediocrità . . . .[19]

The second allusion is found under the words *Paragrandini, parafulmini* on a page of the *Zibaldone* for 1825.[20] These words are followed by an interesting quotation from CESTIAS who lived in the fourth century B.C. The legend tells of a fount of liquid gold the bottom of which was iron. Knives made from this iron had the property of turning aside "clouds, hail, and thunder bolts" and twice, says the narrator, the King had proved their efficacy of which he, CESTIAS, had been a witness, too. And so LEOPARDI draws from his fund of ancient lore a lightning rod which antedates FRANKLIN's by centuries.

FRANKLIN launched his famous kite in 1752. In a few decades the results of the experiment are evident. In 1784 BERNARDIN DE ST. PIERRE refers to "cet art nouveau et encore plus merveilleux de l'électricité, qui écarte le tonnerre de leurs hotels;"[21] and FRANKLIN, returning to America in 1787, notes the increased number of lightning rods and their efficacy. LEOPARDI may have become interested in the subject through some such early reference to it, or he might have been reading some contemporary article, for the invention was still exciting much curiosity in his day. Under the heading *Conduttori frankliniani* in a supplement to the *Biblioteca italiana* is earnestly recommended the use of lightning rods for all tall bel-

fries and cupolas;[22] and the *Moniteur universel*[23] of Paris for 1818 records the invention by BRIZÉ-FADIN of an *échelle-paratonnerre* to be set up against haystacks, thatched cottages and other low country buildings. The article on the *Conduttori frankliniani*, while encouraging the use of the lightning rod, condemns the hail rod or *paragrandini* invented by the Frenchman L'APOSTOLE (sic) because its efficacy had not been sufficiently proved. This invention by the pharmacist LAPOSTOLLE consisted of straw ropes supported by metal-tipped linden rods. It was claimed that this arrangement would protect a sixty-acre tract by drawing the lightning from the clouds and thus impeding the formation of hail. A later invention known as the hail-cloud dispenser or *grandinifugo* consisted of a cannon which, when fired into an approaching cloud, was supposed to scatter the cloud and so protect the fields.

The invention of gunpowder and firearms offers LEOPARDI additional proof that the farther we go from nature and the more complex our civilization becomes, the more we degenerate. Paraphrasing MONTESQUIEU and ROGNIAT, LEOPARDI accuses the invention of having weakened mankind[24] and of having leveled the strong and the weak, the brave man and the coward, so that *virtù* has become useless.[25] A third entry in the *Zibaldone* contains an impressive idea which LEOPARDI had come upon in perusing the *Biblioteca italiana:*[26] by the invention of gunpowder, the energy that men once had has gone into machines, and men have in turn become machines themselves.

Balloons had flown from the eighteenth century into the nineteenth. Popular enthusiasm for them ran high. LEOPARDI succumbs to the new invention and cites aeronautics along with the telescope and gunpowder as among those important discoveries which, so often due to chance, may greatly influence civilization.[27] This in 1821. Five years later he reiterates the probable importance of this invention if ever perfected:

Se i palloni aerostatici, è l'aeronautica acquisterà un grado di scienza, e l'uso ne diverrà comune, e la utilità (che ora è nessuna) vi si aggiungerà . . . .[28]

And finally LEOPARDI, in his *Paralipomeni*, endows Leccafondi and Dedalo with wings, justifying himself with an allusion to the machine of Padre LANA and noting that the "globo aerosta-

[17] *Scritti vari, ed. cit.*, 721.
[18] *Ibid.*, 722.
[19] *Le Operette morali, ed. cit.*, 721.
[20] *Ed. cit.*, II, 1027.
[21] *Etudes de la Nature* (Paris, 1796), III, 107.

[22] *Proposta delle lettere, arti e scienze nell'Italia dal 1821 al 1826*, a supplement to the XIth year of the *Biblioteca italiana*, p. 241.
[23] P. 1128.
[24] *Zibaldone, ed. cit.*, I, 254.
[25] *Ibid.*, 479.
[26] *Ibid.*, 655 and Note.
[27] *Ibid.*, 254.
[28] *Ibid.*, 479.

tico ottien fede/Non per udir ma perchè si vede."[29] In 1837 there appeared a work by RAMBELLI on this Jesuit inventor, Padre LANA, and it is just possible that LEOPARDI may have seen it while composing his Paralipomeni.[30] LANA's airplane of 1670, which was merely theoretical, is described as consisting of a ship to which were attached four light hollow spheres in which a vacuum should be created by draining them of the water they were to contain. It is interesting to note that Padre LANA foresaw the devastating use of airplanes in war and, even while toying with such an invention, declared that God would not allow it to be realized, for it might ultimately menace civilization by dropping bombs on ships and cities.[31]

The MONTGOLFIER brothers, who sent up their first balloon in 1783, were the first to make flying appear really practicable. BENJAMIN FRANKLIN, writing from Passy that same year, says: "We think of nothing here at present but flying and balloons engross all our conversation."[32] The following January FRANKLIN warns a would-be aeronaut to take every precaution lest he fail in his contemplated flight, as the onlookers were very intolerant of failure.[33] A great improvement was made when it was found possibe to replace heated air with hydrogen gas, but public interest seems to have subsided a little until the invention of the parachute, first demonstrated on June 28, 1802, by M. GARNARIN. Flying then took hold of the popular imagination in good earnest, as an article entitled The Universality of Balloons, appearing in November 1802, shows. "Balloons," says the writer "have, during last autumn, absolutely eclipsed the wonted glory of paper-kites in England; nor has the curiosity in regard to them been confined to England solely."[34] In 1816 Mlle GARNARIN "rose like an eagle" in her balloon with firing of guns and waving of flags[35] and GRISCOM in his Year in Europe (1818-1819) describes Mme BLANCHARD as she made her seventy-fourth ascent in 1818, also shooting off fireworks as she arose.[36] Soon attempts were made to remain suspended in the air, and a certain SCARMUCCI of Florence claimed to be able to be aloft a month;[37] and the Cenni storici for January 1825,[38] reports the rumor of a balloon capable of carrying sixty persons and of remaining aloft five or six months. In 1824 a Bolognese, SARTI by name, flew his aereo veliero

over Milan. This was not a balloon but a ship borne up by sails.[39] And the seventh of September 1825, a huge crowd, including all the dignitaries of Bologna, witnessed the ascension of FRANCO ORLANDI, who landed safely some thirty-five miles away at Ferrara.[40] It is small wonder that LEOPARDI, writing in Bologna a year later, should have mentioned balloons among the inventions which, if perfected, might some day affect civilization greatly.

While balloons rose aloft, England first, then France, and later Italy, began to illuminate their streets with gas. The subject is a popuar one in the magazines of the time, and the Cenni storici of 1824[41] contains the fantastic proposal that gas jets be put on the outside of the windows of London houses so that the light might shine into the rooms and thus simulate sunshine. LEOPARDI finds a place for illuminating gas first in his Copernicus of 1827 and later in his Palinodia. When, as LEOPARDI relates in the former, the Sun refuses to continue traveling around the earth, the First Hour urges him not to withdraw his light from the Earth, explaining how expensive it would be, should men be obliged to burn candles and oil lamps all day, and how soon all supplies would be consumed and men be reduced to living in darkness. The light of the Sun might, she continues, be dispensed with if only that "certa aria da servire per ardere, e per illuminare le strade, le camere, ecc." had been discovered, but for that blessing men would have to wait another three centuries.[42] The allusion in Palinodia shows LEOPARDI skeptical of the benefits to be derived from gas-illuminated streets, which, though more brightly lighted, will probably be no safer than before.[43]

LEOPARDI makes short shrift of the telegraph, merely including it in the Zibaldone among the various inventions which may, if improved, alter civilization. Crude telegraphic systems had been in use for several decades, but, when LEOPARDI made his prophecy, these systems were being improved by the application of the ideas of GALVANI and VOLTA.

Steam would per force have a prominent place in any industrial satire of the early nineteenth century, and indeed LEOPARDI includes steam and the express train in the jumble of inventions which the Palinodia contains. He also alludes in the Zibaldone to the future importance of navigazione a vapore. It seems strange that our author, so in-

[29] Edited by ALLODOLI (Turin, 1921), p. 101.
[30] Ibid., See note on stanza 23, verse 6.
[31] Geschichtsblätter für Technik (Berlin, 1914). Vol. I, 140.
[32] The Works of Benjamin Franklin (Federal Edition, N. Y. and London, 1904), X, 215.
[33] Ibid., X, 266.
[34] The Universal Magazine (London, 1802), 334.
[35] Mechanic's Magazine (September 13, 1825), 36.
[36] (New York, Collins and Co., 1823), 254.
[37] Mechanic's Magazine (November 29, 1825), 219.
[38] P. 77.

[39] A. COMANDINI, L'Italia nei cento anni del secolo XIX (1801–1900) 1801–1825 (Milano, 1900–1901), 1274.
[40] Ibid., p. 1332.
[41] P. 222.
[42] Operette morali, ed. cit., 201–202.
[43] I Canti, commentati da A. STRACCALI (Firenze, Sansoni, 1934), 273, 1, 129.

terested in antiquity, should have omitted any allusion to the sporadic steam inventions credited to the Homeric era, to HERO OF ALEXANDRIA, to LEONARDO DA VINCI, to BALASCO DA GARAY, BRANCA, and others. BRANCA's device[44] was the most highly developed, a picturesque contraption in the shape of a head with a pipe issuing from the mouth. This head, filled with water, was set on a kettle containing fire. The steam thus generated, passing through the pipe, struck a wheel which, when rotated, communicated movement to pestles and mortars. A similar kettle was invented by the Marquis of WORCESTER, who is said by MARION DE LORME to have stolen it from a lunatic at Bicêtre in 1663. Such is the story at any rate. LEOPARDI fails to mention any of these inventions but he does include the steamboat, and well he might, as it was already active in Mediterranean waters about the time that LEOPARDI began making entries in his *Zibaldone*. Some thirty years before, FRANKLIN had written from Philadelphia:

We have no philosophical news here at present except that a boat moved by steam-engine rows itself against the tide in our river, and it is apprehended the construction may be so simplified and improved as to become generally useful.[45]

FRANKLIN's prediction had rapidly verified itself, and the *Spettatore* of Milan for 1818, in its section dealing with foreign matters, notes the presence of seven large steamboats on the Mississippi river.[46] In the same year GRISCOM[47] made a memorable voyage on the first public steamboat on the Mediterranean, the *Ferdinando I*, plying between Genoa and Marseilles. The author recounts how the excited inhabitants of the small towns along the coast visited the boat whenever it put in to shore for a load of wood to keep the fires up. As for steam trains, they presented much more of a problem and Italy acquired them slowly. When the *Palinodia* was written, France had already three important railroads.

Other mechanical means of locomotion came into existence in these early decades, but remain unrecorded by LEOPARDI. The *Draisienne*, a wooden velocipede, named for its inventor DRAISINE, became popular in Milan in 1818. The next year appeared a poem in Milanese dialect called *El Gran Cavall Meccanegh*[48] written to celebrate a local invention, the *cavallo meccanico* or *velocimano*, a three-wheeled affair, worked by hand instead of by foot. The *Literary Gazette* of September 16, 1820,[49] quotes from the *Journal de Nancy* the invention of a new type of carriage so constructed that a single person riding in the back

of the vehicle could propel his six passengers at the speed of a trotting horse. LEOPARDI might even have seen in current periodicals allusions to a primitive automobile, the *chariot à vapeur* in use in French mines in 1816.[50] The *Cenni storici* of 1824[51] mentions a *vettura meccanica*, made in Birmingham, which the writer of the article says "possa riuscire anche utile." This invention seems to have been improved by GRIFFITH of Brompton and tried out successfully in Vienna.[52]

Though failing to sense the importance of the nascent automobile, LEOPARDI does mention what was called at the time "il trionfo delle macchine a vapore a grande pressione," that is, the tunnel beneath the Thames under construction from 1825 to 1843. The interest in this enterprise is evident from the plans and suggestions printed in the *Mechanic's Magazine* during those years. LEOPARDI alludes to the long drawn out execution of the project:

> e sotto l'ampie
> Vie del Tamigi fia dischiuso il varco,
> Opra ardita, immortal, ch'esser dischiuso
> Dovea, già son molt'anni.[53]

By far the most humble of all the steam inventions included in *Palinodia* are cooking utensils:

> E nove forme di paiuoli, e nove
> Pentole ammirerà l'arsa cucina.[54]

A reference in an earlier work, the *Scommessa di Prometeo*, 1824, indicates that the kettles referred to were designed to utilize steam. Bacchus and Minerva present mankind with the classic gifts of wine and oil, but Vulcan arrives with "una pentola di rame, detta economica, che serve a cuocere che che sia con piccolo fuoco e speditamente."[55] The *Mechanic's Magazine* for January of that year reveals the invention of a "potatoe steamer" capable of cooking fifty pecks of potatoes in one half hour instead of the usual twenty-four.[56] And *Cenni storici*, for the same year, mentions a "calefactore," apparently a double-boiler.[57]

Much of the inventiveness of the nineteenth century displays itself in musical instruments, and among the many invented it would seem most likely to discover the Romantic machine, in quest of which we set out. LEOPARDI was aware of these new musical inventions. Though he seems nowhere to mention a specific instrument, he alludes in 1823 to the "tante invenzioni e perfezionamenti"

---

[44] *Mechanic's Magazine* (October 11, 1823), 105.
[45] *Op. cit.*, XII, 4.
[46] XI, 126.
[47] *Op. cit.*, I, 509.
[48] COMANDINI, *op. cit.*, 1008.
[49] P. 603.
[50] *Annales des Arts et Manufactures*, (Paris, 1816), III, 75–86.
[51] I, 183.
[52] *Ibid.*, 200.
[53] *Palinodia, ed. cit.*, lines 125–127.
[54] *Ibid.*, lines 120–121.
[55] *Operette morali, ed. cit.*, p. 60.
[56] I, 353.
[57] P. 222.

of musical instruments.[58] The Aeolian harp, romantic par excellence, was still in use; the harmonica, perfected by FRANKLIN in 1759 and so named by him in honor of the musical Italian language, had before reaching the nineteenth century acquired a keyboard and glass tubes in horizontal position. In LEOPARDI's time the brood had greatly increased. Periodicals describe and advertise musical curiosities, most of them with barbaric names. There were pianos of many sorts, upright, square, elliptical. Self-playing pianos appeared, and similar instruments such as the apollino and the apollonicon. There were a combination of harp and guitar, a portable dital harp, a claviharpe. And to mention various other instruments varying slightly in mechanism, the exact nature of which is of no moment here, but whose names are sufficiently descriptive: the melodicon and panmelodicon, the physharmonica and a sort of orchestrion called the panharmonicon; the uranion, the melodion, the polyplectron, the xylosistron, the xylharmonicon; and a tryphon which combined in itself a xylophon, a xylorgan, and a xyloharmonicon. The KAUFMANN musical instruments are worth special attention. They were being displayed in Paris in 1817 and the *Journal général de France*[59] advertises the KAUFMANN musical soirées. The *Literary Gazette*[60] of London describes the instruments at considerable length. The harmonichorde is said to be a sort of celestial piano, a very much improved harmonica, and of more musical importance than the other instruments, as it requires real skill on the part of the performer. The cordaulodion is like many other such inventions to be found in every German city, a kind of mechanical piano containing a flute and flageolet stop and capable of crescendo and diminuendo. The belloneon, likewise mechanical, seems to have been a complete military band which executed marches and flourishes with a unity, precision, and correctness beyond the reach of the most practiced artists. The fourth instrument was an automaton trumpeter, like others previously invented, but more perfect in that it played a distinct chord or executed two parts at once in thirds and fifths. Even more spectacular in its appeal than these KAUFMANN instruments, was the *organo di mare* whose function was to attract whales and large quadrupeds. It seems to have been most efficacious, if we are to believe the account given in the *Cenni storici* of August 1827, which tells how a shipowner had, by means of this instrument, captured fourteen whales and ninety-two polar bears.[61] Even barometers had

become musical thanks to the Swiss;[62] and the Italians, in imitation of the more precocious Germans, had begun making carillons to hang in their belfries.[63]

The color organ, an invention akin to musical instruments, attracted both E. T. A. HOFFMANN and LEOPARDI. Apparently the only such organ known up to September 1821, the date on which LEOPARDI entered a note on the subject in his *Zibaldone*,[64] was the ocular harpsichord which Père CASTEL began constructing about 1725. A discussion of his theories is to be found in *Le Clavessin pour les Yeux*.[65] Sounds, says the writer and inventor, heard alone are insipid: but combine them into melody or harmony and they please; colors can be treated in the same way.[66] CASTEL combined a chromatic scale of twelve colors which were controlled by keys and on which tunes in color could be executed. HOFFMANN scoffs at this invention, saying that color means nothing to us unless it be associated with objects for which we have some sentimental attachment;[67] and LEOPARDI considers the attempt ridiculous because long habit has accustomed us to note shapes so that we are unable to enjoy color apart from form.[68] He objects again on the ground that it is not so much the harmony as the quality of the individual sound that gives pleasure: hence the idea of a color harmony would be futile.[69] LEOPARDI goes on to relate his musical theories to tastes and odors as well as to colors. In this extension of the parent idea he had been preceded by CASTEL who suggests an organ of perfumes (to be imagined in great detail later by HUYSMANS in *A rebours*) and a similar instrument for the tactual sense.[70]

The color organ seems to have been in the public mind during the twenties. There appeared a book by Dr. BUSBY entitled *Assimilation of Colours to Musical Sounds* in which Père CASTEL is ridiculed for having confused music and color. In February of the preceding year a Dr. BUCHANAN of Kentucky advertised as his discovery a "concert for the eye." He offers to execute this machine should a subvention of $1000 be forthcoming.[71]

If not a musical instrument, perhaps our elusive Romantic invention was some one of the clever mechanical toys which abound in the early part

---

[58] *Zibaldone, ed. cit.*, II, 442.
[59] April 2, 1817.
[60] April 5, 1817, p. 167.
[61] VI, p. 199.

[62] *Ibid.*, November 1824, II, 45.
[63] *Ibid.*, February 1829, X, 229.
[64] *Ed. cit.*, I, 1223.
[65] See *Esprits, saillies et singularités du Père Castel*, (Amsterdam-Paris, 1763).
[66] *Ibid.*, p. 304.
[67] *Musikalische Schriften, II*, p. 94 in *E. T. A. Hoffmann's Werke* (Berlin, Bong, 1920) Part XIV.
[68] *Zibaldone, ed. cit.*, I, 1123.
[69] *Ibid.*, I, 1125.
[70] *Op. cit.*, 369.
[71] *Mechanic's Magazine*, February 7, 1824, p. 382.

of the century—old-new inventions, to be sure, inasmuch as the ancient Greeks and Egyptians had contrived to make toys move and gods perform miracles by means of mercury and water power.[72] The literature and the Church of the Middle Ages had their automatons,[73] and figures had been moving on the faces of clocks for centuries. GIOVANNI TORRIANI diverted CHARLES V in his monastic retreat with flying birds and mechanical knights, and as a child LOUIS XIV was entertained by such clever inventions as a tiny mechanical coach drawn by six horses. LEOPARDI was not above drawing his analogies from toyland. His Galantuomo,[74] pleading for variety to enliven the world, asks what a puppet show would be like if all the *burattini* wore identical clothes and made identical gestures. And in the same dialogue he concludes that, in order to endure life, we must be like those toys which children call *saltamartini* and which, turn them any way you will, always get back up on their feet again.

The android appears in our poet's satirical *Proposta di premi fatta dall'Accademia dei Sillografi.*[75] Automatons of this sort fascinate, not only because of their intricate machinery, but because they give to the inventor the sense of god-like power. Did not Pygmalion's statue come to life? Legend and·literature have occupied themselves much with mechanical beings. Legend attributes to DESCARTES an automaton which he is said to have called his daughter Francine. So life-like was this machine that the captain of a vessel on which it was traveling, fearing it the work of magic, threw it overboard.[76] Frankenstein, created by man, thousands of flesh and blood, aroused terror in the nineteenth-century reader; VILLIERS DE L'ISLE-ADAM in his *Ève future* has EDISON make his mechanically perfect Eve to console a young man for his lost love; SAMUEL BUTLER discourses in *Erewhon* on the dangerous possibility that machines may develop minds of their own and eventually surpass mankind and for this reason the men of Erewhon destroy them; and KARL KAPEK in his *R. U. R.* subjugates mankind to the man-made Robots.

In the *Proposta* just mentioned, the Academicians, finding the defects in the human race incurable, decide to replace men with machines, offering three prizes for the best automatons to impersonate a true friend, a good man, a faithful woman. To justify the possibility of such an invention as the true friend, LEOPARDI cites many

famous automatons: those of REGIOMONTANUS and VAUCANSON; the statue of Memnon at Thebes; the famous head (some say man) of brass made by ALBERTUS MAGNUS and destroyed by THOMAS AQUINAS because (says a pious legend) he took it for the work of the Devil; or because (says gossip) he was jealous of the automaton which could make better syllogisms than himself. Finally LEOPARDI cites the artist-writer automaton which at that time in London "disegnava figure e ritratti e scriveva quanto gli era dettato da chiunque si fosse."

Automatons such as those imagined by LEOPARDI were indeed frequently met with in the late eighteenth century. In 1753 FRIEDRICH VON KNAUSS, after twenty years of work, had exhibited his first writing automaton. He perfected this in 1760. Another similar android was made by JOSEPH NEUSSNER in 1783. But most famous, certainly, in LEOPARDI's day, were the inventions of the JAQUET-DROZ, father and son, who, aided by a mechanic, LESCHOT, made and exhibited in 1774 a writer, an artist, and a musician. Replicas of the writer and the artist were made from 1782 to 1787 in Vienna and a second replica was exhibited by HENRI MAILLARDET in London in 1811. It changed hands again and was again shown in 1815, at the Wakefield theater.[77] This figure could both write and draw, and there can be no doubt that LEOPARDI had this one in mind. There are notices of exhibitions of these DROZ figures in Bologna and Milan in the year 1828[78] and considerable enthusiasm is shown for the five *personcine*. One drew with accuracy and grace; another wrote whatever was dictated to her; a third, a young lady, played a small organ; and the last two figures danced. References to musician-androids are to be found among reports of the automatons exhibited at the Foire St. Germain in the eighteenth century; a shepherd and a shepherdess who played thirteen different airs on a flute and a figure the size of an eight-year old child, which played a *cor de chasse.*[79] The *Gazzetta Veneta*, 1760, contains the description of a similar shepherd and shepherdess which had been seen in Venice some years previous.[80] Extremely famous were the flute-player of VAUCANSON and the automaton trumpeter made by MAELZEL in 1808. These were surpassed in turn by the KAUFMANN trumpeter already described. MAELZEL exhibited a new trumpeter in 1818. Among the KAUFMANN inventions was also a piano-playing figure and it is reported that a theater mechanic,

[72] MAGNIN, *Les Marionnettes* (Paris, 1862), *passim.* See also H. R. EVANS, *The Old and New Magic* (Chicago, 1906).
[73] J. W. Spargo, *Virgil the Necromancer* (Cambridge, 1934).
[74] *Galantuomo e mondo* in *Scritti vari, ed. cit.,* II, 339.
[75] *Operette morali, ed. cit.,* 30 ff.
[76] *Magasin pittoresque* (Paris, 1840) 8e année, p. 271.

[77] CHAPUIS et GÉLIS, *Le Monde des automates* (Paris, 1928), II 225 ff.
[78] *Cenni storici*, X, 112; I Teatri, II (II), 305–308.
[79] *Dictionnaire historique des arts* (Paris, 1906): *Automates.*
[80] Edited by ZARDO (Florence, 1915), p. 38.

LAGNAC by name, was also engaged in constructing a woman piano-player when he died in December 1808.[81] The KAUFMANN inventions, when exhibited in Dresden in 1813, were seen by E. T. A. HOFF-MANN and possibly inspired his tale *Die Automate.*

LEOPARDI need have felt no hesitation in requiring speech of his automatons, for not only legend but mechanics had already given them voice. The prototype of the speaking figure, among the inventions mentioned by LEOPARDI, is the statue of Memnon at Thebes. The sounds emitted by this statue were due to changes in temperature occurring as night changed to day. Legend had also accorded speech to the head, or figure, attributed to ALBERTUS MAGNUS, but LEOPARDI might have cited less remote examples. The *Gazzetta Veneta* alludes to a Bacchus astride a keg. The god "salutava con la voce e facea qualche breve complimento ai signori e alle signore che andavano per vederlo."[82] There is also a record of two talking heads made by the abbé MICAL (1778) one of which would say: "Le roi fait le bonheur de ses peuples" and the other: "Et le bonheur de ses peuples fait celui du roi."[83] This loquacious Bacchus and the two sententious heads were probably mere mouthpieces for some human voice. In 1783, however, the abbé MICAL invented two new talking heads which were placed on boxes each containing an artificial glottis on a taut membrane which, when vibrated by air passing through, produced a poor imitation of the human voice. KRATZENSTEIN's talking automaton of 1779, which won a prize offered by the Academy of Sciences of St. Petersburg, could produce only the five vowels. A little later VON KEMPELEN of Vienna succeeded in adding enough consonants so that the words "mamma" and "papa" and a few phrases could be spoken. Interest in the production of speech continued to grow.[84] In 1824 MAELZEL, the inventor of the trumpeter, made a doll into which he put KEM-PELEN's mechanism for saying "mamma" and "papa." The next year was published in *Cenni storici*[85] the description of a wooden soldier automaton invented by an Englishman. This soldier would drill with his musket and would then discharge it, pronouncing distinctly the word "Fire!", while two bells near him sounded an alarm. In 1880 FABER, after twenty-five years of work, greatly interested London with his speaking automaton which could modulate its voice and also sing, though with less success.

LEOPARDI includes among his historical automatons "more than one chess player." KEM-PELEN invented such a machine for MARIA THERESA of Austria in 1769. It became very famous, was shown in London in 1819, and brought to America by MAELZEL in 1824, was accorded an essay by E. A. POE, and was finally destroyed in the Philadelphia fire of 1854. This chess player was not, however, a true automaton. To what other invention of the sort LEOPARDI refers is not clear.

The second machine, the noble man, imagined by our poet, is to be an *uomo di vapore.* The Academy concludes that steam (since other means are lacking) should serve to move an automaton to the exercise of *virtù* and the acquisition of glory. Here LEOPARDI's imagination seems to have worked unaided, for there has come to light no evidence of an android propelled by steam, until that made by GEORGE MOORE years later.

The third automaton, a faithful wife, is inspired by Pygmalion's statue and CASTIGLIONE's portrait of a court lady.[86]

The popularity enjoyed by mechanical toys and automaton figures was shared by mechanical pictures and theaters. Possibly LEOPARDI had one of these latter inventions in mind when describing his Romantic machine. It appears that mechanics had invaded painting as early as 1498. Among the possessions of ANNE OF BRITTANY was found "Ung tableau de Hercule paint, les sourcilz et yeux branlans."[87] But the vogue for such pictures did not develop until the eighteenth century when Père TRUCHET made pictures of various trades in which the artisans were detached from the painting itself. A picture of 1820 which was run by clock work is also described by CHAPUIS and GÉLIS. It showed the Pont de St. Maurice between Switzerland and Piedmont done in oils and animated by groups of figures.[88] Such pictures were often accompanied by music.

Closely related to these animated paintings are the toy theaters run by some mechanical device and dating, like the mechanical toy, back at least to HERON OF ALEXANDRIA. The eighteenth century was familiar with such theaters. No historian of the subject fails to mention the toy opera, made by Père TRUCHET for the future LOUIS XIV, in which figures moved through five acts and the set shifted itself four times. Toward the middle of the century the central grotto of Hellbrunn near Salzburg was filled with two hundred and fifty-six figures of which one hundred and thirteen were articulated and performed various movements suitable to the trades they represented. An organ

[81] *Geschichtsblätter für Technik* (Berlin, 1914), Vol. V, 283.
[82] *Ed. cit.,* 38.
[83] *Dictionnaire historique de France, ed cit.: Automates.*
[84] W. NIEMANN, "Sprechende Figuren" in *Geschichts-blätter für Technik,* VII (1920), pp. 2 ff.
[85] III, 43.

[86] CIMADORO's *Pimmalione, o la statua animata* was popular in Europe about this time.
[87] CHAPUIS et GÉLIS, *op. cit.,* I, 319.
[88] *Ibid.,* 326.

accompanied their gestures and the mechanism was run by water power.[89] MAGNIN describes an elàborate mechanical theater which was displayed at the Foire St. Germain in 1741 and which included not only ·moving figures but also vessels wrecked by storms at sea.[90] In the *Gazzetta Veneta* is described a mechanical show by ALBERT WINDERFINGH of Flanders which was to be exhibited in Venice the following year. It represented a hunting scene in which a life-size hunter goes with his dog in quest of partridges, shoots a bird which the dog retrieves; the hunter then, seating himself beneath a tree, would play on a flute handed him by the inventor, and to the air played by the hunter a life-size couple would dance gracefully. ZARDO alludes in the preface of this edition of the *Gazzetta Veneta* to "una macchina di figure movibili," the work of a French portrait painter, who offered to furnish other such sets of moving figures on order.[91]

These mechanical exhibitions not only amused but edified the public. In 1775 was shown a *Jugement universel* composed of three thousand five hundred figures in low relief which would move as desired. Two years later the public enjoyed a "spectacle de peinture, de mécanique et de musique, en cinq actes, tiré du *Paradis perdu* de MILTON."[92] Nor did the vogue for such edifying entertainments cease in the next century. London had, in 1811, the opportunity of witnessing SANGER's Mechanical Collection of Alabaster Figures and Moving Wax Works, the object of which was to instruct the young: Moses was shown striking the rock and it is said that the "just proportion and mechanical movement of this figure surpasses everything of the kind that has hitherto been attempted."[93] Popular Italian periodicals express their wonder at similar ingenious contrivances. An organist at Bayreuth, says the *Cenni storici*, has filled a cage with fifty different birds made of silver and covered with feathers. These birds sing most naturally and the inventor asks 60,000 lire for his invention.[94] *I Teatri* of 1827 praises the mechanical theater of S. RADEGONDA which consists of a series of *vedute pittoriche* representing sunrise, sunset, and the various seasons, having exquisitely painted scenes and filled with moving mechanical figures.[95] And in the *Cenni storici* we again find mention of a similar invention. This time it is a forty-two piece puppet orchestra made and exhibited in Boston by the brother of the famous MAELZEL.

The little violinists are said to perform wonders with their fingers and their bows and the orchestra to execute the overtures of *Don Giovanni*, *Iphigenia*, *The Vestal*, closing with *God Save the King*.[96]

LEOPARDI was doubtless as unconscious as his contemporaries that out of various inventions then familiar was to develop a century later an invention as tremendously important as the motion picture. One of the earliest steps in this direction, the magic lantern, was well known. Indeed it seems to date back beyond ATHANASIUS KIRCHER to JOHN OF FONTANA who, in the fifteenth century, used some such device to throw pictures of terrifying demons on the walls of besieged cities in order to frighten the assailants.[97] And it was apparently a magic lantern which was used to convince BENVENUTO CELLINI of the existence of ghosts. LEOPARDI refers to the magic lantern in the seventh canto of *Paralipomeni*. Dedalo and Count Leccafondi having reached the hereafter of the animal world, are able to distinguish ghosts in the darkness, ghosts which would have been invisible in daylight just as "spariscono al Sol quelle figure/Che la lanterna magica dipinge." The popularity of the invention in Germany is attested by MAX HUFNAGL's sentimental account of the introduction of the Lanterna Magica into his German home before the days of the kaleidoscope and the "Spielringe." To the delight of the children pictures of religious processions, soldiers, and dances, were thrown on the wall to the accompaniment of a musical clock from the Black Forest.[98]

LEOPARDI also alludes to the *camera lucida*, a kindred invention. Impressed by a lonely tower seen against a blue sky, he jots down in his notes "Torre isolata in mezzo all'immenso sereno, come mi spaventasse con quella veduta della camerottica per l'infinito . . ."[99] This invention, which is a prismatic arrangement by which a reduced virtual image of an object could be apparently cast on a drawing board (a convenience for tracing outlines), was no novelty, having been invented by LEONE BATTISTA ALBERTI; but a new, simplified, and more practical form of it had been invented early in the nineteenth century by WOLLASTON. A sister invention, that is the *camera oscura*, credited to LEONARDO DA VINCI, is not mentioned by LEOPARDI. It is to be numbered also among the diversions of the day, as is proved by GRISCOM's description of a *camera oscura* located at the top of a

[89] *Ibid.*, 77.
[90] MAGNIN, *op. cit.*, 169.
[91] *Ed. cit.*, 38.
[92] MAGNIN, *op. cit.*, 115.
[93] RAMSAYE, *A Million and One Nights* (N. Y., 1926), 4 T.
[94] October 1825, IV, 5.
[95] 1827, I (II), 851.

[96] October 1829, XII, 21.
[97] F. M. FELDHAUS, *Die Technik der Vorzeit* (Leipzig-Berlin, 1914), 823.
[98] "Zauberlaterne" in *Zeitspiegel* (München, 1831), I, 81–87.
[99] *Appunti e ricordi* in *Scritti vari, ed. cit.*, II, 267.

turret of the Royal Observatory in London. On a table was produced

an elegant miniature picture of the various objects surrounding the Observatory . . . . The waving foliage of the majestic trees, the deer grazing in the park, the river whitened with sails, and all the varieties of a most luxuriant landscape, were suddenly thrown before us in a living picture, upon a table in a dark room, where a moment before, all was bland and colorless.[100]

While LEOPARDI pored over the books in his father's library at Recanati, the public of European capitals patronized with enthusiasm any form of pictorial diversion which inventors had up to then been able to devise. In 1802 a Mr. PHILIPSTAL began projecting ghosts to the accompaniment of thunder and lightning, and we find E. G. ROBERTSON making a fortune with his Phantasmagoria and his Phantoscope in Paris in 1817 and 1818. Berlin had its first panoramas in 1800, and the next year a Panstereorama, which made the pictures shown look plastic, was opened in Paris and was still popular in 1817. And from 1807 to 1815, the "optisch-perspektivischen Gemälde" (either a panorama or a panstereorama) made by KARL FRIEDRICH SCHINKEL played an important part in Berlin life.[101] Periodicals of 1817 and 1818 make mention of a panorama of Paris to be seen in Berlin; of one of London on display in Paris; and of one of "classic interest" at the Strand. Pleasure and instruction were also to be had from the Cosmorama which made an appearance in Italy at about this time and furnished views of Athens, Paris, Vienna, and St. Petersburg, as well as views of PERRY's expedition to the North Pole. The Cosmorama of the Palais-Royal showed excavations of Pompei and oriental subjects. Still more realistic effects were gained by the diorama which DAGUERRE and BOUTON invented in 1822. The audience sat on a moving platform and gazed at a transparent picture with light behind it and color screens between the picture and the light. Later, shifting screens were used to produce the effect of movement.[102] Still greater realism was procured in the pleorama of KARL FERDINAND LANGHANS who invented a device whereby citizens of Berlin could take the Rhine trip or view Capri seated in gently moving boats. This was about 1832, at which time the moving picture was practically born with the invention by PLATEAU of the Phenakistoscope and STAMPFER's Stroboscopic Disc. Drawings on one disc viewed through slits in another were made to produce the effect of continuous motion by the twirling of the discs. But the combination of these

discs with the magic lantern came well after LEOPARDI's death.[103]

As we have seen, the public flocked enthusiastically to see any form of panorama, but it seems to have developed an actual craze for the kaleidoscope and of this the periodicals of the time give abundant proof. There is, however, no apparent echo of this in LEOPARDI's work. Dr. BREWSTER patented the invention in July 1817, but there were many disputes as to the justice of his claim. Whoever the inventor, the success was tremendous. The Moniteur universel, Paris, 1818, claims that high society has abandoned all other pastimes in favor of this lunette in which exquisite designs are formed in reflecting mirrors and which, it is added, may serve in the future not only to amuse but to afford designs for the manufacturing world. The article goes on to say that the invention, which so well merits its succès fou, is being manufactured in quantities under such names as multiplicateur français and transfigurateur.[104] A kaleidoscope universel, de société or magique.[106] made of precious stones and destined for a foreign court, is mentioned, and its value set at 20,000 francs.[105] A certain M. FABRI, living at the corner of the Passage des Panoramas, promises his customers the best quality of toy whether it be a kaleidoscope universel, de société or magique.[106] It is also reported that this new toy has found its way to Constantinople where it is delighting the beauties of the harem; and it is hailed in the Literary Gazette of London as the realization of the ocular harpsichord, for only when color is combined with form does it truly delight the eye.[107] It is described at tiresome length in a poem entitled The New Mania. The poet says the invention has come at an opportune moment. Society is languishing for a topic, Lord BYRON's fourth canto being still in the press. Everyone carries the toy about and it has replaced lorgnettes at the opera. The beauty of its design is indescribable; it has surpassed in popularity bilboquet, the monarch of toys.[108] The Italians seem to have succumbed likewise to the charm of this irresistible bauble. In a long madrigal in the Spettatore italiano of 1818, a poet presents to lovely Flora, goddess of flowers, the wonderful new invention which we owe to British genius: a tube of colored blossoms so real as to attract bee and butterfly:

> Guarda, o Flora gentile,
> Entro quel tubo . . . (ah! già lo sdegno esprimi
> De' tuoi vanti gelosa?)
> Attraverso ad un triplice cristallo

100 Op. cit., I, 118.
101 Geschichtsblätter für Technik, ed. cit., I, 213.
102 Mechanic's Magazine, (September 9, 1826), p. 289.
103 See T. RAMSAYE, op. cit., passim.
104 P. 618.
105 Ibid., p. 689.
106 Ibid., p. 867.
107 May 30, 1818, p. 345.
108 Ibid., May 16, p. 315.

Guarda l'onor d'aprile,
Vedi l'azzurra violetta e il giallo
Tulipano e i ligustri ed i giacinti.
Gira in tua mano il tubo e all'occhio pinti
Scorgi, se il vero estimi,
Gigli, narcisi, anemoni, e la rosa
Tua prima cura e affetto.
Nell'ugual moto con diverso effetto
L'ordine ammira onde si forma e intreccia
Or palma ed or ghirlanda
Che non disconverrebbe anco a tua treccia.[109]

A rival of the kaleidoscope called an *opticono-grapte* appeared in France in 1818. It was a portable affair showing views illuminated with prismatic colors which could, by turning a knob, be doubled at will.[110] A similar invention, the *kaleidophone*, 1827, made linear illuminated figures on a screen.[111] And one with a still more formidable name, the *polymorphoscope*, Paris, 1820, consisted of a mirror so combined with colors that members of the fair sex could view themselves arrayed in any tint they might choose and thus, with this "preview" of themselves so arrayed,

select their new dresses of the most becoming shades.[112]

Such were some of the popular mechanical inventions with which the early nineteenth century was familiar. Is the Romantic machine to be found among them? Was it some form of musical instrument, some mechanical theater or toy, some phantasmagoria accompanied by sound? Or did LEOPARDI, on the analogy of such inventions, imagine a similar one and attribute it to the Romanticists as he seems to have imagined a steam man on the analogy of other such automatons? The riddle still remains unsolved. But though the actual machine referred to by LEOPARDI remains obscure, the quest for it has resulted in showing that the Romantic poet of despair and suicide, the brilliant philologist and stylist, was not a little interested in mechanical inventions whether for utilitarian purposes or for amusement, and that he philosophized about them, satirized them, and introduced them into both his prose and his poetry, identifying himself in this way with the newly born mechanical age.

[109] *Spettatore italiano*, No. XV, IX(II) (Milano, 1818), pp. 430–431.
[110] *Moniteur universel*, 1818, p. 1444.
[111] *The Literary Gazette* (April 15, 1827), p. 254.
[112] *Mechanic's Magazine* (August 11, 1827), p. 49.

The University of Chicago

THE BACKGROUND OF TENNYSON'S "AIRY NAVIES"

By Clark Emery

The situation of the prophet is not an enviable one: in his own time, he is more often than not ignored—or, at best—derided; and a century later, if his prophecies have by chance come true, he is either misconstrued by the gullible or maligned by the sceptical. A case in point is Tennyson. With the publication of the 1842 volume of poems, Tennyson rose to a position of eminence among English poets, and few poems in the volume achieved more rapid popularity than *Locksley Hall*, a poem notable for its forecast of the shape of things to come. Significantly, however, the *Westminster Review,* which reprinted the poem almost entire in its critical review, deleted the now famous prophetic lines. And the *Quarterly Review,* which reprinted them, referred to them as "his more indistinct and wider notions."[1]

Now, a hundred years later, the devastating role which aircraft of various types are playing in this time of the breaking of nations has focussed attention on those lines to the exclusion of the rest of the poem:

For I dipt into the future, far as human eye could see,
Saw the vision of the world, and all the wonder that would be;

Saw the heavens fill with commerce, argosies of magic sails,
Pilots of the purple twilight, dropping down with costly bales;

Heard the heavens fill with shouting, and there rain'd a ghastly dew

[1] LXX (1842), 412.

From the nations' airy navies grappling in the central blue.[2]

So amenable are they to interpretation in terms of B-19's, P-38's, Spitfires, and so forth, that the uncritical reader newly introduced to Tennyson and unacquainted with the forms and conditions of aeronautics in Tennyson's time must almost certainly be persuaded that the poet indeed possessed uncanny prophetic powers.

This point of view has quite properly been called in question. For example, Professor De Vane, in a popular anthology, has annotated the passage as follows:

Some commentators fancy that Tennyson was in these lines predicting the coming of modern aviation. . . . This is most unlikely. Tennyson only thought of the extension of balloon activity—new to England in the Thirties. He had no conception of the heavier-than-air machine.[3]

But perhaps Professor De Vane goes a step too far. In the first place, balloon activity was not really new to England in the Thirties. By the Thirties, after a history of fifty years, balloons—because they underwent so little change and improvement—had become almost as commonplace as in the past thirty years the airplane has

[2] ll. 119–24.
[3] William Clyde De Vane and Mabel Phillips De Vane, *Selections from Tennyson* (1940), p. 431. Since writing this paper, I have received a letter from Professor W. D. Paden, who agrees with De Vane that "Tennyson wasn't thinking prophetically of airplanes; he was thinking about balloons . . ."

become. In the second place, there is certainly reason to doubt that TENNYSON had *no* conception of heavier-than-air machines—that conception dates from antiquity. After all, what was Icarus, or MILTON's Lucifer, or TENNYSON's own crag-clasping eagle, if not a heavier-than-air machine? When early experimenters cast about for means of getting their feet off earth, it was not the balloon they thought of—it has no counterpart in Nature; no animal flies because it is lighter-than-air. What they contemplated was the ornithopter, a device which imitates the flapping wings of a bird.

In the thirteenth century, for example, ROGER BACON predicted "instruments to flie withall, so that one sitting in the middle of the Instrument, and turning about an Engine, by which the winges being artificially composed may beate the ayre after the maner of a flying bird."[4] Two hundred years later, LEONARDO DA VINCI turned his attention to the mechanics of bird flight, and on the basis of his observations made drawings of a flying machine with jointed wings intended to be driven by a man's arms and legs.

In 1648 JOHN WILKINS, Bishop of Chester, considering the future of flight, fixed upon four possible means:

1. By spirits, or angels.
2. By the help of fowls.
3. By wings fastened immediately to the body.
4. By a flying chariot.[5]

Of these, he selects the last—the flying chariot —as promising greatest hope for the future, but regarding winged men he is not pessimistic.

Those things that seem very difficult and fearful at the first, may grow very facil after frequent trial and exercise: and therefore he that would effect any thing in this kind, must be brought up to the constant practice of it from his youth; trying first only to use his wings, in running on the ground, as an ostrich or tame goose will do, touching the earth with his toes; and so by degrees learn to rise higher, till he shall attain unto skill and confidence.[6]

He recognizes that the weakness of man's arms presents a problem and accordingly suggests that the legs be made to do the work:

. . . in which contrivance the wings should come down from the shoulders on each side . . . but the motion of them should be from the legs being thrust out, and drawn in again one after another, so as each leg should move both wings; by which means a man should (as it were) walk or climb up into the air; and then the hands and arms might be at leisure to help and direct the motion, or for any other service proportionable to their strength.[7]

[4] In *The Myrour of Alchymy*, the English translation (1597) of *De mirabile potestate Artis et Naturae* (1250).
[5] *The Mathematical and Philosophical Works*, II (1802), 199.
[6] *Ibid.*, pp. 201-2.
[7] *Ibid.*, pp. 203-4.

In 1678 a French locksmith named BESNIER constructed a kind of gliding machine which was described and illustrated in the *Journal des Sçavans* and in the *Philosophical Transactions*. The latter describes it as follows:

It consists of 2 poles or rods, which have at each end of them an oblong chassie or wing of taffety, which folds from above downwards, as the frame of a folding window. . . . When the person designs to fly, he fits these poles upon each shoulder, so that 2 of the chassies may be before him, and the other 2 behind him. Those chassies or wings which are before him, are moved or struck downwards by the strength of his arms and hands, by which the hinder chassies are lifted up, and those hinder wings are pulled or struck downwards by the legs, which pull them down by the 2 strings which are fastened both to the legs and hinder wings.[8]

He is said to have been able to glide from roof to roof—and even over a river. He eventually sold the contrivance to a traveling showman who was less successful in its operation and was shortly killed. A few years later (1742) the Marquis DE BACQUEVILLE is reported to have glided, using artificial wings, from his home some distance across the Seine; he fell (to paraphrase Scriptures) among laundresses on a float, injuring several of them and breaking his leg.

A flying machine like BESNIER's made a literary appearance in the eighteenth century in Cambridge's *The Scribleriad*. In Book IV occurs an aerial race between a German and a British youth:

They spread their wings, and with a rising bound,
Swift at the word together quit the ground,
The Briton's rapid flight outstrips the wind:
The lab'ring German urges close behind.[9]

During the race the Briton's wings come undone, but in falling, he grasps the foot of his rival and both crash. In the 1751 edition this scene is the subject of a BOITARD engraving, and the contrivance pictured is clearly that invented by BESNIER.[10]

The Scribleriad, of course, was a satire upon the pretensions of quack-scientists; and scarcely less satirical was the chapter of JOHNSON's *Rasselas* entitled "A Dissertation on the Art of Flying"

[8] *The Philosophical Transactions, Abridged* (1809), II, 476-7.
[9] CHALMERS, *English Poets*, XVIII, 268.
[10] A curious book entitled *République Universelle, ou l'Humanité Ailée, Réunie sous l'Empire de la Raison* has an interesting plate showing the harness and wings whereby men were, in this Utopia, to fly. It was published in Geneva in 1788 and appears to be (I have not seen the book) in the tradition of those romances so popular in the eighteenth century of which PALTOCK's *Life and Adventures of Peter Wilkins* and the imitative *Life and Astonishing Adventures of John Daniels* are outstanding examples. The flying machine in the latter book is a particularly interesting one. It consists of a kind of "flying wing," in the middle of which is a stationary platform; the "pilot," standing on the platform, manipulates a pump-handle which raises and lowers the surrounding wings, causing the craft to ascend or descend. BOITARD also did an engraving of this device.

which presents arguments for and against man-manipulated wings, arguments resolved by the optimistic aeronaut's later plunge into a nearby lake. But less literary and less sceptical persons continued experimentation. SWEDENBORG, the great mystic and scientist, invented a flying machine consisting of a light frame covered with strong canvas and provided with two large oars or wings moving on a horizontal axis, and so arranged that the upstroke met with no resistance while the downstroke provided the lifting power. SWEDENBORG knew that the machine would not fly but suggested it as a start and was confident that the problem would be solved. In 1781 JEAN-PIERRE BLANCHARD designed and built what he called the "Vaisseau-Volant"—a flying chariot with four large wings moved by hand and foot levers by the operator, who sat inside. This was a failure, but BLANCHARD, who later became a famous balloonist, made some effort to adapt to the balloon the wings and rudder of the chariot.

In brief, TENNYSON must have been both unimaginative and illiterate to have had *no* conception of the heavier-than-air machine.[11]

There is, of course, the possibility that he had neither the balloon nor the heavier-than-air machine in mind. A complete sceptic might conceivably take the following position: When TENNYSON speaks of "airy navies," he is not speaking metaphorically but literally and means not air-ships but clipper-ships. The navies are "airy" simply because the masts are tall and the ships propelled by air in motion; the "central blue" represents merely the ocean, and the allusion to heavens filled with commerce is a poetic pictorialization of ships coming into sight, sail-first, over the curve of the sea. This is certainly a quixotic interpretation; nevertheless it can be maintained with some degree of success by anyone possessed of sufficient forensic agility. The argument will be based on the premise that TENNYSON was essentially a literal-minded rather than imaginative poet; evidence for this premise might be adduced from lines in the same poem—for example, the famous error in the line

Let the great world spin forever down the ringing grooves of change[12]

[11] It seems improbable, too, that TENNYSON could have been unaware of the seventeenth and eighteenth century romances and poems which, in their prophecies that England would someday colonize the moon, make his forecast seem modest indeed. GRAY's Latin poem, *Luna Habitabilis*, is a good example, and it deserves especial note because a translation of the last few lines has appeared in the recent *A Book of Prophecy from the Egyptians to Hitler*, ed. by JOHN COURNOS (New York, 1942). The excerpt in this book is misleading because, out of context, it seems to prophesy aerial battle alone instead of aerial battle for possession of the moon, which is more properly fancy than prophecy, though some eighteenth century writers took the idea seriously.

[12] l. 182.

of which TENNYSON remarked: "When I went by the first train from Liverpool to Manchester (1830), I thought that the wheels ran in a groove. It was a black night and there was such a vast crowd round the train at the station that we could not see the wheels. Then I made this line."[13]

But ingenuity rather than reason and evidence will best support this point of view, and it may be taken as certain that TENNYSON had in mind some kind of aircraft. What kind, it is impossible to say, for he was nowhere more specific than in the *Locksley Hall* passage. However, a brief résumé of the rise and progress of aerostation from 1782 to 1842 and of the impress it made on the minds of scientific and literary men will at the same time give a clearer idea of what TENNYSON *might* have had in mind and suggest the extent to which he was truly a prophet.

It was in June of 1783 that centuries of speculation came to fruition. In that year and month at Annonay, the MONTGOLFIER brothers, STEPHEN and JOSEPH, displayed the first practicable balloon. It was made of paper, with a wooden frame at the mouth, and was filled with some 22,000 cubic feet of hot air produced by burning straw under the mouth. It flew, for only about ten minutes, but in that time ascended a good 5,000 feet, to the joy and amazement of the crowd of observers. Public interest was immediate and intense. As one rather elegant writer later put it:

In those halcyon days, during the transient calm of political turmoils, and the happy absence of all military events, the prospect of navigating the atmosphere excited a very general ferment, and engrossed the conversation of all ranks. Yet the tale appeared so extraordinary as to leave some doubts of its veracity. . . . To dispel the suspicions which infected the subject, it was necessary to repeat the experiment in every large capital.[14]

Two months later the experiment was repeated in Paris by the brothers ROBERT and the physicist M. CHARLES. An advance was made by inflating the balloon with hydrogen gas—then newly discovered—instead of hot air. Of this flight BENJAMIN FRANKLIN wrote to Sir JOSEPH BANKS, President of the Royal Society, as follows:

It is supposed that not less than five thousand people were assembled to see the experiment; the Champ de Mars being surrounded by multitudes, and vast numbers on the opposite side of the river.

At five o'clock notice was given to the spectators, by the firing of two cannon, that the cord was about to be cut. And presently the globe was seen to rise, and that as fast as a body of twelve feet diameter, with a force only of thirty-nine pounds, could be supposed to move the resisting air out of the way. There was some wind, but not very strong. A little rain had wet it, so that it shone, and made an agreeable appearance. It diminished in apparent magnitude as it rose, till it entered the clouds, when it seemed

[13] In *Alfred Lord Tennyson, A Memoir*, by his Son (1897), p. 195.

[14] *Encyclopedia Britannica*, 8th ed., "Aeronautics."

to me scarce bigger than an orange, and soon after became invisible, the clouds concealing it.

The multitude separated, all well satisfied and delighted with the success of the experiment, and amusing one another with discourses of the uses it may possibly be applied to, among which many were extravagant. But possibly it may pave the way to some discoveries in natural philosophy of which at present we have no conception.[15]

FRANKLIN was both an interested and acute observer; in a postscript to the same letter he forwarded some of the conjectures which circulated about Paris regarding the new invention's possible utility.

Among the pleasantries conversation produces on this subject, some suppose flying to be now invented, and that since men may be supported in the air, nothing is wanted but some light handy instrument to give and direct motion. Some think progressive motion on the earth may be advanced by it, and that a running footman or a horse slung and suspended under such a globe, so as to have no more of weight pressing the earth with their feet than perhaps eight or ten pounds, might with a fair wind run in a straight line across countries as fast as that wind, and over hedges, ditches, and even waters. It has been even fancied that in time people will keep such globes anchored in the air, to which by pulleys they may draw up game to be preserved in the cool, and water to be frozen when ice is wanted; and that to get money, it will be contrived to give people an extensive view of the country, by running them in an elbow chair a mile high for a guinea, etc., etc.[16]

To this letter Sir JOSEPH replied:

. . . . I consider the present day, which has opened a road into the air, as an epoch from whence a rapid increase of the stock of human knowledge must take its date; and that it will have an immediate effect upon the concerns of mankind, greater than any thing since the invention of shipping, which opened our way upon the face of the water from land to land.[17]

By November FRANKLIN was able to write:

. . . The improvement in the construction and management of the balloons has already made a rapid progress, and one cannot say how far it may go. A few months since the idea of witches riding thro' the air upon a broomstick, and that of philosophers upon a bag of smoke, would have appeared equally impossible and ridiculous.[18]

And to JOHN INGENHOUSZ he wrote of the effect of the discovery upon international relations:

It appears as you observe, to be a discovery of great importance, and what may possibly give a new turn to human affairs. Convincing sovereigns of the folly of wars may perhaps be one effect of it, since it will be impracticable for the most potent of them to guard his dominions. Five thousand balloons, capable of raising two men each, could not cost more than five ships of the line, and where is the prince who can afford so to cover his country with troops for its defence as that ten thousand men descending from the clouds might not in many places do an infinite deal of

mischief before a force could be brought together to repel them?[19]

One thinks of the present bombing of Germany and re-reads this passage with mixed emotions. Within a year PILATRE DE ROZIER became the first human being to ascend in a lighter-than-air craft. The ascent was of no great extent, but not long after, Professor CHARLES and M. ROBERT made an aerial journey of almost thirty miles. From that time there was no doubt in the minds of French experimenters that the balloon was "here to stay." In England, meanwhile, acceptance of the new contrivance was slower. POPE'S injunction to his countrymen to

Be not the first by whom the new are tried,
Nor yet the last to lay the old aside

was not in this instance ignored, as indeed— witness Dunkirk and Singapore—it has not been more recently.[20]

Another year, however, produced the first flights from Britain. From Edinburgh JAMES TYTLER made two ascents in August of 1784, thereby earning the cognomen of "Balloon" TYTLER.[21] And a month later VINCENZIO LUNARDI[22] made the first flight from actual English soil. *The Gentleman's Magazine* made the following report:

The aerial voyage, which had been much talked of, and long expected, at length took place. It drew an innumerable multitude, of all ranks, together, to the ground from whence the balloon was to be launched, and many thousands occupied the eminences round the metropolis. . . . It was really curious to listen to the discourse, and to observe the different traits of so many vacant faces, who, though assembled, had no conception of what they came to see, or perhaps, more properly speaking, what they had pronounced beforehand was impossible to be seen. The notions and opinions of this motley multitude were certainly as various as their situations in life were different. The populace . . . were sure the *thing* could not be done by day-light, for no *Christian* could fly through the air, and Goblins and Sprits [sic] were not permitted to ramble till the dead hour of night. The next class to these had very little more faith than their fellows; "they could not think as *how* it *could be* that a bubble could carry a *man*. . . ." The middle ranks were doubtful, but not without hope. The more enlightened were anxious for the event, and were not without sharing in that concern which every sensible mind could not but feel for the issue of so hazardous an enterprise.[23]

[15] Dated from Passy, 30 August, 1783. BENJAMIN FRANKLIN, *Works*, ed. JOHN BIGELOW (1904), X, 155–158.
[16] *Ibid.*, p. 161.
[17] *Ibid.*, p. 159.
[18] *Ibid.*, pp. 207–8.

[19] *Ibid.*, pp. 267–8.
[20] VINCENZIO LUNARDI is quoted as saying in 1784: "Philosophers in England have attended to aerial voyages, with a silence and apparent indifference not easily to be accounted for." Cf. *The Critical Review*, LVIII (1784), p. 417.
[21] TYTLER was an acquaintance of BURNS, and editor of the *Encyclopedia Britannica*.
[22] LUNARDI became a very popular figure in England and Scotland, to the extent that a kind of woman's hat was named after him. In BURNS's famous poem *To a Louse*, it was a Lunardi whose unblemished beauty the insect was so wantonly violating.
[23] LIV (1784), pt. 2, 711.

Despite this ballast of doubtful public opinion, the balloon sailed:

... on a sudden a cannon was heard ... and the machine was seen to move, but in a reeling course, expressive of some defect. A few moments passed in dreadful apprehension, from which, however, the friends of Lunardi were soon relieved, and the balloon was seen to rise, with all the majesty that heart could wish, to the astonishment of millions, who, scarcely open to conviction, beheld it with a kind of awful terror, which rather closed their lips in stupid silence, than prompted them to rend the air, as might have been expected, with joyful acclamation.[24]

The response from literary men was immediate and, as might be expected, positive, negative, and mixed. COWPER was enthusiastic:

I know not how it fares with you at a time when philosophy has just brought forth her most extraordinary production, not excepting, perhaps, that prodigy, a ship, in all respects complete, and equal to the task of circumnavigating the globe. My mind, always frequently getting into these balloons, and is busy in multiplying speculations as airy as the regions through which they pass. . . . The invention of these vehicles is yet in its infancy, yet already they seem to have attained a degree of perfection which navigation did not reach, till ages of experience had matured it, and science had exhausted both her industry and her skill, in its improvement. I am aware, indeed, that the first boat or canoe that was ever found ... was a more perfect creature in its kind than a balloon at present; the single circumstance of its manageable nature giving it a clear superiority both in respect of safety and convenience. But the atmosphere, though a much thinner medium, we well know, resists the impression made upon it by the tail of a bird, as effectually as the water that of a ship's rudder. Pope ... says beautifully—

Learn of the little nautilus to sail,
Spread the thin oar, and catch the driving gale.

It is easy to parody these lines, so as to give them an accommodation and suitableness to the present purpose.

Learn of the circle-making kite to fly,
Spread the fan-tail, and wheel about the sky.

It is certain, at least, that nothing within the reach of human ingenuity will be left unattempted to accomplish, and add all that is wanting to this last effort of philosophical contrivance. The approximating powers of the telescope, and the powers by which the thunderstorm is delivered of its contents peaceably and without mischief, were once, perhaps in appearance more remote from discovery, and seemed less practicable, than we may now suppose it, to give direction to that which is already buoyant; especially possessed as we are of such consummate mechanical skill, already masters of principles which we have nothing to do but apply, in the similar case of navigation, and having in every fowl of the air a pattern, which now at length it may be sufficient to imitate.[25]

But religious scruples led him from this abstract affirmation to pragmatic negation; he says of Man that this invention will prove a judgment upon him because, first:

... if a power to convey himself from place to place, like a bird, would have been good for him, his Maker would

[24] *Loc. cit.*
[25] *The Correspondence of William Cowper*, ed. THOMAS WRIGHT (1904), II, 132 ff. Letter to the Rev. JOHN NEWTON, Dec. 15, 1783.

have formed him with such a capacity. . . . Secondly, I think it will prove a judgment, because, with the exercise of very little foresight, it is easy to prognosticate a thousand evils which the project must necessarily bring after it; amounting at last to the confusion of all order, the annihilation of all authority, with dangers both to property and persons, and impunity to the offenders.[26]

SAMUEL JOHNSON, as one might expect, was rather more sceptical than COWPER:

On one day I had three letters about the air-balloon: yours was far the best, and has enabled me to impart to my friends ... an idea of this species of amusement. In amusement, mere amusement, I am afraid it must end, for I do not find that its course can be directed so as that it should serve any purposes of communication; and it can give no intelligence of the state of the air at different heights, till they have ascended above the height of mountains, which they seem never likely to do . . . .[27]

In a letter to Mrs. THRALE, he mentions, with mild irony, an improvement on the balloon.

You observe, Madam, that the ballon [sic] engages all mankind, and it is indeed a wonderful and unexpected addition to human knowledge; but we have a daring projector, who, disdaining the help of fumes and vapours, is making better than Daedalean wings, with which he will master the ballon and its companions as an eagle masters a goose. It is very seriously true that a subscription of eight hundred pounds has been raised for the wire and workmanship of iron wings; one pair of which, and I think a tail, is now shown in the Haymarket, and they are making another pair at Birmingham. The whole is said to weigh two hundred pounds—no specious preparation for flying, but there are those who expect to see him in the sky.[28]

WALPOLE, as excerpts from several letters reveal, was in some quandary whether to take the new invention seriously—he wrote to HENRY SEYMOUR CONWAY that "I have, at last, seen an air-balloon. . . . It seemed to light on Richmond Hill; but Mrs. HOBART was going by, and her *coiffure* prevented my seeing it alight"[29]—but he made some rather interesting remarks and conjectures.

To Sir HORACE MANN he wrote:

. . . . I cannot fill my paper ... with air-balloons; which, though ranked with the invention of navigation, appear to me as childish as the flying kites of schoolboys.[30]

And again:

How posterity will laugh at us, one way or another! If half a dozen break their necks and balloonism is exploded, we shall be called fools for having imagined it could be brought to use: if it should be turned to account, we shall be ridiculed for having doubted.[31]

To the Countess of UPPER OSSORY he pro-

[26] *Ibid.*, II, 135.
[27] To Dr. BROCKLESBY. *Boswell's Life of Johnson*, ed. G. B. HILL (1891), IV, 412.
[28] JOHNSON, *Letters*, ed. G. B. HILL (1892), II, 272.
[29] WALPOLE, *Letters*, ed. Mrs. PAGET TOYNBEE (1905), XIII, 64.
[30] *Ibid.*, XIII, 191.
[31] *Ibid.*, XIII, 279.

claimed that he had no occasion "for divining
with what airy vehicles the atmosphere will be
peopled hereafter, or how much more expeditiously
the east, west, or south will be ravaged and
butchered, than they have been by the old-fash-
ioned clumsy method of navigation."[32] But to
CONWAY he had written a week before:

. . . I chiefly amused myself with ideas of the change that
would be made in the world by the substitution of balloons
to ships. I supposed our seaports to become *deserted villages;*
and Salisbury Plain, [and] Newmarket Heath . . . arising
into dockyards for aerial vessels. Such a field would be
ample in furnishing new speculations. But to come to my
ship-news:—

   'The good balloon Daedalus, Captain Wing-ate, will fly
in a few days for China; he will stop at the top of the
Monument to take in passengers . . . .'

In those days Old Sarum will again be a town and have
houses in it. There will be fights in the air with wind-guns
and bows and arrows; and there will be prodigious increase
of land for tillage, especially in France, by breaking up all
public roads as useless. . . .[33]

THOMAS MARTIN, in his *Hints of important
Uses, to be derived from Aerostatic Globes,* saw
the possibilities of the balloon as a reconnoitering
agency in wartime, but his reviewer in *The
Critical Review* was less sanguine: "The idea of
reconnoitering in the gallery of a balloon, is too
ridiculous to excite a moment's attention."[34] As
a matter of fact, military balloons were used by the
French in 1794 just before the battle of Fleurus,
and their use is said to have won the battle for the
French, not only because of the information they
obtained, but also because of their effect upon
Austrian morale. And as early as 1850, the city
of Venice was bombed by five balloons when the
Austrian army found it impossible to draw its
heavy artillery over the marshes in the vicinity.[35]
But to revert to the eighteenth century, ballooning was so much the craze in 1784 that a Mr.
PILLON successfully wrote and produced a
farce-comedy entitled *Aerostation; or The Tem-
plar's Stratagem,* in the prologue to which he
wrote:

   I make no doubt to entertain you soon
   With a new theatre in a *stage-balloon.*
   No more in garret high shall poets sit,
   With rival spiders spinning cobweb wit;
   Like ancient barons future bards shall fare,
   In *their own castles* built up *in the air.*[36]

But in the mind of ERASMUS DARWIN, one of
the great, neglected optimists of all time, there
was no question—and no hint of ridicule; in that

amazing compendium, *The Botanic Garden,* he
wrote bombastically:

   Soon shall thy arm, Unconquer'd Steam! afar
   Drag the slow' barge, or drive the rapid car:
   Or on wide-waving wings expanded bear
   The flying-chariot through the fields of air.
   —Fair crews triumphant, leaning from above,
   Shall wave their fluttering kerchiefs as they move,
   Or warrior-bands alarm the gasping crowd,
   And armies shrink beneath the shadowy cloud.[37]

In America, where flights were also being made,
PHILLIP FRENEAU, as befitted the poet of a new
world, was no less ebullient:

   At sea let the British their neighbors defy—
   The French shall have frigates to traverse the sky,
   In this navigation more fortunate prove,
   And cruise at their ease in the climates above.
   If the English should venture to sea with their fleet,
   A host of balloons in a trice they shall meet.
   The French from the zenith their wings shall display,
   And souse on these sea-dogs and bear them away . . .
   Yet more with its fitness for commerce I'm struck;
   What loads of tobacco shall fly from Kentuck . . .
   To markets the farmers shall shortly repair
   With their hogs and potatoes, wholesale thro' the air,
   Skim over the waters as light as a feather,
   Themselves and their turkies conversing together.[38]

Some years later SHELLEY contemplated the
balloon with characteristic missionary fervor.
HOGG reports him as saying:

   The balloon has not yet received the perfection of which
it is surely capable; the art of navigating the air is in its
first and most helpless infancy; the aerial mariner still swims
on bladders, and has not mounted even the rude raft; if
we weigh this invention, curious as it is, with some of the
subjects I have mentioned, it will seem trifling, no doubt—
a mere toy, a feather in comparison with the splendid
anticipations of the philosophical chemist; yet it ought not
altogether to be contemned. It promises prodigious facilities
for locomotion, and will enable us to traverse vast tracts
with ease and rapidity, and to explore unknown countries
without difficulty. Why are we still so ignorant of the interior of Africa?—why do we not despatch intrepid aeronauts
to cross it in every direction, and to survey the whole
peninsula in a few weeks? The shadow of the first balloon,
which a vertical sun would project precisely underneath it,
as it glided silently over that hitherto unhappy country,
would virtually emancipate every slave, and would annihilate
slavery forever.[39]

The impressive fact about almost every one of
the preceding quotations, positive or negative, is

[37] Canto I, ll. 289–296.
[38] *The Progress of Balloons.*
[39] THOMAS JEFFERSON HOGG, *Life of Percy Bysshe Shelley*
(1858), I, 62–3. SHELLEY, of course, above all other poets
was able to put into words the poetry of flight. It is interesting, though possibly irrelevant, to encounter in *The
Revolt of Islam,* in the description of the aerial battle
between the Eagle and the Serpent, the following analogue
to TENNYSON's "there rain'd a ghastly dew." SHELLEY's lines
are:

   For, from the encounter of those wondrous foes,
   A vapor like the sea's suspended spray
   Hung gathered. . . . (Canto I, ll. 93–5.)

[32] *Ibid.,* XIII, 202.
[33] *Ibid.,* XIII, 199–200.
[34] LVIII (1784), 424.
[35] *Cf. Annual of Scientific Discovery,* ed. DAVID A. WELLS
and GEORGE BLISS (1850), I, 47.
[36] Quoted in WRIGHT's *England under the House of Han-
over,* II, 328.

this: they make clear that no sooner had man burst the fetters which chained him to earth than he began to make forecasts—to look into the future as far as human eye could see. As one writer said in 1836:

The fancies of the time [the 1780's and '90's] were so elated with the discovery of the balloon that the gravest philosophers talked like children in a nursery at the first sight of a rocking horse. They thought that they could ride round the universe. The moon, the sun, the stars, were to be visited with the regularity of the 'London dilly, carrying six insides. . . .'[40]

This enthusiasm began to dissipate, however, as all attempts to bring the balloon under complete control ended in failure. To quote again the foregoing writer: "It is remarkable . . . that the balloon, of all the showy contrivances of the last half century, is that which, with the most tempting capabilities, has been the least improved."[41]

This is not to say that experimentation did not go on. It did. Lack of success served only as a challenge. In Spain, Dom JOSEPH PATINHO invented a dirigible in the shape of a sword-fish, the fins serving as oars and the tail as a rudder, with two oarsmen and a steersman riding it as on a horse;[42] in a letter to FRANKLIN May 24, 1784, FRANCIS HOPKINSON proposed a spindle-shaped balloon driven by a wheel at the stern, the wheel to consist of vanes or fans of canvas whose planes should be inclined with respect to the plane of its motion;[43] THOMAS JEFFERSON mentioned a "screw which takes hold of the air and draws itself along by it," and remarks that "perhaps it may be used . . . for the balloon";[44] in France Baron SCOTT invented a sausage-shaped dirigible to be lifted by small gas-balloons or ballonets, on each side fore and aft, the machine to be inclined up or down by inflating or deflating the ballonets;[45] JACOB KAISERER of Vienna, THOMAS MACKINTOSH of London, and others proposed that birds be used to draw and steer balloons as horses draw and steer wagons;[46] someone suggested carrying small cannon in the balloon and firing them in the hope that the recoil would drive the balloon forward; the Comte DE LENNOX created a great

stir in London with his dirigible "The Eagle," 160 feet long, 50 feet high, and 40 feet wide, to be navigated by large oars or paddles and constructed for "Establishing direct Communication between the several Capitals of Europe";[47] PIERRE FERRAND attempted to propel a cylindrical dirigible on the rotary principle of the screw propeller—around the barrel of the balloon was a spiral screw, which was to be rotated and thus force the contrivance forward;[48] Sir GEORGE CAYLEY proposed a cigar-shaped, hydrogen-filled dirigible with propellers driven by a steam-engine;[49] CHARLES GREEN exhibited in London a model supplied with a clock-work driven propeller —"By touching a stop in the mechanism, Mr. GREEN immediately communicated a rapid rotatory motion to the fans [propellers], when the machine rose steadily to the ceiling, from which it continued to rebound until the clock-work had run out . . ."[50] And so on. And so on.

In spite of all this activity *The English Cyclopedia* was able to say in 1859 that "Although much has been suggested, scarcely anything has been accomplished towards rendering balloons available for any practical use. Little has been done towards guiding a balloon. . . . Much ingenuity continues to be unprofitably wasted on ballooning. . . ."[51]

Such abject pessimism was much less the order of the day in 1836. In November of that year CHARLES GREEN,[52] MONCK MASON, and ROBERT HOLLAND flew from London to Weilburg, Germany, a distance of almost 500 miles in 18 hours. MASON, an artist of some talent, made aerial sketches—perhaps the first in the air—and wrote an account of the voyage. The review of the latter in *Blackwood's Magazine* comments: "This was altogether an extraordinary achievement. It was almost the first instance, in which the balloon has not been used as a mere toy, but has been directed to practical utility. The narrative says that the means of the machine were so entirely *un*-exhausted, that if they had been so inclined, they might have circumnavigated the globe."[53]

Elsewhere in this same volume of the magazine a writer comments thus optimistically:

We understand that Mr. Green doubts of the future possibility of steering the balloon. That it is beyond our power at present, is admitted. But what steers a bird? . . . . What steers and carries the wild swan, as heavy as an infant, a

[40] *Blackwood's Magazine*, XL (1836), 624.
[41] *Loc. cit.*
[42] FRANCIS TREVELYAN MILLER, *The World in the Air* (1930), I, 175. This book is subtitled "The Story of Flying in Pictures," and in its pictures the book is good. The running text, however, is not always accurate. Most of the citations in this paragraph are also to be found in MAGGS Brothers' *Descriptive Catalogue of Books, Engravings, and Medals illustrating the Evolution of the Airship and the Aeroplane* (1930).
[43] *Cf.* GEORGE EVERETT HASTINGS, *The Life and Works of Francis Hopkinson* (1926), p. 338.
[44] THOMAS JEFFERSON, *The Writings*, ed. H. A. WASHINGTON (1853), I, 445–6.
[45] MILLER, *op. cit.*, p. 202.
[46] *Ibid.*, pp. 226 and 275.
[47] *Ibid.*, p. 277.
[48] *Ibid.*, p. 280.
[49] *Loc. cit.*
[50] *The American Eclectic*, II, 188, reprinted this account from the *Year-Book*, 1841.
[51] Vol. I (1859), Arts and Sciences section.
[52] It was with Mr. GREEN that R. MONCKTON MILNES, friend of HALLAM and TENNYSON and member of "The Apostles," made a balloon flight in 1830.
[53] XLI (1837), 333–4.

thousand miles through the tempest and *against* the tempest? The united action of the wings and tail. The buoyancy of the balloon would render the wings unnecessary, except for addition to the steerage power. The true and only difficulty to be mastered is that of enabling the balloon to go faster or *slower* than the wind; for it is only in such cases that the rudder can have any thing to act upon . . . . the requisite would be a rudder of such length and force as at once to accelerate (or retard) and guide. This rudder might be a long frame, with a wheel or vane kept in rapid motion at the end. For this some modification of the steam-engine would be required. . . .[54]

While the improvement of the balloon and the dirigible were thus engaging the attention of ingenious mechanists, it was not to the exclusion of the heavier-than-air craft. In 1807 JACOB DEGEN, a Viennese clockmaker, invented a "Flugmaschine" consisting of umbrella-like taffeta wings attached by small cords to a central stick. The taffeta was loosely fashioned, in imitation of a bird's feathers. DEGEN was supposed to have raised himself some 50 feet in Vienna, but he required the assistance of a balloon, and his attempts in Paris were complete failures.[55] In 1810 THOMAS WALKER of Hull drew plans for a kind of mechanical bird, which he never built; but his *Treatise upon the Art of Flying by Mechanical Means* (Hull 1810) went through more than one edition in America and was re-published in England in 1831. This contained "instructions and plans for making a flying car with wings, in which a man may sit, and, by working a small lever, cause himself to ascend and soar through the air."[56] As early as 1809 GEORGE CAYLEY had planned a combination of helicopter and aeroplane—an aircraft built with slightly oblique planes to furnish the lift, fitted with two propellers to force the wheeled chassis forward, horizontal and vertical rudders, and a steam engine for power. CAYLEY was far in advance of his times; it is quite possible that his failure to go beyond theory to actual experiment retarded the invention of a working airplane by a hundred years.[57] In 1827 GEORGE POCOCK wrote on *The aeropleustic art; or navigation in the air by the*

use *of kites or buoyant sails.* Next to CAYLEY's apparatus, however, the most remarkable invention was WILLIAM SAMUEL HENSON's Aerial Steam Carriage, a monoplane of the "pusher" type intended to "convey Passengers, Troops, and Government Despatches to China and India, in a few days."[58] This machine came to public notice (and it attracted great attention) in 1842, too late to have had effect on TENNYSON's *Locksley Hall.* The optimism of its projectors, the attention which it received, and the hope it assured, however, more than suggest that the heavier-than-air machine was definitely *not* beyond the possibility of a poet's conception the few years before, when *Locksley Hall* was being composed.

This paper might with the greatest of ease— to employ a notorious aeronautical phrase—have been extended to greater length. But I have already a fairly good-sized mountain of evidence, and the conclusion to be produced is a very small mouse indeed. My only excuse for such disproportion is that it has proved a most delectable mountain. The conclusion seems fairly obvious. First: the value of TENNYSON's "prophetic" lines, when seen in their proper context, does not consist in their prophetic insight at all but in their apt distillation of (by his time) relatively trite ideas. They exemplify simply another case of "What oft was thought, but ne'er so well expressed."[59] And second: there is no reason save TENNYSON's lack of explicitness to assume that in this passage he was thinking only of the balloon. It might have been the ornithopter. This device had had a long literary history, and, as we have seen, the well-known MONCK MASON, as late as 1838, had suggested that it might prove more practicable to experiment in that direction than to continue with the balloon—and this immediately after the amazing flight to Weilburg. (*Cf.* footnote 54.) It might have been a kind of flying chariot, like BLANCHARD's or CAYLEY's, or WALKER's. The one thing holding back mechanical flight, as CAYLEY remarked, was the difficulty of finding a prime mover capable of "providing sufficient power with the requisite lightness." Experimenters had been tinkering with steam

[54] *Ibid.,* pp. 43–4. MONCK MASON, GREEN's collaborator in the famous voyage to Weilburg, was also dubious: ". . . when we consider the nature and amount of the forces required to the propulsion of the balloon, it becomes a matter of question whether the same exertions would not be sufficient to enable us to dispense with its services altogether, and transport ourselves through the air by the simple exercise of wings alone." (*Aeronautica; or Sketches illustrative of the Theory and Practice of Aerostation, etc.,* London, 1838, p. 330.) This passage is footnoted with an account of the winged flight of the Marquis DE BACQUEVILLE.

[55] MILLER, *op. cit.,* p. 237.

[56] See the MAGGS Brothers' catalogue (p. 52) for a picture of this machine.

[57] CAYLEY's letters to *The Mechanics' Magazine, Museum, Register, Journal and Gazette,* Vols. XXVI and XXXVIII are of extreme interest to anyone interested in the history of aviation.

[58] MILLER, *op. cit.,* p. 204. In commenting on HENSON's machine, JOHN WISE (*A System of Aeronautics, etc.,* Philadelphia, 1850, pp. 84–89) mentions two American airplanes, invented but not constructed, apparently in the '20's, and quotes *Newton's Journal of Arts and Sciences* to the effect that many such projects had been promulgated (in England and elsewhere).

[59] THACKERAY is rarely thought of as a prophet, but in his *Irish Sketches* (1843) he wrote that "Future Cockneys setting off after breakfast from London Bridge in an *Aerial Machine* may come to hear the morning service here [in the Armagh Church] and not remark the faults which have struck a too susceptible tourist of the Nineteenth Century." (THACKERAY found the church in need of a century's mellowing.)

engines, carbonic acid motors, clock-work devices, and so on; and CAYLEY said (in 1844) that "I have for some time turned my attention to the use, as a power, of common atmospheric air expanded by heat, and with considerable success."[60] The material for TENNYSON was there; all he needed to do was to consider the problem solved— exactly the same imaginative feat necessary to the visualization of balloon-navies. It might more probably have been a steam-powered, propeller-driven dirigible, something on the order of the modern zeppelin, which is not, strictly speaking, a balloon. Or perhaps his imaginative navy comprised all three. CAYLEY wrote, a few years later: "Elongated balloons, of large dimensions . . . offer greater facilities for transporting men and goods through the air, than mechanical means alone, inasmuch as the whole weight is suspended in the air without effort. . . ." But—"mechanical flight seems more adapted for use on a much

[60] *The Mechanics' Magazine, etc.,* XXXVIII, 276.

smaller scale, and for less remote distances; *serving, perhaps, the same purpose that a boat does to a ship, each being essential to the other.*"[61]

The point is, of course, that, acknowledging the amount of literature on the subject (and one must agree that back of that literature there must have been a vast amount of verbal conjecture), it is unwise to deny the possibility that TENNYSON did indeed visualize something after the fashion of twentieth century aircraft. That he did, no one can say with certainty. But, on the other hand, no one can say, with finality, that he did not. In either case, he was only one, and a late one at that, of many prophets.

Indiana University

[61] *Ibid.,* XXXVIII, 276. In the '30's and '40's CAYLEY was repeating ideas conceived and expressed much earlier in his career. The occasion of the articles quoted in this paper was the revival of public interest in aviation resulting from GREEN's flight to Weilburg, and the ensuing experiments of GREEN, MASON, HENSON, *et al.*

J. Clerk Maxwell's first attack on the problem of governor instability was based on H. C. Fleeming Jenkin's governor used in the British Association for the Advancement of Science experiments for the determination of the ohm in 1863. (Courtesy of the Whipple Science Museum, University of Cambridge.)

Maxwell and the Origins of Cybernetics

By Otto Mayr*

We have decided to call the entire field of control and communication theory, whether in the machine or in the animal, by the name *Cybernetics*, which we form from the Greek χυβερνήτης or *steersman*. In choosing this term, we wish to recognize that the first significant paper on feedback mechanisms is an article on governors, which was published by Clerk Maxwell in 1868, and that *governor* is derived from a Latin corruption of χυβερνήτης.[1]

—NORBERT WIENER

INTRODUCTION

SINCE 1948, when Norbert Wiener wrote these words, James Clerk Maxwell (1831–1879) has been widely celebrated as the father of the theory of automatic control; in the eighty years prior to 1948, Maxwell's paper "On Governors"[2] was almost entirely ignored. This contrast in estimation has never been analyzed, probably because the paper itself is in part incomprehensible.[3] The purpose of the following discussion is to supply such historical data as are required for a full understanding, to offer a more objective appraisal than is implied in the early neglect or the recent enthusiasm, and to relate Maxwell's interest in a technological subject such as governors to his scientific thought in general.

The paper "On Governors" stems from the period between 1865 and 1871 when, between appointments at King's College, London, and Cambridge University, Maxwell

* Museum of History and Technology, Smithsonian Institution, Washington, D.C. 20560. I am indebted to Dr. Thomas K. Simpson, St. John's College, Annapolis, Dr. C. W. F. Everitt, High Energy Physics Laboratory, Stanford University, and Dr. I. B. Hopley, Clifton College, Bristol, for a number of valuable suggestions, and to Dr. William Levine, Department of Electrical Engineering, University of Maryland, for a critical reading of the manuscript.

[1] Norbert Wiener, *Cybernetics, or Control and Communication in the Animal and the Machine* (Cambridge, Mass.: M.I.T. Press, 1948), pp. 11–12. Wiener had not coined a new word. In 1834 A. M. Ampère had referred to the science of government as *la cybernétique*, in *Essai sur la philosophie des sciences* (Paris, 1843), Pt. 2, pp. 140–141.

[2] *Proceedings of the Royal Society of London*, 1867/1868, *16*:270–283; in all further references I will use the pagination of this first publication. The paper also appeared in the *Philosophical Magazine*, 4th Ser., 1868, *35*:385–398; in Maxwell's *Scientific Papers*, W. D. Niven, ed., 2 vols. (Cambridge, 1890), Vol. II, pp. 105–120; and more recently in *Mathematical Trends in Control Theory*, R. Bellman and R. Kalaba, eds. (New York: Dover, 1964), pp. 5–17.

[3] A detailed discussion of Maxwell's governor paper is given in A. A. Andronov and I. N. Voznesenski, *J. C. Maxwell, I. A. Vyshnegradskii, A. Stodola: Teoriia avtomaticheskogo regulirovaniia* (Moscow: Akademia Nauk SSSR, 1949), to which I, not reading Russian, am unable to do justice. Judging from externals, mathematics, and illustrations, there seems to be no significant duplication between the Russian work and the present study.

lived in semi-retirement at Glenlair, his country seat in southwestern Scotland, working chiefly on his *Treatise on Electricity and Magnetism*. One of the diversions that would break up this secluded life was an annual visit to London.[4] In 1868 this visit lasted from the beginning of the year well into spring.[5] Among the scientific meetings which he attended, two are of specific interest. On January 23 at the London Mathematical Society Maxwell gave two papers ("The Construction of Stereograms of Surfaces" and "On Reciprocal Diagrams in Space, and their Relation to Airy's Function of Stress") and then asked the members present for help in a mathematical difficulty he had come across "in studying the motion of certain governors for regulating machinery."[6] He received an answer from Professor W. K. Clifford which, as shall be shown, seems to have proven helpful. Four weeks later, on February 20, 1868, his paper "On Governors" was received by the Royal Society; Maxwell read it there on March 5. It seems then that the paper was begun in Glenlair but completed in London.

To some extent Maxwell's interest in governors reflects a contemporary vogue. At the height of the age of steam the mechanism responsible for controlling the speed of every steam engine was afflicted by problems of inaccuracy and instability that seemed to foil the efforts of both theory and practice. In the 1860s and 1870s practitioners invented scores of new governors. Scientists, too, especially of Maxwell's direct acquaintance, responded to the challenge by inventing new mechanisms and by seeking analytical solutions.[7]

But Maxwell also drew on personal experience. In 1863, as a member of a British Association for the Advancement of Science committee on electrical standards, he determined experimentally, together with Balfour Stewart and H. C. Fleeming Jenkin, the absolute measure of electrical resistance. The apparatus, designed by William Thomson, consisted of a circular coil of wire rotating about a vertical axis driven by a falling weight. Constant speed, a crucial condition, was maintained by a centrifugal governor invented by Fleeming Jenkin which made a great impression upon Maxwell.[8] Later, incidentally, in Cambridge Maxwell once more returned to the subject of governors.[9]

Concerning Maxwell's motives, the paper shows a gap between his ostensible aim and the actual course of his argument: although he had set out "to direct the attention of engineers and mathematicians to the dynamical theory of . . . governors,"[10] his actual interest in helping the engineers did not go far. He discussed no practical governors; the paper deals with mechanisms devoid of industrial significance, inventions of scientists who were all Fellows of the Royal Society. More unhappily yet, the

[4] Lewis Campbell and William Garnett, *The Life of James Clerk Maxwell* (London, 1882), p. 324.

[5] For a *terminus ante quem*: on Mar. 27, 1868, Maxwell wrote to W. R. Grove from a London address; *Scientific Papers*, Vol. II, p. 121.

[6] *Proceedings of the London Mathematical Society*, 1866–1869, 2: 57–61.

[7] For a sampling of practical governor designs, see Otto Mayr, *Feedback Mechanisms in the Historical Collections of the National Museum of History and Technology* (Washington, D.C.: Smithsonian Institution Press, 1971), Ch. 3; the scientist's involvement in the problem I have treated more generally in "Victorian Physicists and Speed Regulation: An Encounter between Science and Technology," *Notes and Records of the Royal Society* (in press).

[8] *Reports of the Committee on Electrical Standards* (London, 1873), esp. pp. 96–99.

[9] I. B. Hopley has discovered in the Whipple Science Museum, University of Cambridge, a pendulum governor designed by Maxwell presumably while at the Cavendish Laboratory. It is described extensively in I. B. Hopley, *Clerk Maxwell's Contributions to Physics*, Ph.D. thesis, University of London, 1957, Vol. II, pp. 368–379.

[10] Maxwell, "On Governors," p. 271.

mechanisms that indeed were treated were neither adequately explained nor identified. The paper could be fully understood only by insiders who knew these mechanisms through personal information.

Maxwell's own interest in governors had nothing to do with their practical utility: he was attracted by two features that are related to the subject in very different ways. The governor mainly provided him with an occasion for a general discussion of the issue of *dynamic stability*, which was to occupy most of the paper. On the last two pages he turned to *differential gears*, a machine element—rarely used on governors—that had fascinated him for years as a mechanical model of electrical phenomena.

DYNAMIC STABILITY

The paper's main theme is introduced by way of a classification scheme which divides all existing governors simply into two groups, *moderators* and *governors* proper. The reader is startled to learn that the oldest and best known of the species, the centrifugal governor of James Watt, is no governor at all but only a moderator, like the simple friction governors employed in the weight drives of various scientific instruments or the "water-break [*sic*] invented by Professor J. Thomson."[11] What these all have in common is that their corrective action (increase of resistance or reduction of steam supply) is directly proportional to overspeed. They are inherently unable to maintain constant speed. A lasting change in equilibrium conditions requires a lasting change in the governor action, which in turn would be impossible without a certain, if small, error in output speed (referred to by modern control engineers as proportional offset).

Genuine governors, according to Maxwell, are only those that are in principle free of this shortcoming. They must possess an additional mechanism that translates any output error into a corrective action that increases steadily until the output error has entirely disappeared. As examples Maxwell cites devices by Fleeming Jenkin, W. Thomson, L. Foucault, the Astronomer Royal (G. B. Airy), and C. W. Siemens (inconsistently, for the devices of Thomson and Foucault, by Maxwell's own standard, are only moderators!).

The distinction between moderators and governors is not only described in words, it is also tested by a mathematical criterion: the equation of motion of the device in question is subjected to steady-state conditions, so that time derivatives of speed vanish.[12] If, in the resulting steady-state equation, speed remains a function of such independent variables as power or resistance, the device is a moderator. In a genuine governor the equilibrium speed would be independent of these disturbances. Thomson's and Foucault's governors could slip through this test only because Maxwell omitted in their equations of motion[13] a term for the force (due to springs or gravity) that draws the flyweights back to their rest position.

The dichotomy *moderator–governor*, which Maxwell adopted from Siemens,[14] attracted much attention in the 1860s and 1870s, although under different names. The German literature instead spoke of *static* and *astatic* governors (terms coined by Franz

[11] *Ibid.* This device, which is no speed regulator, has not been identified; it is not identical with the one described in James Thomson, "On the Friction Break Dynamometer," *Report of the British Association for the Advancement of Science*, 1855, *25*:209–210.

[12] "On Governors," pp. 274–275.

[13] *Ibid.*, p. 278, Eq. 10.

[14] Charles William Siemens, "On Uniform Rotation," *Philosophical Transactions of the Royal Society*, 1866, 657, and "On an Improved Governor for Steam Engines," *Proceedings of the Institution of Mechanical Engineers*, 1853, 76.

Reuleaux in 1859), while Foucault distinguished between *nonisochronous* and *isochronous* regulators.[15] In modern engineering usage this all corresponds to "controllers with *proportional* response" versus those with *"integral* response." In retrospect, Maxwell's limitation of his study to governors of this narrow definition must be considered unfortunate, for he thus excluded most of the governors used in industry.

Instability Maxwell defined by a governor's response to disturbances: a governor is unstable if its output (the controlled speed) instead of returning to equilibrium will either increase continuously or enter into an oscillation of growing amplitude. "This condition is mathematically equivalent to the condition that all the possible [real] roots, and all possible parts of the impossible [imaginary] roots, of a certain equation shall be negative." With regard to his success he added, "I have not been able completely to determine these conditions for equations of a higher degree than the third; but I hope that the subject will obtain the attention of mathematicians."[16] This sums up the state of the problem before and after his own contribution.

The problem already had a considerable history. The first mathematical investigation had been published in 1840 by the Astronomer Royal George Biddell Airy (1801–1892), who had encountered instability on the friction governors regulating the weight drives of equatorial telescopes.[17] Airy's approach had been dictated by his astronomical background: he described the path of the unstable centrifugal pendulum, similar to a planetary orbit, as an ellipse with superimposed sinusoidal oscillations. In his analysis he failed to employ a crucial trick, namely to linearize the resulting differential equations. The solutions of these equations, obtained only with difficulty, gave little insight into the behavior of his governors or into the stability problem in general. The approach was not used again, either by himself or by anyone else. His follow-up article ten years later (1850) was essentially a report on practical progress,[18] but it also contained a hint of a more promising mathematical approach: if the differential equation could be linearized—Airy suggested adding to the apparatus a damping element with linear characteristics—then it could be solved easily, with the signs of the roots indicating instability or stability.

When Maxwell first attacked this "very general and very important problem in Dynamics" in his Adams Prize essay "On the Stability of the Motion of Saturn's Rings" (1856),[19] he followed probably unwittingly this suggestion of Airy's (Airy in turn praised this paper as "one of the most remarkable applications of Mathematics to Physics that I have ever seen"[20]). For each of his hypothetical models of the rings of Saturn Maxwell followed the same procedure: by assuming all disturbances to be small he reduced the equations of motion to linear differential equations with constant coefficients which could be solved with relative ease. Reasoning that the motion could

[15] Franz Reuleaux, "Zur Regulatorfrage," *Zeitschrift des Vereins deutscher Ingenieure,* 1859, *3*:165–168. Léon Foucault, "Sur une solution de l'isochronisme du pendule conique," *Comptes Rendus de l'Académie de Sciences, Paris,* 1862, *55*:135–136. See also Foucault's extensive writings on speed regulation in the *Recueil des travaux scientifiques de Léon Foucault,* ed. C.-M. Gariel (Paris, 1878), pp. 435–514.

[16] "On Governors," pp. 271–272.

[17] George Biddell Airy, "On the Regulator of the Clock-work for effecting uniform Movement of Equatorials," *Memoirs of the Royal Astromical Society,* 1840, *11*:249–267.

[18] "Supplement to a Paper on the Regulation of the Clock-work for effecting Uniform Movement of Equatorials," *Mem. Roy. Astr. Soc.,* 1851, *20*:115–119.

[19] J. C. Maxwell, "On the Stability of the Motion of Saturn's Rings," *Scientific Papers,* Vol. I, p. 295.

[20] Campbell and Garnett, *Life of Maxwell,* p. 513.

be stable only if the solution converged—that is, if all real roots and all real parts of the imaginary roots were negative—he derived from these solutions conditions for the stability of the rings. In this procedure he was favored by good luck; the characteristic polynomials turned out to be biquadratic and therefore solvable by elementary algebra.[21] In the general case—that is, if they had been anything but quadratic, cubic, or biquadratic—this would not have been possible. It was this general case to which he addressed himself in the governor paper.

Dynamic stability interested some illustrious contemporaries as well. W. Thomson and P. G. Tait, in their *Treatise on Natural Philosophy*, introduced a lengthy section on *kinetic stability* with the dictum "There is scarcely any question in dynamics more important for Natural Philosophy than the stability or instability of motion."[22] Their approach, probably devised by Tait,[23] was based on Hamiltonian dynamics: a general criterion of stability was outlined in terms of the *principle of varying action*. Maxwell, although a close friend of both Thomson and Tait, did not adopt this method. Perhaps he distrusted it; perhaps he did not have time to examine it. On December 11, 1867, he wrote to Tait regarding the latter's sensational new book: "I shall not see it till I go to London."[24] By the following February 20 the governor paper was in the hands of the Royal Society.

Maxwell's attack on governor instability was organized in two stages. The first, based upon a discussion of Fleeming Jenkin's governor of 1863, led to an equation of motion that was merely cubic and hence lacking in generality. Therefore Maxwell made a new attempt, with a far more elaborate notation and based on a second, more complex, governor by Fleeming Jenkin, which yielded an equation of the fifth order.

Fleeming Jenkin's first governor, constructed to regulate the apparatus of the ohm-determination experiments of 1863, is by Maxwell's definition a genuine governor—a controller with integral response.[25] It consists of two rotating mechanisms capable of moving entirely separately (see the frontispiece). The main part, a traditional centrifugal pendulum with a brake drum above it, mounted together on a vertical shaft, is driven through belt and pulley by the weight-powered machine which the governor is meant to regulate. The integral response is produced by the second mechanism, driven by the idler pulley rotating loosely on the main shaft between the flyweights and the brake drum. This pulley is connected through a worm gear to the band brake and to a counterweight (suspended in a viscous fluid in the narrow upright cylinder, center) which tends to release the band brake. A connection between the two systems is established whenever the speed of the main system exceeds the desired value, that is, whenever due to excessive centrifugal force the spring-loaded rocker arm connected to the flyweights is pressed against the idler pulley. Then the integral response mechanism

[21] "On the Stability of the Motion of Saturn's Rings," e.g., pp. 299–302, or 331–333.

[22] William Thomson and Peter Guthrie Tait, *Treatise on Natural Philosophy* (Oxford, 1867), p. 282.

[23] C. G. Knott, *Life and Scientific Work of Peter Guthrie Tait* (Cambridge: Cambridge Univ. Press, 1911), pp. 194 and 197.

[24] *Ibid.*, p. 189.

[25] Henry Charles Fleeming Jenkin (1833–1885), after an association with William Thomson in the laying of the Atlantic telegraph cable, became professor of engineering at University College, London (1865), and at the University of Edinburgh (1868) (*DNB*, Vol. XXIX). Fleeming Jenkin apparently never published the invention of this governor. Credit for rediscovering the device in the Whipple Science Museum, Cambridge University, belongs to I. B. Hopley, who has described it in "Maxwell's Work on Electrical Resistance: 1. The Determination of the Absolute Unit of Resistance," *Annals of Science*, 1957, *13*:267–268, Plt. 13.

is set in motion, tightening the belt brake to reduce the speed of the main system. It will continue to increase the braking torque on the main shaft until the centrifugal pendulum has released the idler pulley, that is, until the speed error has entirely disappeared. The magnitude of the braking torque is thus proportional to the time integral of the speed deviation.

For each of the two rotating systems of this governor, equations of motion are obtained by summing the forces (driving forces, resistances, inertia, etc.). Presumably for reasons of simplicity Maxwell employs the notation of linear motion. Accordingly, the equation of motion[26] of the main system of the governor is written as

$$M\frac{d^2x}{dt^2} = P - R - F\left(\frac{dx}{dt} - V_1\right) - Gy, \qquad (276:10)$$

where M is the moment of inertia of the main shaft, P the driving torque, R the external resistances, V_1 the equilibrium speed, dx/dt the actual speed, $F(dx/dt - V_1)$ the braking torque due to the centrifugal pendulum pressing against the idler pulley; y is the variable of motion of the second system; Gy, the retarding torque of the band brake, increases as the second system is kept in motion. The force of the centrifugal pendulum, actually a function of the square of speed, is linearized on the grounds that (1) in this particular governor, by design, the angle of the pendulum is constant, and (2) variations of velocity are small.

The motion of the second system, the integral response mechanism, is described by the equation

$$B\frac{d^2y}{dt^2} = F\left(\frac{dx}{dt} - V_1\right) - Y\frac{dy}{dt} - W, \qquad (275:6)$$

where B is the moment of inertia, $Y(dy/dt)$ the resistance of the dashpot, and W the counterweight; $F(dx/dt - V_1)$, the term that couples the two systems, here represents the driving force. Combining Equations (275:6) and (276:10) leads to a differential equation of the third order in (dx/dt),

$$MB\frac{d^3}{dt^3}\left(\frac{dx}{dt}\right) + (MY+FB)\frac{d^2}{dt^2}\left(\frac{dx}{dt}\right) + FY\frac{d}{dt}\left(\frac{dx}{dt}\right) + GF\left(\frac{dx}{dt}\right) - GFV_1 + GW = 0.$$

This equation, being linear and having constant coefficients, has a solution of the form

$$x = A_1 e^{n_1 t} + A_2 e^{n_2 t} + A_3 e^{n_3 t},$$

where n_1, n_2, and n_3 are the roots of the characteristic polynomial

$$MBn^3 + (MY+FB)n^2 + FYn + GF = 0. \qquad (276:12)$$

This solution, as has been stated earlier, will describe stable motion if all real roots and all real parts of the imaginary roots are negative. The task then is to discover a criterion that will show whether this condition is fulfilled without requiring the actual solution of the characteristic polynomial (which at best, in special cases, would be laborious, and in general, impossible). Without explanation or proof Maxwell presents

<hr />

[26] "On Governors," p. 276, Eq. 10. Equations   number; e.g., (276:10).
will hereafter be identified by page and equation

as the required stability condition the inequality

$$\left(\frac{F}{M}+\frac{Y}{B}\right)\frac{Y}{B}-\frac{G}{B}>0.$$

In general notation, for a characteristic polynomial $p_3n^3+p_2n^2+p_1n+p_0=0$, this is equivalent to

$$\begin{vmatrix} p_1 & p_0 \\ p_3 & p_2 \end{vmatrix}>0,$$

namely the Hurwitz criterion (see below) for cubic polynomials. The derivation of the above stability condition is elementary but not trivial: E. J. Routh, an eminent mathematical technician, judged it worthy of a footnote.[27]

If the first stage of Maxwell's attack on governor instability was successful, its results lacked generality. The second stage not only uses a far more elaborate notation, it also dispenses with the assumption of a linearized centrifugal pendulum. The quadratic nature of centrifugal force is accepted, and so is the fact that with increasing speed a centrifugal pendulum swings outward (changes its moment of inertia).

First Maxwell deals with the centrifugal pendulum alone. Combining the equation of *rotary* motion

$$\frac{d}{dt}\left(A\frac{d\theta}{dt}\right)=L \qquad\qquad (276:1)$$

with the energy equation

$$\tfrac{1}{2}A\left(\frac{d\theta}{dt}\right)^2+\tfrac{1}{2}B\left(\frac{d\phi}{dt}\right)^2+P=\int L\,d\theta, \qquad\qquad (277:2)$$

Maxwell obtains the expression

$$\frac{d}{dt}\left(B\frac{d\phi}{dt}\right)=\tfrac{1}{2}\frac{dA}{d\phi}\left(\frac{d\theta}{dt}\right)^2+\tfrac{1}{2}\frac{dB}{d\phi}\left(\frac{d\phi}{dt}\right)^2-\frac{dP}{d\phi} \qquad\qquad (277:4)$$

(where θ is the angle of rotation about the vertical axes, ϕ the pendulum's angle of deflection from the vertical, A and B the corresponding moments of inertia, L the driving torque, P the potential energy). This equation describes the *centrifugal* motion of the pendulum: the first two right-hand terms represent the centrifugal, the third the centripetal force. Assuming all disturbances to be small, Maxwell reduces the two equations of rotary and centrifugal motion to the linear form

$$A\frac{d^2\theta}{dt^2}+\frac{dA}{d\phi}\,\omega\,\frac{d\phi}{dt}=L \qquad\qquad (277:7)$$

and

$$B\frac{d^2\phi}{dt^2}-\frac{dA}{d\phi}\,\omega\,\frac{d\theta}{dA}=0 \qquad\qquad (277:8)$$

(where ω is the constant average speed of the governor). How the second of these has

[27] "If the roots of the cubic $ax^3+bx^2+cx+d=0$ be $x=a\pm\beta\sqrt{(-1)}$ and γ, we have $-b/a=2a+\gamma$, $c/a=2a\gamma+a^2+\beta^2$, $-d/a=(a^2+\beta^2)\gamma$, whence we easily deduce $(bc-ad)/a^2=-2a\{(a+\gamma)^2+\beta^2\}$; hence $bc-ad$ and a have always opposite signs." Edward John Routh, *Dynamics of a System of Rigid Bodies*, Pt. 2 (5th ed., London, 1892), p. 76. Routh's procedure is based upon a theorem concerning the relations between roots and coefficients of equations, stated in W. S. Burnside and A. W. Panton, *The Theory of Equations* (Dublin/London, 1881), p. 37.

been arrived at is not made clear. It is significant, however, that the term $dP/d\phi$ for the centripetal force has been lost. This force, the force of a spring or of gravity, is responsible for returning the flyweights toward the axis; it increases with the centrifugal displacement and could be represented, in the simplest case, by an expression of the form $C\phi$ added to the left side of the second equation. The combination of these two equations leads to a second-order linear differential equation analogous to that of an undamped spring-mass system with the natural frequency (not period, as Maxwell wrote) per revolution of $dA/d\phi\,(AB)^{-\frac{1}{2}}$.

This centrifugal pendulum is next fitted into a full-fledged governor. Underlying Maxwell's analysis are two mechanisms, both weight-driven friction governors, invented by Foucault and W. Thomson. Thomson's was extremely simple (Fig. 1): it consisted of two centrifugal weights held back by spring force, constrained to move solely in the horizontal plane. At overspeed the centrifugal weights would press outward against a stationary ring, thus producing the required braking action.[28] The Foucault governor (Fig. 2) incorporated a centrifugal pendulum of traditional form. Instead of mechanical friction, it employed an air brake: with increasing speed, the governor sleeve caused an increase in the airflow and hence in the power consumption of a centrifugal fan driven by the machine to be regulated.[29] In both cases the corrective action is directly proportional to the speed deviation, which means that the devices are proportional governors, or, in Maxwell's terms, *moderators*.

To expand the equations of the centrifugal pendulum into a mathematical representation of a complete governor, Maxwell adds the term $G\phi$ representing the control action (of the friction brake in Thomson's, or of the air brake in Foucault's governor) to the first equation, and terms for viscous friction to both equations. They become then

$$A\frac{d^2\theta}{dt^2} + X\frac{d\theta}{dt} + K\frac{d\phi}{dt} + G\phi = L \qquad (278:9)$$

and

$$B\frac{d^2\phi}{dt^2} + Y\frac{d\phi}{dt} - K\frac{d\theta}{dt} + [C\phi] = 0, \text{ where } K = \frac{dA}{d\phi}\omega. \qquad (278:10)$$

(The term $C\phi$, added by the present author, is explained below.)

Combining these two equations leads to a third-order linear differential equation which is tested for stability, as in the previous section, by means of the third-order stability condition. These equations involve a curious contradiction. Intended to describe the action of genuine governors (devices with integral response), they were derived from the physical models of Thomson's and Foucault's governors—moderators that Maxwell mistook for governors. Apparently, in the course of the analysis, purpose overshadowed reality: the resulting equations indeed describe governors with integral response. To describe proportional control, the second equation would have

[28] Described in William Thomson, "On a New Form of Centrifugal Governor," *Transactions of the Institution of Engineers and Shipbuilders in Scotland*, 1868, *12*:67–71, Plt. 3. Since this paper was read and published after Maxwell's governor paper, Maxwell must have known Thomson's governor from personal information.

[29] This is the first of the numerous governors invented by Foucault (1819–1868) in the last years of his life. It is described in Gariel, ed., *Recueil des travaux scientifiques de Léon Foucault*, pp. 435–441, 501–503, Plts. 16.1 and 16.2, and 19.1 and 19.2. The governor was protected by French Patent No. 60642, of Aug. 23, 1862, and English Patent No. 1862:3479, of Dec. 30, 1862.

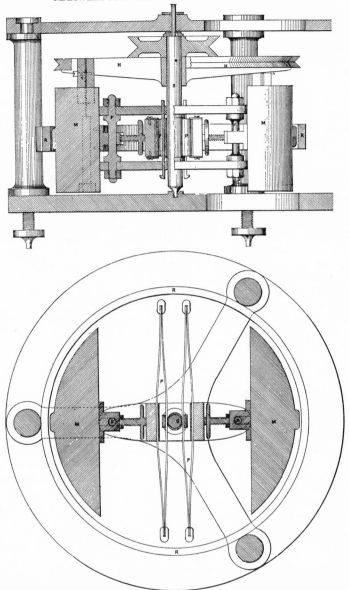

FIGURE 1. *William Thomson's friction governor, 1868, used to regulate the speed of weight-driven apparatus. At overspeed, the rotating weights M, restrained by the leaf springs P, press against the stationary ring R. (From* Transactions of the Institution of Engineers and Shipbuilders in Scotland, *1868, 12, Plt. 3.)*

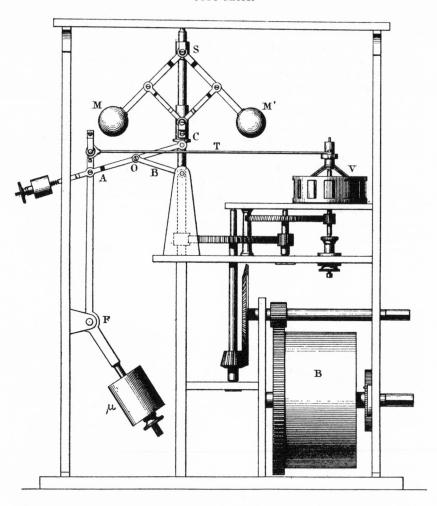

FIGURE 2. *Leon Foucault's governor of 1862, used to regulate the speed of the spring motor B. The centrifugal pendulum is linked to the centrifugal fan V in such a manner as to increase, with rising speed, the flow rate and hence the load resistance of the fan. The complicated arrangement of linkages and counterpoises on the left is designed merely to linearize the relationship between speed and output motion of the governor.* (*From* Recueil des travaux scientifiques de Léon Foucault, *C.-M. Gariel, ed., Paris, 1878, Plt. 19.*)

to include an additional term of the form $C\phi$ which, as noted, was lost earlier in the derivation.[30]

So far the more elaborate mathematical treatment has brought no returns: combining the two equations of motion merely leads to another third-order linear differential equation which is tested for stability in the same manner as in the previous case. Therefore Maxwell turns to a more complicated device which he terms a "compound governor"; actually it is no more than a governor by his own definition (a governor with integral response). The compound governor is shrouded in some mystery. Maxwell did not name its inventor, and he described it only briefly: "the break of Thomson's governor is applied to a moveable wheel, as in Jenkin's governor, and . . . this wheel works a steam valve, or a more powerful break," adding that "this compound governor has been constructed and used."[31] These points are corroborated by Thomson in his own account (given over half a year later); he added, however, that this modification of his governor was due to Fleeming Jenkin.[32] Jenkin seems never to have patented or publicly described the device. It may be visualized as seen in Andronov's reconstruction[33] (Fig. 3), except that the flyweights were arranged not as pendula but exactly as in Thomson's governor.

Since the device incorporates a third separately moving mechanism—the external ring with its attachments—Maxwell introduces for its mathematical description a

[30] That Eqs. (278:9) and (278:10) indeed represent an *integral* control system, whereas they would represent *proportional* control if the term $C\phi$ were added to (278:10), is best demonstrated by expressing the equations in block diagram notation. By introducing the differential operator $p \equiv d/dt$, Eq. (278:9) becomes

$$Ap^2\theta + Xp\theta + Kp\phi + G\phi = L,$$

or, solved for the controlled variable, governor speed,

$$p\theta = \frac{L - \phi(Kp + G)}{Ap + X},$$

which can be represented graphically as

$$\phi \longrightarrow \boxed{Kp + G} \overset{+}{\underset{-}{\longrightarrow}} \bigcirc \longrightarrow \boxed{\frac{1}{Ap + X}} \longrightarrow p\theta$$

Likewise, Eq. (278:10) becomes

$$Bp^2\phi + Yp\phi - Kp\theta + [C\phi] = 0.$$

Written in Maxwell's original form, i.e., without the term $C\phi$, this is equivalent to

$$\phi = \frac{\theta pK}{p(Bp + Y)} \quad \text{or} \quad \theta p \longrightarrow \boxed{\frac{K}{p(Bp + Y)}} \longrightarrow \phi.$$

If both equations are combined, the whole system presents itself as a closed feedback loop:

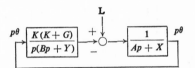

The factor p in the denominator of the left-hand block identifies this as a control system of integral type (see, e.g., Francis H. Raven, *Automatic Control Engineering*, New York: McGraw-Hill, 1961, pp. 57–59), or as a "type 1 system" (J. J. D'Azzo and C. H. Houpis, *Feedback Control System Analysis and Synthesis*, New York:McGraw-Hill, 1960, pp. 114–115). If Eq. (278:10) is expanded by the additional term $C\phi$, shown above in brackets, the block diagram takes the form

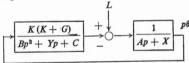

which is characteristic of proportional or "type 0" systems (Raven, *Automatic Control Engineering*, pp. 52–57, D'Azzo and Houpis, *Feedback Control*, pp. 114–115).

[31] "On Governors," pp. 278–279.

[32] Thomson, "On a New Form of Centrifugal Governor," p. 69.

[33] Andronov and Voznesenski, *J. C. Maxwell*, p. 371.

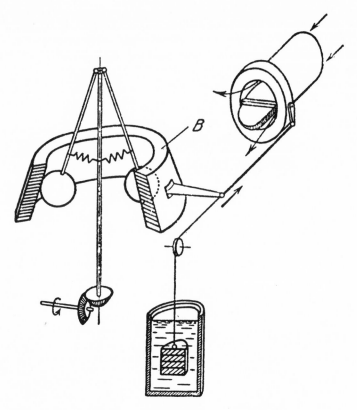

FIGURE 3. *H. C. Fleeming Jenkin's modification of William Thomson's governor, 1868; conjectural reconstruction. (From A. A. Andronov, I. N. Voznesenski, et al., J. C. Maxwell, I. A. Vyshnegradskii, A. Stodola:* Teoriia avtomaticheskogo regulirovaniia, *Moscow: Akademia Nauk SSSR, 1949, p. 371.)*

third independent variable (the ring's angular position ψ) and a third equation of motion:

$$A\frac{d^2\theta}{dt^2} + X\frac{d\theta}{dt} + K\frac{d\phi}{dt} + T\phi + J\psi = P - R,$$

$$B\frac{d^2\phi}{dt^2} + Y\frac{d\phi}{dt} - K\frac{d\theta}{dt} = 0, \qquad (278:13)$$

$$C\frac{d^2\psi}{dt^2} + Z\frac{d\psi}{dt} - T\phi = 0.$$

The two equations of motion of the previously discussed governor are retained, the second unchanged, the first in slightly expanded form (added are the term $J\psi$ for the control effect of the steam valve and R for external resistances); the form of the additional third equation follows that of the second. Combining these by elimination of ϕ and ψ leads to a linear fifth-order differential equation in θ with constant coefficients, which has the characteristic polynomial

$$n^5 + n^4\left(\frac{X}{A}+\frac{Y}{B}+\frac{Z}{C}\right) + n^3\left[\frac{XYZ}{ABC}\left(\frac{A}{X}+\frac{B}{Y}+\frac{C}{Z}\right)+\frac{K^2}{AB}\right] + n^2\left(\frac{XYZ+KTC+K^2Z}{ABC}\right)$$

$$+ n\frac{KTZ}{ABC}+\frac{KTJ}{ABC}=0. \tag{278:15}$$

Now the crucial question is reached: when will a polynomial that is principally insolvable have only negative roots? Maxwell's answer is this:

> I have not succeeded in determining completely the conditions of stability of the motion from this equation; but I have found two necessary conditions, which are in fact the conditions of stability of the two governors taken separately. If we write the equation $n^5+pn^4+qn^3+rn^2+sn+t$ [(279:16)], then, in order that the possible parts of all the roots shall be negative, it is necessary that $pq>r$ and $ps>t$ [(279:17)]. I am not able to show that these conditions are sufficient.[34]

Maxwell did not prove or explain his conclusions. His approach can only partly be reconstructed. As mentioned earlier, a few weeks before completing the paper, on January 23, 1868, Maxwell had attended a meeting at the London Mathematical Society. After giving two papers himself and hearing one by J. J. Walker, "On the Anharmonic-Ratio Sextic," Maxwell asked

> ... if any member present could point out a method of determining in what cases all the possible parts of the impossible roots of an equation are negative. In studying the motion of certain governors for regulating machinery, he had found that the stability of the motion depended on this condition, which is easily obtained for a cubic, but becomes more difficult in the higher degrees. Mr. W. K. Clifford said that, by forming an equation whose roots are the sums of the roots of the original equation taken in pairs and determining the condition of the real roots of this equation being negative, we should obtain the condition required.[35]

The extremely concise form into which Clifford's advice is here condensed makes it difficult to judge whether the advice was useful. That indeed it was may be inferred from another consideration. E. J. Routh, who at last presented a definitive solution (see below) of Maxwell's instability problem, in 1874, also at the London Mathematical Society, read a paper on "Stability of a Dynamical System with two Independent Motions" in which he used Clifford's suggestion successfully to obtain complete stability criteria for biquadratic and quintic systems.[36]

Maxwell's study of governor stability ends with a section on "Mr. C. W. Siemens's Liquid Governor,"[37] which adds nothing of substance to the previous results. Siemens,

[34] "On Governors," p. 279. Eqs. (279:16) and (279:17) are indeed only part of the stability conditions for this particular case; they are equivalent to the second and fourth of the four Hurwitz criteria for quintic polynomials.

[35] Discussion of J. J. Walker's paper "On the Anharmonic-Ratio Sextic," *Proc. Lond. Math. Soc.*, 1866–1869, 2:60–61.

[36] E. J. Routh, "Stability of a Dynamical System with two Independent Motions," *Proc. Lond. Math. Soc.*, 1873–1874, 5:97–99.

[37] Siemens has described this device in "On Uniform Rotation," *Phil. Trans.*, 1866, 657–670, which Maxwell has cited, and in "Description of an Improved Chronometric Governor for Steam Engines," *Proc. Inst. Mech. Engrs.*, 1866, 19–42.

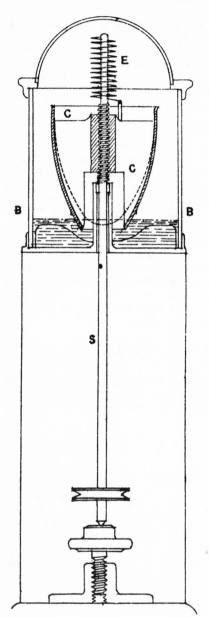

FIGURE 4. *William Siemens' liquid governor, 1866. (From* Philosophical Transactions, *1866, Plt. 29.)*

successful industrialist and stalwart of the Royal Society, had repeatedly published during the past twenty years on the subject of governors. His "liquid governor" of 1866 (Fig. 4) was of particular, albeit academic, interest, because as a sensor of speed it employed an ingenious alternative to the centrifugal pendulum. Its speed-sensing element may be compared to the impeller of a centrifugal pump, rotating on a vertical shaft with its inlet side immerged in a liquid. The impeller is attached to the drive shaft in a peculiar manner: it is not connected rigidly but only loosely by means of a screw thread, while its weight is supported by a spring. In case of overspeed, the rotation of the impeller falls behind that of the drive shaft; forced downward by the thread, the impeller immerges more deeply into the liquid, thus pumping at a higher rate and exerting an increasing resistance torque upon the drive shaft. The opposite takes place when the machine runs too slowly. By applying the moments of momentum equation and the energy equation to a stream tube along the impeller, Maxwell obtained two equations of motion which proved to be nonlinear. He did not carry the analysis to a conclusion as in the previous cases. After discussing various mathematical assumptions and modifications of design by means of which the equations of motion might be linearized, he turned to a new subject.

DIFFERENTIAL GEARS

Read by itself, the concluding chapter, "Theory of Differential Gearing," will appear cryptic. No longer concerned with the stability problem, it concentrates upon a machine element that was a peculiarity of the governors of Siemens. Differential gears had struck Maxwell's fancy a good deal earlier. In his paper "On Physical Lines of Force" (1861) he had referred to the differential gears in Siemens' governor as a mechanical model for a certain feature of his theory of molecular vortices.[38] If now in the context of governors he studied the dynamics of differential gears, his unacknowledged motive was the mechanical representation of electrical phenomena.

Once more he changed the paper's mathematical language. So far he had written equations of motion in the traditional form of Newton's Second Law. Now he shifted to the formalism of Lagrange, perhaps under the influence of Thomson and Tait's *Treatise*, which he must have first read at the very time when he wrote this chapter (see above). He based his treatment upon the intermediate form of Lagrange's equation of motion[39] (i.e., without generalized coordinates)

$$\varXi\delta\xi+H\delta\eta-\varSigma m\left(\frac{d^2x}{dt^2}\delta x+\frac{d^2y}{dt^2}\delta y+\frac{d^2z}{dt^2}\delta z\right)=0, \qquad (281:2)$$

where ξ is the angle of rotation of the intermediate wheel about its horizontal axis and η the angular position of the latter wheel's horizontal axis about the vertical axis (see Fig. 5). (The angular positions of the upper and lower vertical shafts are called ϕ and θ; see Eq. 282:12 below.)

First, the differential gear is studied by itself. The only forces acting on it are the bearing friction $\varXi$ and the weight H connected to the valve linkage (Fig. 5 left).

---

[38] J. C. Maxwell, "On Physical Lines of Force," *Phil. Mag.*, 4th Ser., 1861, *21*:283:

The only conception which has at all aided me in conceiving of this kind of motion is that of the vortices being separated by a layer of particles, revolving each on its own axis in the opposite direction to that of the vortices, so that the contiguous surfaces of the particles and of the vortices have the same motion.

In mechanism, when two wheels are intended to revolve in the same direction, a wheel is placed between them so as to be in gear with both, and this wheel is called an "idle wheel." The hypothesis about the vortices which I have to suggest is that a layer of particles, acting as idle wheels, is interposed between each vortex and the next so that each vortex has a tendency to make the neighbouring vortices revolve in the same direction with itself.

In mechanism, the idle wheel is generally made to rotate about a *fixed* axle; but in epicyclic trains and other contrivances, as, for instance, in Siemens' governor for steam-engines, we find idle wheels whose centres are capable of motion. In all these cases the motion of the centre is the half sum of the motions of the circumferences of the wheels between which it is placed. Let us examine the relations which must subsist between the motions of our vortices and those of the layer of particles interposed as idle wheels between them.

[39] Thomson and Tait, *Treatise on Natural Philosophy*, p. 204.

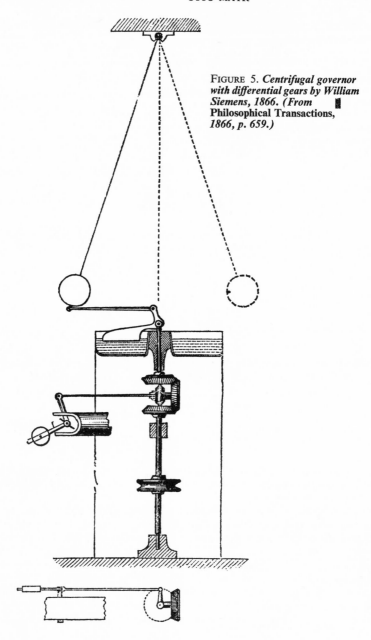

FIGURE 5. *Centrifugal governor with differential gears by William Siemens, 1866. (From* **Philosophical Transactions,** *1866, p. 659.)*

Expressing x, y, and z by coordinate transformation in terms of ξ and η, the equation of motion then becomes

$$\left(\varXi - \Sigma mp^2\frac{d^2\xi}{dt^2} - \Sigma mpq^2\frac{d^2\eta}{dt^2}\right)\delta\xi + \left(H - \Sigma mpq\frac{d^2\xi}{dt^2} - \Sigma mq^2\frac{d^2\eta}{dt^2}\right)\delta\eta = 0. \quad (282:5)$$

Substituting $L = \Sigma[m(p_1^2 + p_2^2 + p_3^2)]$, $M = \Sigma[m(p_1q_1 + p_2q_2 + p_3q_3)]$, and $N = \Sigma[m(q_1^2+q_2^2+q_3^2)]$ (where $p_{1,2,3}$ and $q_{1,2,3}$ are the transformation coefficients), and stipulating that both halves of the equation must be independently equal to zero, Maxwell obtains for the simple differential gear the equations of motion

$$\varXi = L\frac{d^2\xi}{dt^2} + M\frac{d^2\eta}{dt^2}, \quad (282:7)$$

and

$$H = M\frac{d^2\xi}{dt^2} + N\frac{d^2\eta}{dt^2}. \quad (282:8)$$

What is of interest here to Maxwell is only one feature: the two equations describe motions in ξ and η that generally interact; they will be mutually independent only if $M = 0$.[40]

If the differential gear is coupled with an engine (driving torque Θ) on one side and with a centrifugal pendulum (reaction torque Φ) on the other, the original equation of motion (282:5) expands to

$$\Theta\delta\theta + \Phi\delta\phi + \left(\varXi - L\frac{d^2\xi}{dt^2} - M\frac{d^2\eta}{dt^2}\right)d\xi + \left(H - M\frac{d^2\xi}{dt^2} - N\frac{d^2\eta}{dt^2}\right)\delta\eta = 0. \quad (282:9)$$

Following the same procedure as before (eliminating θ and ϕ, simplifying the coefficients, and separating) leads to the equations of motion for the whole system:

$$\Theta + P\varXi + QH = L'\frac{d^2\theta}{dt^2} + M'\frac{d^2\phi}{dt^2},$$

and

$$\Phi + R\varXi + SH = M'\frac{d^2\theta}{dt^2} + N'\frac{d^2\phi}{dt^2}. \quad (282:12)$$

Again Maxwell emphasized the point that motion in θ and ϕ will be independent only if $M' = 0$. He concludes the paper with a few words on the physical implications of this result for practical governors.

From the point of view of the mechanical engineer, Maxwell's concern for the independence of motion of differential gears is rather puzzling: not only were differential gears seldom used in this application, but in practice the problem of interaction simply never presented itself. The puzzle's answer is that Maxwell's interest stemmed from another root. To him the interaction between the separate motions of a set of differential gears was analogous to the mutual induction between separate electrical circuits. Later he had an actual model of this built for classroom demonstration (Fig. 6), of which he wrote in 1876, "I have been making a mechanical model of an induction coil, in which the primary and the secondary currents are represented by the

[40] "On Governors," p. 282.

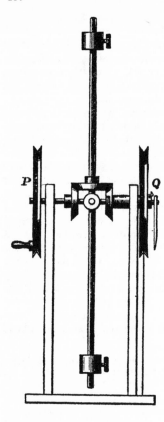

FIGURE 6. *Maxwell's differential gear model,
c. 1876, used for the demonstration of
electrical induction. The two outer flywheels
P and Q represent the primary and secondary
circuits; an increase of the moment of inertia of
the flywheel in the middle illustrates the effect
of placing an iron core between the two circuits.
(From James Clerk Maxwell, A Treatise on
Electricity and Magnetism, 3rd ed., Oxford,
1892, Vol. II, p. 228.)*

motion of wheels, and in which I can symbolise all the effects of putting in more or
less of the iron core, or more or less resistance and Leyden jars in either circuit."[41]

INFLUENCE OF MAXWELL'S PAPER

If Maxwell's paper "On Governors" did not present a finished theory of automatic
control, and if it contained a number of inconsistencies, it is nevertheless true that
modern systems engineers will find its language and approach eminently congenial,
especially when compared with the style of the vast governor literature produced at

[41] Letter of Maxwell to Lewis Campbell,
Christmas 1876, in Campbell and Garnett, *Life
of Maxwell*, pp. 396–397. Descriptions of this
model are also given on pp. 551–554, and by
J. J. Thomson as a footnote in the 3rd ed. of
Maxwell's *Treatise on Electricity and Magnetism*
(Oxford, 1892), Vol. II, p. 228.

This story has an amusing sequel. Ludwig
Boltzmann, the Viennese physicist who pro-
selytized Maxwell's electrodynamics on the
Continent, was so fascinated with differential
gears as a mechanical analogy of electrical
induction that he based a good part of his
*Vorlesungen über Maxwell's Theorie der Elek-
trizität und des Lichtes* (Leipzig, 1891) upon this
device (pp. 2–49 and Plts. 1 and 2). He also had

the same time on the Continent. Implicitly or explicitly, Maxwell had anticipated a great deal of the conceptual framework of modern feedback control engineering.[42]

The paper did not lack publicity: originally published in the *Proceedings of the Royal Society* in 1868, it was reprinted in full the same year in the *Philosophical Magazine* and later in Maxwell's collected *Scientific Papers* (1890). It was the paper's form, however, that rendered it inaccessible: its mathematical language, at once concise and casual, was difficult to follow; the mechanisms discussed were without practical interest and, to make matters worse, inadequately described. As a result, in the world of engineering the paper was ignored. Surveying the British, French, German, and American engineering literature up to World War I, I have found no reference to it with the exception of a few works on rational mechanics.

The paper's influence was limited to Maxwell's direct scientific circle, or rather, to one of its members. E. J. Routh (1831–1907),[43] a son-in-law of Airy, the Astronomer Royal, was an insider in this exclusive group. He had been a rival of Maxwell's in their student days at Cambridge (they had shared the Smith Prize of 1854, after Routh had been graduated as Senior Wrangler, with Maxwell taking second place). Later, as chief mathematical coach at Cambridge, Routh set records in preparing successful candidates for mathematical examinations. Maxwell's challenge to the mathematicians that they should discover a general stability criterion spurred Routh on to his best work. We recall that subsequent to Maxwell's paper Routh had presented the missing derivation of Maxwell's stability condition for cubic systems and complete stability conditions for quintic systems. When the problem for the 1877 Adams Prize was chosen to be "The Criterion of Dynamic Stability" (Maxwell was one of the four members of the prize committee), Routh presented a definitive solution in an essay

---

an elaborate model built. Arnold Sommerfeld, his successor to the chair of theoretical physics in Munich and heir to the model, reported, in *Lectures on Theoretical Physics: Mechanics*, trans. Martin O. Stern (New York: Academic Press, 1952), p. 225:

In 1891 Boltzmann gave a series of lectures on Maxwell's electromagnetic theory at the University in Munich. He devoted the first lectures to the detailed consideration of a doubly cyclic mechanical system in order to illustrate the mutual inductive effect between two electrical circuits. The carefully worked mechanical model, consisting mainly of two pairs of beveled gears with centrifugal governors, is preserved in the museum of our Institute. To us it seems much more complicated than Maxwell's theory which it was intended to illustrate. Hence we shall not use it to clarify this theory, but instead take advantage of it in an exercise on the differential of an automobile, to which it is similar in its essential features.

[42] An important exception is the concept of the *closed feedback loop* which seems to have been foreign to Maxwell. Apparently he saw the governor as an oscillatory system comparable to though more complex than a vibrating spring-

mass system. In the introduction to the paper (p. 277, top) he suggested correctly that the "governing power" (open loop gain?) was directly related to the system's stability; in the mathematical analysis he did not return to this idea. Lacking the concept of the closed loop, he could not appreciate the effect upon stability of the time lags experienced by a signal travelling around the loop. Stability, he believed, could be achieved only by a sufficient amount of viscous damping (p. 273, bottom). This belief, expressed already in 1851 by Airy, which is correct within limits, led Routh to this extreme conclusion: "The defect of a governor is therefore that it acts too quickly, and thus produces considerable oscillation of speed in the engine. . . . It will be presently shown that this fault may be very much modified by applying some resistance to the motion of the governor" (Routh, *Dynamics of a System of Rigid Bodies*, p. 75). This generalization, a patent absurdity, has evoked appropriate comments from practical engineers; see, e.g., W. Trinks, *Governors and the Governing of Prime Movers* (New York: Van Nostrand, 1919), p. xviii.

[43] *DNB*, 2nd Suppl. (London: Smith, Elder, 1912), Vol. III, *s.v.*

On the Stability of a Given State of Motion, which won him the prize and a place in the history of mechanics.[44]

Continental developments continued independently. Between 1876 and 1879 I. A. Vishnegradskii, engineering professor in St. Petersburg and later Russian Minister of Finance, carried the governor problem to a stage comparable with that of Maxwell's paper.[45] The task was continued by two professors at the Swiss Federal Polytechnicum in Zurich—the engineer Aurel Stodola and the mathematician Adolph Hurwitz, whose collaboration led to the Hurwitz stability criteria (1895), which have been shown to be equivalent to Routh's.[46]

Routh's book *Dynamics of a System of Rigid Bodies* (1860), later editions of which made reference to Maxwell's governor paper, was translated into German in 1898.[47] As a result, the paper was cited in two monographs on speed regulation, the only citations in its first half-century apart from Routh's that I have been able to discover. Neither author discussed it in depth: Wilhelm Hort's comments were that "Unfortunately Maxwell neglected to express himself in detail on the mechanisms in question, so that it is impossible to gain full insight into his derivations,"[48] while Richard von Mises remarked on some externals of Maxwell's paper—such as the distinction between governors and moderators—and ignored the rest.[49]

---

[44] Edward John Routh, *A Treatise on the Stability of a Given State of Motion, Particularly Steady Motion* (London, 1877), p. vi.

[45] J. Wischnegradski, "Über direktwirkende Regulatoren," *Civilingenieur*, 1877, 28:95–132, and "Mémoire sur la théorie générale des régulateurs," *Revue Universelle des Mines*, 1878, 4:1–38, 1879, 5:192–227.

[46] Hurwitz formulated his criteria as follows:

A necessary and sufficient condition that the equation

$$a_0 x^n + a_1 x^{n-1} + \ldots + a_n = 0,$$

with real coefficients in which the coefficient a_0 is assumed to be positive, have only roots with negative real parts, is that the values of the determinants

$$\Delta_1 = a_1, \Delta_2, \Delta_3, \ldots, \Delta_n$$

all be positive.

The determinants in question are defined as

$$\Delta = \begin{vmatrix} a_1, a_3, a_5, \ldots, a_{2\lambda-1} \\ a_0, a_2, a_4, \ldots, a_{2\lambda-2} \\ 0, a_1, a_3, \ldots, a_{2\lambda-3} \\ \cdot \quad \cdot \quad \cdot \quad \cdot \quad \cdot \\ \cdot \quad \cdot \quad \cdot \quad \cdot \quad a_\lambda \end{vmatrix}$$

Adolph Hurwitz, "On the Conditions under which an Equation has only Roots with Negative Real Parts," trans. H. G. Bergmann, in Bellman and Kalaba, eds., *Mathematical Trends in Control Theory*, p. 73. The original paper appeared under the title "Über die Bedingungen, unter welchen eine Gleichung nur Wurzeln mit negativen reellen Theilen besitzt," *Mathematische Annalen*, 1895, 46:273–284.

[47] E. J. Routh, *Die Dynamik der Systeme starrer Körper*, trans. A. Schepp, with a preface by Felix Klein (Leipzig, 1898).

[48] Wilhelm Hort, "Die Entwicklung des Problems der stetigen Kraftmaschinenregelung nebst einem Versuch der Theorie unstetiger Regelungsvorgänge," *Zeitschrift für Mathematik und Physik*, 1904, 50:233–279, esp. p. 244.

[49] Richard von Mises, "Dynamische Probleme der Maschinenlehre," *Encyklopädie der Mathematischen Wissenschaften*, Felix Klein and Conrad Müller, eds. (Leipzig: Teubner, 1911), Vol. IV.2, pp. 255 and 257.

HERTZ AND THE TECHNOLOGICAL SIGNIFICANCE OF
ELECTROMAGNETIC WAVES

By Charles Süsskind *

On reviewing the manuscript of my monograph on the origins of radio-telegraphy,[1] a British colleague — a Fellow of the Royal Society who had studied in Germany — asked me whether I knew that Heinrich Rudolf Hertz (1857–1894) had, on his death bed, stated that he did not think that the electromagnetic waves whose existence he had confirmed would ever be of any technological significance. I had heard the anecdote before, though in less elaborate form and never from so well-qualified a source, and I now determined to track down the story.

Its first appearance evidently dates back to the publication of an early text on radiotelegraphy by Karl Friedrich Braun (1850–1918), the inventor of the cathode-ray tube, in 1901:

Schon im Jahre 1889 erhielt HERTZ vom Civilingenieur HUBER in München die Anfrage, ob sich seine Wellen nicht zu einer drahtlosen Telegraphie wür-den verwenden lassen. HERTZ verneinte die Frage. Wäre sie zwei Jahre später an ihn ergangen, vielleicht hätte er sie bejaht.[2]	As early as 1889, Hertz was asked by an engineer in Munich, Huber, whether his waves could not be employed for wireless telegraphy. Hertz answered in the negative. If the question had been put to him two years later, perhaps his answer would have been in the affirma-tive.

The English literature on the subject echoes this view. In another early account, Story says: " Huber questioned Hertz as to the possibility of making use of the electro-magnetic waves as a means of telegraphing without wires. Hertz threw cold water on the idea. He had not grasped the full significance of his own discovery." [3]

Huber's letter and Hertz's reply are preserved in the Deutsches Museum in Munich. In 1930, Appleyard published a photographic reproduction of the letter, together with a rather inaccurate translation, and added the following comment:

It can be definitely stated that concerning the future employment of Hertzian waves for telegraphy and telephony he had no premonitions. For there exists a letter written by him to one, Herr Huber, who wanted to know whether

* University of California, Berkeley.
[1] Charles Süsskind, *Popov and the Beginnings of Radiotelegraphy* (San Francisco: San Francisco Press, 1962).
[2] K. F. Braun, *Drahtlose Telegraphie durch*

Wasser und Luft (Leipzig: Veit & comp., 1901), p. 15. English translations have been made by the author of this article.
[3] A. T. Story, *The Story of Wireless Telegraphy* (London, 1904).

there was a prospect in that direction. Hertz regarded it as impracticable. His reply, which is reproduced in Fig. 13, was to the effect that the application of such a mode of electrical communication to practical telegraphy or telephony would need a mirror as large as a continent.[4]

Further evidence that the story continues to have literary currency appears in the biographical collection *Die grossen Deutschen*. Max Theodor Felix von Laue (1879–1960), who contributed the article on Hertz, wrote in 1957 that Hertz " himself never gave a thought to the technological utilization " of his waves (*an deren technische Verwendung er selbst nie gedacht hat*).[5]

The simplest way to set the record straight is to quote Huber's inquiry and Hertz's reply in original and in English translation.

Huber to Hertz, 1 December 1889:

Schon von verschiedenen Seiten habe ich von Ihren grossartigen Erfolgen auf dem Gebiete der Electricitätslehre gehört ohne aber genau erfahren zu haben, um was es sich speciell handelte. Heute erst komme ich in die glückliche Lage einige Details zu erhalten & mir genauere Aufklärung durch Ihre Originalberichte zu verschaffen. Meine Hochachtung Ihnen gegenüber, Herr Professor, ist eine so grosse, dass *ich* es gar nicht wage, Ihnen von Herzen Glück zu Ihren weittragenden Entdeckungen zu wünschen; denn der Unterschied ist ein zu grosser. In Nachstehendem erlaube mir nur eine Frage an Sie zu stellen, mit der höfl. Bitte um gelegentliche gefl. Beantwortung durch einige Zeilen.

Es würde mich sehr interessiren zu hören, ob es nicht auch möglich wäre, nach Ihrer Theorie, die magnetischen Kraftlinien (die unsichtbaren natürlich) in die Ferne zu übertragen? Ich habe hier Transformatoren & das Telephon in erster Linie in Betracht gezogen.

Auf der einen Station würde z. B. im Brennpunkte eines Hohlspiegels ein Pol eines Electromagnets erregt. Die magnet. Linien (das magnet. Feld) werden dann vom Spiegel der andern Station aufgenommen & erzeugen mit

I had previously heard from various sources about your magnificent successes in the field of electrical knowledge, but without having learned exactly what the particular subject was. Not until today do I find myself in the fortunate position of having obtained some details and of having achieved more exact understanding through your original reports. My respect towards you, Sir, is so great that *I* do not even dare to wish you luck with all my heart in your far-reaching discoveries; for the difference between us is too great. In the following, I take the liberty of putting only one question to you, with the respectful request that you might favor me with a few lines in reply at your convenience.

I should be very interested to hear whether it would not be possible, according to your theory, to transmit the magnetic lines of force (the invisible ones, of course) over a distance? I am thinking in the first instance of transformers & the telephone.

One could, for instance, excite a polepiece of an electromagnet at the focal point of a convex mirror. The magnetic lines (the magnetic field) are then received by the mirror of the second station & produce induction (sec-

[4] Rollo Appleyard, *Pioneers of Electrical Communication* (London: Macmillan, 1930), p. 140.

[5] Herrmann Heimpel, ed., *Die grossen Deutschen* (Berlin: Propyläen-Verlag, 1957), Vol. 4, pp. 103–112.

CHARLES SÜSSKIND

Benützung einer Inductionsspule Inductions- (secundäre) Ströme.[6]

ondary) currents by means of an induction coil.

The letter, which was sent to Hertz in Bonn from the Netherlands, is signed " Heinrich Huber aus München, Electriker." It contains a sketch of two facing parabolic mirrors, one with the top of an electromagnet at its focal point and the other, an air-core coil. There is no mention of telegraphy (let alone " wireless " telegraphy) whatsoever. Huber, who was employed at the power station that provided The Hague with electric light, manifestly had only electric power and the telephone in mind.

Hertz replied immediately.

Hertz to Huber, 3 December 1889:

Auf Ihre freundlichen Zeilen vom 1 ds antworte ich ganz ergebenst das folgende: Magnetische Kraftlinien lassen sich ebenso gut wie die elektrischen als Strahlen fortpflanzen, wenn ihre Schwingungen nur schnell genug sind, denn in diesem Falle gehen sie überhaupt mit den elektrischen zusammen, und die Strahlen und Wellen um welche es sich in meinen Versuchen handelt könnte man ebenso gut magnetische als elektrische nennen.

Aber die Schwingungen eines Transformators oder eines Telephons sind viel zu langsam. Nehmen Sie tausend Schwingungen in der Sekunde, was doch eine hohe Zahl ist, so würde dem doch im Aether schon eine Wellenlänge von 300 Kilometern entsprechen, und von der gleichen Grössenordnung müssten also auch die Brennweiten der benutzten Spiegel sein. Könnten Sie also Hohlspiegel von der Grösse eines Continents bauen, so könnten Sie damit die beabsichtigten Versuche sehr gut anstellen, aber praktisch ist nichts zu machen, mit gewöhnlichen Hohlspiegeln würden Sie nicht die geringste Wirkung verspüren. So vermuthe ich wenigstens.[7]

In regard to your friendly lines of the 1st inst. I beg to reply as follows: Magnetic lines of force can be propagated as rays just as well as electric lines as long as their oscillations are sufficiently fast, for in that case they altogether coincide with the electric lines, and the rays and waves that occur in my experiments could be equally well called magnetic as electric.

But the oscillations of a transformer or a telephone are much too slow. Take a thousand oscillations per second, which is surely a high figure, yet the corresponding wavelength in the aether would be 300 kilometers, and the focal lengths of the mirrors employed would have to be of the same order of magnitude. If you could thus build convex mirrors as large as a continent, you might very well be able to set up the proposed experiments, but in practice nothing can be done, you would not perceive the slightest effect with ordinary convex mirrors. At least that is what I suppose.

[6] MS No. 2939, Deutsches Museum, Munich.
[7] MS No. 573, Deutsches Museum, Munich. Appleyard's translation (*op. cit.*) renders *eines Transformators oder eines Telephons* as " of a

' Transformator ' or telegraph " and omits the final sentence; the substitution of " telegraph " for " telephone " and the omission of the mild disclaimer serve to compound the confusion.

This reply is technically flawless. The proposal was to propagate electromagnetic waves at audio frequencies, and Hertz quite rightly pointed out that they would not propagate and that antennas of stupendous size would be in any case required for their generation. The various technical solutions of the problem, such as detection of the keying or of low-frequency modulation of a high-frequency carrier, which led to radiotelegraphy and radiotelephony, did not come until after Hertz's death.

Accordingly, the story that Hertz (whose first technical training was in engineering) had no head for practical matters may be safely laid to rest, together with the implication that his reply to Huber delayed the development of radiotelegraphy by several years. First, the above correspondence received no circulation at the time. Second, as I pointed out in my monograph,[8] at least three other proposals to employ electromagnetic waves for communications were independently made during the following three years, by Richard Threlfall (1861–1932) in 1890;[9] in an editorial in *The Electrician* in 1891;[10] and by William Crookes (1832–1919) in 1892.[11] The first publication to describe a radiotelegraphic system was Marconi's patent application in 1896.[12] Third, it is possible that radiotelegraphy might have developed independently, from the efforts of the inventors whose observations of electromagnetic-wave propagation before Hertz I described in a recent paper.[13]

There is a curious postscript to the story. In 1906, the Deutsches Museum authorities corresponded with Huber (then back in Munich) to establish whether he was the one who had written the letter to Hertz, which his family had contributed to the Museum's manuscript collection. Huber confirmed that he was their man,[14] and added that the primitive experimental configuration that he had proposed " for wireless telegraphy and telephony " derived from the discoveries that had been made in 1879 by David Edward Hughes (1830–1900). He went on to cite the extract from Braun's book that I have quoted.[15]

However, the observations that Hughes made in 1879 were not published until 1899, ten years *after* Huber's correspondence with Hertz, as I noted in the above-mentioned paper;[16] until then, Hughes' observations were known only to a handful of his colleagues in the Royal Society, men with whom Huber could scarcely have had any contact. It would thus appear that Huber, whose memory had evidently played him the familiar trick of reversing the sequence of two events (his letter to Hertz and his reading about Hughes' experiments a decade or more later), was himself an early victim of the false belief that he had proposed radiotelegraphy to Hertz and had received a " wrong " answer.

[8] Susskind, *op. cit.*
[9] Richard Threlfall's presidential address, *Report of the Australasian Association for the Advancement of Science*, 1890, 2:27–54.
[10] Unsigned editorial, *Electrician*, 1891, 26: 685. The editor at that time was A. E. Trotter (1857–1947).
[11] William Crookes, " Some Possibilities of Electricity," *Fortnightly Review* (London),

1892, 51:173–181.
[12] British Patent No. 12,039; 1896.
[13] C. Süsskind, " Observations of Electromagnetic-Wave Radiation Before Hertz," *Isis*, 1964, 55:32–42.
[14] MS No. 572, Deutsches Museum, Munich.
[15] Braun, *op. cit.*
[16] Süsskind, " Observations of Electromagnetic-Wave Radiation Before Hertz."